Y0-CBD-399

AMERICAN ASSOCIATION OF TEACHERS
OF SPANISH AND PORTUGUESE

Teaching Cultures of the Hispanic World: Products and Practices in Perspective

Vicki Galloway, Editor
Georgia Institute of Technology

CENGAGE
Learning

Australia • Brazil • Japan • Korea • Mexico • Singapore • Spain • United Kingdom • United States

Teaching Cultures of the
Hispanic World: Products and
Practices in Perspective
Vicki Galloway

Editor: Tim Spurlock

Production Manager: Staci
Powers

Production Coordinator: Spring
Greer

Marketing Coordinator:
Sara I. Hinckley

© 2001 Wadsworth, Cengage Learning

ALL RIGHTS RESERVED. No part of this work covered by the
copyright herein may be reproduced, transmitted, stored or used
in any form or by any means graphic, electronic, or mechanical,
including but not limited to photocopying, recording, scanning,
digitizing, taping, Web distribution, information networks, or
information storage and retrieval systems, except as permitted
under Section 107 or 108 of the 1976 United States Copyright Act,
without the prior written permission of the publisher.

For product information and technology assistance, contact us
at **Cengage Learning Academic Resource Center,**
1-800-423-0563

For permission to use material from this text or product, submit
all requests online at **www.cengage.com/permissions**
Further permissions questions can be emailed to
permissionrequest@cengage.com

ISBN-13: 978-0-759-30766-7

ISBN-10: 0-759-30766-0

Delmar
5191 Natorp Blvd.
Mason, Ohio 45040
USA

Cengage Learning products are represented in Canada by Nelson
Education, Ltd.

For your course and learning solutions, visit
academic.cengage.com

Notice to the Reader

Publisher does not warrant or guarantee any of the products described herein or
perform any independent analysis in connection with any of the product information contained herein. Publisher does not assume, and expressly disclaims, any
obligation to obtain and include information other than that provided to it by
the manufacturer. The reader is expressly warned to consider and adopt all safety
precautions that might be indicated by the activities described herein and to avoid
all potential hazards. By following the instructions contained herein, the reader
willingly assumes all risks in connection with such instructions. The publisher
makes no representations or warranties of any kind, including but not limited to,
the warranties of fitness for particular purpose or merchantability, nor are any such
representations implied with respect to the material set forth herein, and the publisher takes no responsibility with respect to such material. The publisher shall not
be liable for any special, consequential, or exemplary damages resulting, in whole or
part, from the readers' use of, or reliance upon, this material.

Printed in the United States of America
2 3 4 5 6   16 15 14 13 12

FD059

Teaching Cultures of the Hispanic World: Products and Practices in Perspective

Table of Contents

Acknowledgements 2

Giving Dimension to *Mappaemundi*: The Matter of Perspective 3
Vicki Galloway, Georgia Institute of Technology

Deepening Cross-Cultural Learning in the Classroom 65
Olgalucía G. González, Washington and Jefferson College

Perspectives in Practices: Teaching Culture Through Speech Acts 95
Carmen García, Arizona State University

Analyzing Cultural Products in Practice 113
Nancy A. Humbach, Miami University, Ohio

Understanding Culture Through Music: Products and Perspectives 137
Paula R . Heusinkveld, Clemson University

The Five C'S of Legends and Folktales 161
Susan M. Bacon, University of Cincinnati
Nancy A. Humbach, Miami University, Ohio

Building on Our Experiences 181
Núria Vidal, Education Office, Embassy of Spain

Challenging Perspectives: Lessons From and For the Changing Spanish Classroom 197
Zena Moore, University of Texas, Austin

About The Authors 218

Acknowledgements

This volume is dedicated to Lynn A. Sandstedt for the vision and leadership he has provided Spanish teachers and the foreign language teaching profession during his tenure as Executive Director of the American Association of Teachers of Spanish and Portuguese. As one of our profession's strongest proponents of culture teaching, his efforts have had a tremendous impact on our classrooms and his guidance and support during the preparation of this book have been invaluable to its authors. We express our sincere appreciation to Lynn for his untiring dedication to the improvement of foreign language teaching.

Chapter 1

Giving Dimension to *Mappaemundi*: The Matter of Perspective

Vicki Galloway
Georgia Institute of Technology

En este imperio, el Arte de la Cartografía conoció una Perfección tal que el Mapa de una sola Provincia ocupaba toda una ciudad y el Mapa del Imperio toda una Provincia. Con el tiempo, esos Mapas Desmesurados dejaron de constituir una satisfacción y los Colegios de Cartógrafos elaboraron un Mapa del Imperio que tenía el Formato del Imperio y que coincidía con él punto por punto. Menos apasionadas por el estudio de la Cartografía, las Generaciones Siguientes pensaron que ese Mapa Dilatado era inútil y, no sin impiedad, lo abandonaron a la Inclemencia del Sol y los Inviernos. En los Desiertos del Oeste subsisten Ruinas muy deterioradas del Mapa. Animales y mendigos las habitan. En todo el país, no hay otras huellas de las disciplinas geográficas.

Jorge Luis Borges
"Del rigor de las ciencias"

The *Ser* and *Estar* of "Worlds"

The class was Intermediate Spanish, and I had planned a grammar lesson that would review uses of *ser/estar/haber* while introducing the next grammatical item on the agenda, the *"se pasivo."* Since the chapter vocabulary was geographical terms *(río, lago, océano, montaña, frontera, etc.)*, I had posted a large "classroom" map obtained from the campus bookstore. The students' first task was to generate questions a map could answer: *¿Dónde está? ¿Cómo es? ¿Quién(es) son de...? ¿Qué ... hay?* and so on. We then moved quickly to the second task: Students were to look at the map and express any and all observations they could make, using *ser, estar, hay* and the passive constructions *se ve(n), se encuentra(n)*. Each student was asked to make one statement of observation and then join to this statement an explanation or logical expansion, selecting from a list of connectors, such as *sin embargo, por ejemplo, porque, por eso*, and so on. For example:

> Initial statement: *Se ven los nombres de los países.*
> Expansion: *Sin embargo, los nombres están en inglés, no en español.*

However, as I looked at the map with the students and listened to their statements, I sensed a culture lesson emerging. I began to jot down some of their rather startling observations [the ? indicates a teacher prompt for clarification or expansion].[1]

Student 1:   *Se ve el tamaño de los países. (?) Por ejemplo, Estados Unidos, con Alaska, es como Sudamérica.*

Student 2:   *Se ve dónde están los países. Por ejemplo, Estados Unidos está en el centro* (laughter). *Canadá está al lado de Estados Unidos; México está bajo...debajo de nosotros.*

Student 3:   *Sí y... también hay...fronteras. (?) Por eso, se ve la separación de los países. (?) Por ejemplo, México es no...no es como los Estados Unidos.*

Student 4:   *Se ve el...la...forma de los países. Por ejemplo, Chile es como una ... serpiente...Además, Centroamérica.*

Student 5:   *Se ve el agua...mucho agua...mucha? Por ejemplo, hay océanos. (?) Cuba está rodeada de agua. También Puerto Rico.*

Student 6:   *Se encuentran los continentes.. Por ejemplo, Norteamérica es mucho más grande que Sudamérica ...(?) Aquí Africa también, pero no es verdad. Además Europa es...se ve más grande que Sudamérica. ¡Pobre Sudamérica!*

Student 7:   *Se ven los colores de los países* (laughter). *Por ejemplo, Perú es verde, Colombia es amarilla... muy feliz.*

Student 9:   *¡Es las drogas!* (more laughter)

The expressions on students' faces indicated that even as they were speaking they were aware that some of the things they were saying about the world were simply not "true." Yet, here were the facts—concrete, standardized and graphically displayed—courtesy of the 16th-century Flemish cartographer, Gerardus Mercator. Indeed, still hanging in many U.S. schoolrooms, for the consumption of all learners in all disciplines, may be some Mercator-like map, in which Alaska appears three times the size of Mexico, in which Europe is larger than South America, and in which center stage belongs to the United States.

As flat, textureless depictions of the world, maps of necessity give deceptive lessons in geography. To show the form of landmasses, size must be compromised; to display accurately the size of territories, trueness of form must be sacrificed. Likewise, on the rotating sphere where we reside, there are no north, south, east or west edges; it is only human selection that designates one pole as North and the other as South, putting Australia "down under" rather than "up above."[2] It is human selection as well that gives maps their focal points, targeting some parts of the planet for central position and others for the periphery of our vision. Maps are ways of seeing and, as such, they are themselves a powerful lesson in the *ser* and *estar* of the world.

I then invited students to consider what they did not see, what was missing from the map:

Student 1:   *No se ven...estados en Estados Unidos... [?] Porque el mapa es muy general....[?] Es importante porque los estados son importantes. [?]Son diferente...diferentes. [?] Yo no soy de Georgia...por ejemplo. Soy de Nueva York. Soy diferente. Todos son diferentes en Estados Unidos.*

Student 2:   *¡No hay gente en el mapa!* (laughter) *[?] Porque... personas son el mundo.*

Student 3:   *No hay lenguas...no sé la lengua...por ejemplo, no sé la lengua en ...*[I want to say I don't know what language people speak in different countries...] *No sé qué idioma se habla en....India...o idiomas porque hay muchos en India. El mapa no dice...No se dice.*

Student 4:   *No hay acción...¿Cómo se dice* movement? *Todo... no movimiento... No hay movimiento. Todo es... ¿cómo se dice* static?

On our map there was no indication of life—no sense of movement, interaction, change. There were no histories, no traditions, no cultures. There really was, in fact, no "world" at all, merely a bland surface sectioned off into political entities. On our map, of course, there were no people. We could not see, for example, that regardless of territorial size, the population of North America (including Mexico, Central America and the Caribbean) only exceeds that of South America by twenty percent. And while students had been quick to point out their distinctiveness within the borders of their own country, on this world map– the kind we have all looked at throughout our lives— the color fill of separate countries lures the viewer into assuming homogeneity inside, heterogeneity outside, the borders of political territories. Indeed, we would require a very different map, one with a very different purpose, to see the rainbow of nations and mosaic of communities that lie inside the boundaries of a given country. Even then, we might only be able to imagine the rich cultural and linguistic variation that resides therein, visually uncapturable. It is perhaps only from our personal experiences that we would be able to know, deeply, that peoples inside the boundaries of a country are as diverse and resistant to generalization as those outside that country's boundaries, or that borders themselves do not confine or separate people as cultures migrate, interact and continually modify each other. And deeper still than the level of peoples, on our map, as students had observed, there were no *persons*—there was no way of capturing the diversity that lies inside a particular "culture" within a country, or inside a particular gathering of individuals within that culture. It is indeed such realizations that complicate any culture-learning mission, for "cultures" are in essence 'organizations of their diversity.'

Y es que cada individuo tiene una versión particular de todo aquello que le rodea, una versión particular de la cultura a la que decimos que pertenece (si es que se puede hablar de pertenecer a una única cultura), mostrándose en sus comportamientos o puntos de vista particulares divergen-

cias con respecto a lo que aparece como norma establecida en el discurso homogeneizador...Cada miembro tiene una versión personal de cómo funcionan las cosas en un determinado grupo y, de este modo, de su cultura. Lo que se presenta ante nosotros como la cultura de ese grupo no es otra cosa que una organización de la diversidad, de la heterogeneidad intragrupal inherente a toda sociedad humana. (García Castaño et al. 3)

While every map teaches something in its depiction of the planet, each also is inherently biased, conflictive and incomplete for more (or less) than simple geography, maps reflect theories, values, specific purposes—not "world" but "worldview." Maps, as culture products, are projections, each impelling outward a (one) "reality"—that of the beliefs, priorities and perspectives of their cartographers. Maps are interpretations that need to be interpreted (Smith).

It was this 'interpretation' that I sought from students in the next class session, when I removed the Mercator and replaced it with a Peters' Projection.[3] This map, devised by the German historian Arno Peters, surrenders conformity or accuracy of shape to portray all areas—countries, continents, oceans – according to their actual size, proportion and position in the world. On this map, students could see that the "South" is in reality over twice the size of the "North" and that those areas they had referred to as "Third World" actually *dominate* the planet in size. Hence, I asked them to explain what they meant by *tercer mundo*, a term of European origin:

1. *Es los países de África, de Latinoamérica, de Asia... algunos de Asia, no todos...No tienen desarrollo.*

2. *Quiere decir que son pobres. (?) ¿Pobres? Es no tener dinero. (?) Y no tienen educación. (?) Sí, porque si no se tiene educación no se puede trabajar. (?) Es necesario* ambition... *¿ambición? Aquí si no trabaja... si no se trabaja significa no tener ambición.(?) Ambición es ... determinación. (?) Cuando quieres ser mejor. (?) Para ser...proud ...¿cómo se dice? (?)* Proud *significa sentir muy bien...(?)...cuando haces bien... (?)... ¡Ah, no sé! No puedo describir. Es imposible.*

3. *No hay progreso. No se usa la tecnología... (?) Se encuentra la tecnología, pero no como nosotros. (?) Televisores, computadoras, teléfonos celulares, cosas así. (?) No es pobre no tener tecnología.. no... pero no es desarrollo.*

4. *Las personas no tienen cosas que tenemos... No se encuentran (?) Vida moderna... no se encuentra vida moderna. Cosas típicas...electrodomésticos. (?) Sí, quieren las cosas. Pero no tienen...(?) No todos tienen las cosas aquí, pero pueden...si trabajan.*

5. *No soy de Estados Unidos, pero para mí, pobreza no significa educación o tecnología. Significa que no hay agua, no hay comida, no hay medicina...y no hay...hope...espera...esperanza. Aquí no existe pobreza, realmente, no se ve pobreza en Estados Unidos.*

6. *Para mí, tercer mundo quiere decir que no tienen democracia, no tienen libertad. (?) Con*

democracia se puede votar. (?) Libertad para...hacer cosas, ganar dinero (?)...porque hay competition *y eso es bueno (?)* Competition... *¿cómo se dice? Cuando quieres ser mejor que la otra persona y ... por eso tratas mucho.*

7. *Eso es capitalismo... no democracia. Cada democracia no tiene capitalismo. No es necesario.*

8. *En esos países hay muchas peleas y no se puede hablar. Hay mucha discriminación. (?) Sí, aquí hay discriminación...un poco, pero no mucho ahora. (?) Hay mucha diversa...diversidad pero está tolerancia aquí....hay tolerancia (?) Porque la ley dice...se dice en la ley.*

9. *Es por qué todos quieren vivir aquí. (?) En Estados Unidos. (?) todos de otros países. (?) Sí... todos quieren el "sueño americano." (?) El sueño americano es .... hmmmm. No sé... se dice tener casa y coche y todo. Para mí es ser millonario.*

In these discussions (only fragments of which are reported here), students found themselves resorting constantly to several key threads that contribute to the fabric of U.S. individualistic culture: work, ambition, competition, pride. In their use of *ambición*, they wished to connote meanings of diligence and entrepreneurship that lie within the semantic field of their word "ambition" (certainly not the connotations of *codicia* or *avidez* that the Spanish word may evoke). "Competition" was a word for which they repeatedly sought translation in varied contexts. Yet, there is no easy way to package into Spanish such U.S.-meritocracy-based meanings as "peer competition," "grade competition," or acquisitive competition. Though times are changing and the corporate tentacles of *McMundo* are grabbing hold and digging deep, the semantic fields of *competitividad* and *competencia* tend to be much more confined in Hispanic cultures to the politics, sports and world-trade arenas. Moreover, while "competition" has enormously positive connotations in the U.S. mainstream, competitividad, especially amongst classmates, may evoke other sorts of images, such as those captured by two advisors of Madrid's *Consejería de Educación*.

El obscurantismo que ha dominado tantos años...ha dejado secuelas difíciles de erradicar, ha potenciado "ad nauseam" el individualismo y la competitividad fomentando un comportamiento inconscientemente insolidario...la utilización de los demás y el ver en los otros al enemigo o, cuando menos, al competidor molesto. (Chazarra Montiel and Cilleruelo López)

In short, in defining *tercer mundo*, students had revealed some of the structure of their own mental maps. They had identified some of the OECD's so-called indicators of development[4] in economic and social well being but, although living in a country that consumes nearly one-quarter of all fossil fuels and creates fifty percent of the world's solid waste (Karliner), they were unaware of those developmental indicators that lay in the areas of environmental sustainability and regeneration. Wrapped up in their use of the word "technology" was the idea of a clean, fresh, rapid road to "progress" and, in fact, absence of visible technology in its most ubiquitous U.S. forms was for them the most obvious sign of *tercermundismo*. "Poverty"—equated with absence of "U.S. lifestyle" and a low level of education (which in turn was related to lack of initiative or desire to work) was not perceived to exist on any large scale in the U.S.; yet, Karliner has noted that the U.S. now has the widest gap between rich and poor of any industrialized nation in the world. "Democracy" (not one of OECD's specific development indicators) was linked to freedom of voice, but was also confused with the capitalist system and freedom to "earn." And "discrimination" was viewed as a problem of the past in the U.S., where a newfound "tolerance of diversity" (as mandated by law) now beckons *todos* to climb our shores in search of the (it-is-what-I-want-it-to-be) "American Dream."

Indeed, the notion that "everyone wants what we have in the U.S." has surely echoed in every U.S. classroom and is in large part the foundation of many a cross-cultural conflict as more students travel abroad to mingle with foreign nationals. Data reported by González (this volume) indicate, in fact, that students' *patriotismo cerril* displayed on foreign soil can not only offend with its perceived air of arrogance but effectively impede self-awareness in intercultural communication. Implicit in the soulless labels "Third World" and "underdeveloped" is a certain worldview that societies all cherish the same things, share the same notions, pursue the same model. Perhaps the word "pride," whose meaning of resplendent self-actualization students found so impossible to convey, captures a different dimension of the term *desarrollo*—one best expressed in the words of the late Octavio Paz:

> *Desarrollo y subdesarrollo con conceptos exclusivamente socioeconómicos con los que se pretende medir a las sociedades como si fuesen realidades cuantitativas. Así no se toman en cuenta todos los aspectos rebeldes a la estadística y que son los que dan fisonomía a una sociedad: su cultura, su historia, su sensibilidad, su arte, sus mitos, su cocina, todo eso que antes se llamaba el alma o el genio de los pueblos, su manera propia de ser.*

To summarize our class discussions, I transcribed some of the comments students had made and asked them to separate each pair of statements in terms of "observation" or "interpretation" of observation, with the caveat that both might be considered observations, or both interpretations. The following is a fragment of the class handout, which was given in Spanish.

	Observation	Interpretation
Mexico is a territory separate from the U.S. Mexicans are not like "Americans."		
"Drugs" enter the U.S. from Colombia. Colombians are drug addicts.		
That person doesn't have a job. That person is lazy.		
That person does not have a computer. That person is poor.		
That city does not look modern. That city is underdeveloped.		
There is tolerance for diversity in that country. There are laws against discrimination in that country.		
That person does not seem competitive. That person has no pride.		

In the two class sessions of Intermediate learners sketched here, we used maps as metaphors to find our place—where and who we think ourselves to be, what we see and how we see it—and to begin to identify some of the pitfalls that would await our cross-cultural journey. Our "culture" lesson did not come attractively packaged in a pre-planned module; in fact, it was rather messy and unstructured-looking. It did not deal with "topics" one might typically associate with a classroom culture lesson (see Moore, this volume); in fact, it focused only on us as a class group and on our "truths" in their multiple versions. But to accept and appreciate that, as individuals and members of cultures, we carry inside our heads our own constructed realities – frames of awareness, ways of perceiving self and others, sets of assumptions and expectations, beliefs and values and meanings– is a quite important step in acknowledging the truth of different realities for which, rather than an attitude of absolutism, what is needed is a *theory of relativity*.

> There may be something we can call the truth if we keep it so simple it doesn't matter… Frankly, life is hard enough already without pretending it [life] is only one true thing. (Kaiser & Wood).

In these two class sessions, no effort was made to support or counter the views expressed by students. For learners to develop the capacity to analyze their individual perspectives as well as the values and norms that, to greater or lesser extents, have become institutionalized in their society, they must have the opportunity both to express these and to hear them expressed openly and unsanctioned. To criticize, counter or feign insult at what learners are, of their own volition, revealing about what they think will likely serve only to raise defensive shields and result in reticence, fabrication, or even hypercritical backlash at the other culture. If we take the whole culture mission seriously, view it in whole and as a long-term mission, our very first step is to plot where we are—where our learners are—in their awareness of self and attitudes toward others. Indeed, squelching expression at this or any other stage may send a message contrary to the one we are most intent on delivering:

> We cannot strip people of their common sense constructs or routine ways of seeing. They come to us as whole systems of patterned meanings and understandings. We can only try to understand, and to do so means starting with the way they think and building from there. (Trompenaars, et al. 19)

Bennett contends that intercultural sensitivity emerges through stages of personal growth ranging from denial, in which one's own culture is experienced as the only real one, to integration, the state in which one's experience of self is expanded to include the movement in and out of different cultural worldviews. He asserts that each stage indicates a particular cognitive structure that is expressed in certain kinds of attitudes and behaviors related to cultural differences and further, that as an individual progresses through different stages, different kinds of activities are better or worse suited to taking the learner to the subsequent stage. **Table 1** summarizes both the stages and the types of cross-cultural activity recommended at each.

Table 1. Bennett's Developmental Model of Intercultural Sensitivity		
Stage		**Activity**
Ethnocentrism		
Denial	Distance, disinterest, view of own culture as only real one	Exposure to difference
Defense	Denigration or resistance of difference as threatening; hyper-criticism; sense of own superiority	Building, but not overemphasizing cultural pride, self-esteem coupled with objective information about other culture
Minimization	Own cultural assumptions viewed as universal; expectation of sameness; difference interpreted from own perspective, trivialized or romanticized; insistence on correcting other's behavior	Discussion to place own behavior in cultural context; self-discovery; clarifying values, examining dilemmas from different viewpoint
Ethnorelativism		
Acceptance	One's own acknowledged as one perspective; Notice of profound differences; curiosity, respectfulness. Acceptance of own and other worldview; values and assumptions seen as creative processes	Focus on behaviors relative to perspectives; cross-cultural simulations to improve relations
Adaptation	Ability to experience or imagine other cultural reality and understand another perspective; attitudes and skills to function in another cultural frame of reference; willingness to adapt to another style	Intensive or prolonged real-life interaction; fostering empathy without betraying cultural roots
Integration	Ability to analyze situations from different cultural perspective, shift cultural context and self –awareness to exercise choice, engage in on-going creation of worldview that is not dependent upon a single culture perspective	

According to this model, in the Intermediate classroom depicted here, learners' stages of inter-cultural sensitivity ranged from the *ethnocentric* defense stage to the *ethnorelative* acceptance stage, thus suggesting types of culture-learning tasks that would focus on self-awareness and values reflec-tion in their own culture while providing rich information and opportunities for examining different viewpoints of other cultures. It should be noted that models such as Bennett's, however, cannot specifi-cally prescribe what needs to take place in the classroom. Nor can such models truly capture a learner's "cognitive framework" for cross-cultural understanding as, in truth, individuals move up and down in their stages of intercultural sensitivity with the encounter of each novel experience. Especially given the myriad and very distinct cultures of the Hispanic world, a learner may achieve the "acceptance stage" in interacting with one, yet find herself at the "defense stage" in confronting another.

As development of a cross-cultural mind is ongoing and never-ending, what takes place in the classroom can only be considered priming for the real events of intercultural encounters. Trompenaars and colleague remind us that culture is not a physical substance, a set of formulae or a finite body of knowledge. Culture "is made by people interacting, and at the same time determining further interaction" (24) and thus: "It is our belief that you can never understand other cultures…it is impossible to ever completely understand even people of your own culture" (1). Such a realiza-tion, rather than provoke defeatism, should serve to energize us with the importance of the culture-teaching mission and, rather than deter our efforts, inspire us to go as far as we can in purposeful and individually meaningful activity. To respect the complexity of culture teaching yet not be daunted by it constitutes a tremendous challenge, one that requires dedication and planning. As Lessard-Clouston advises, a laissez-faire approach is not adequate—just as we are intentional in our grammar instruction, we must also be systematic about our culture teaching.

In this chapter, we will look at the many kinds of maps that exist to aid (or derail) our impor-tant culture-teaching mission. Some of these are "pocket maps" that attempt to harness and encap-sulate culture for ease of delivery, making us feel immediately smarter without provoking the slightest internal change. Others of these maps are teacher maps, intended to guide us in our very difficult journey as lesson-planners and curriculum-developers; yet, as with all maps, their value lies only in what we feed into them in interpretation and use. And still others of these are perceptual maps that aim to expose the similar and different ways people see and make sense of the world; their value will lie in how we use them not to stereotype communities of people, but to deepen awareness of our own perspectives and, ultimately, to expand *intercultural* discourse. Along the way, we will look at how, as Kramsch says, we can not only teach language *and* culture, but language *as* culture. The question of language *or* culture, however, is simply no longer an option for, as one student puts it:

> This is what I want to learn—what it feels like to be someone else (even though I know I can never feel that exactly) and what we look like to others and why. I really want to understand and I know that's going to take knowing a lot more about myself than I do, than I think I do. I know it will take forever. (Kara, Intermediate Spanish student)

The Map vs. the Territory: Pocket Guides and Thin Descriptions

When map-makers hit just the main points—ignoring all the tiny twists and turns of a coast-line, for example—they call it generalization (Smith) and for some non-navigational purposes a generalized view of the terrain may be appropriate or even precisely what is required. Like these generalized maps, however, attempts to describe a culture – any culture– in terms of general territory, will not serve the needs of our students as intercultural navigators. Such "culture maps" abound in tourist guidebooks and executive-training manuals and typically consist of handy phrases accompanied by brief sketches of customs and strikingly different behaviors. They also, unfortunately, tend to characterize current foreign language textbooks and, to a great extent, foreign-language classrooms (see Moore, this volume). The following is one such culture map of Mexico, for example, taken from a website for students of International Studies. It is prefaced by the admonition that "all cultures have variability within them, perhaps even more than the differences between them." Indeed, as Octavio Paz has said of this same Mexico:

> ...*lo español no está menos vivo en México que lo indio. En nada parecen lo indio y lo español salvo en la complejidad: lo indio es una pluralidad de culturas y sociedades y lo mismo ocurre con lo español...*

MEXICO[5]

Social Customs

Greetings customarily include smiles, nod of the head and\or handshake. Close male friends may embrace; women embrace and kiss the cheek. Common greetings are *¡Buenos días!* (Good morning), *¿Cómo está?* (How are you?), and the casual *¡Hola!* (Hello).

Unannounced visits are common, and hospitality is welcomed and includes refreshments (which would be rude to refuse). When eating, keep both hands above the table. Gifts are not customary in exchange for hospitality, but may be appreciated. Avoid flowers that are yellow (symbolic of death for some classes), red (cast spells), and white (cancel spells).

Appropriate conversational topics include art, parks, museums, fashion, travel, and weather. Avoid unpleasant topics such as the Mexican-American War and illegal aliens. Relationships are important and one may stop for a conversation even if it means being late for an appointment. The theme of death is common and celebrated, and may seem unusual to Americans.

Most business meetings occur during the two to three hour lunch break, but relationships are built before business begins. *Respeto* (respect) is important and may involve a mixture of fair play, democratic spirit, power pressure, and love-hate affections. Status is important (social, age, class), and you may be told what makes you happy rather than objective facts.

The gesture for "no" is shown by extending the index finger with palm outward and shaking the hand side to side. Items should not be tossed to a person, but handed. Sneezing is responded to by *¡Salud!* (Good health). Only an animal's height is shown using the whole hand; use the index finger.

But what "Mexico" is this depicted here? Assuming we could even consider such a vast, lush and incredibly diverse terrain to hold one homogenous culture, it is easy to see how this type of map would cast a rather freakish image of it. The random, decontextualized mix of *saludos*, spells and sneezes presents not Mexico itself, but an imaginary land, a hybrid "culture" construed from the most striking strangeness. Is this information wrong? Yes and no. Yes, for example, one may greet with *¡Hola!* and *Buenos días, ¿cómo está?* And, in fact, this is where the issue of *saludos* may even be left in our textbooks and classrooms. Indeed, we have in this information, some icons of a short-hand map—if we know the territory in which they are referenced, we can perhaps navigate certain rudimentary situations as a passing tourist—perhaps. But what happens if we do not know the "lay of the land?" Are we not likely to assume the environment of our own culture, simply superimposing these Spanish-language icons upon it?

There are, in this example, some issues that require reflection of every Spanish teacher: When we claim to teach culture in our classrooms, are we really teaching culture, or are we merely disseminating a map—one so referenced to our own ways that difference looms monstrously and inexplicably large, one that joins and compacts parts of many unique cultures under the label "Hispanic," one that projects more of its cartographer than of the authentic territory? Throughout the past few decades, it has been popular to condemn foreign language textbooks for just such treatment of culture as that represented here in the "Mexico culture" map for, in truth, we would want our textbooks to do it all, to give us the "language and culture of the Hispanic world" in 460 attractive, colorful pages. Yet, if textbook publishers' readings of teacher-consumer surveys are correct, the cry is that there not be "too much culture" mixed into "language" lessons, because there is "not enough time for both." It would appear that we want "culture" extricated from language and delivered as a side dish, so that we know where it is and may take it or leave it as time and interest permit. Publishers, hence, convey to authors this teacher perspective: that "culture" must be separate, brief and unobtrusive, for change is too risky when the old formula sells. The fact is that even the best textbook can only be a springboard. Teaching is not the textbook's job—it is ours, and if such a thing as "Hispanic culture" existed and if, additionally, it were no more than a set of behavioral inventories, our culture-teaching job would be easy indeed. Yet, as Firth reminds us, in "culture" we are dealing with a massively encompassing and complex term comparable to such concepts as gravity in physics, disease in medicine, or evolution in biology.

Learning a new territory involves raising issues beyond the basic "what to say and do" generalities to sensitize learners to phenomena that may have no coordinates on their mental maps, may lie outside the perceptual field of their own culture's reality. Often overlooked in our introductory Spanish lesson on greetings, for example, are such things as *where* does one greet, and *whom* does one greet, and *why* does one greet? What is implicitly communicated by a particular greeting, done in a particular way, between two particular people in a particular context of a particular culture? How is the greeting used to signal in-group status or power distance in both social and business contexts? [See García, this volume.] How does one greet "in passing," and what is the proximity in standing face to face? How important are greetings in general, what role do they play, and what assumptions and expectations are packaged into them in particular interactions? In this regard, even being a member of the Spanish-speaking world does not ensure comfortable navigation through its multitude of cultures, as the following webchat comment of a Spaniard in Argentina illustrates:[6]

> *Todo es diferente, la ciudad, la gente, incluso el idioma. Y aunque hablamos la misma lengua, existen muchísimas diferencias, no sólo en ciertas palabras o frases, sino también en la entonación. Hay veces en las que me hablan y no entiendo nada. Lo mismo me pasa al saludar, es decir, dar un beso en vez de dos ...ya me he quedado más de una vez con la cara puesta sin saber qué hacer...*

Indeed, just on the issue of whom to greet, data collected by González (this volume) indicate that U.S. students' apparent lack of attention to the *saludo* on entering the home was a primary source of irritation to their Spanish host families. In the U.S., for example, one enters an office, a store, a restaurant, with a certain purposeful tunnel vision and moves directly toward a specific goal—to consult with a person, to make a particular purchase, to seat oneself at a table. Greeting and leave-taking are not commonly part of the mental script for these occasions. Greeting, in fact, may not be perceived as having a critical role in many contexts of our students' lives, even in their own homes. In how many of the following situations, for example, would our students say they always greet? In which of these might it almost never occur to them to greet? (The same questions may be asked of leave-taking.)

_____ your family members immediately on entering the house, before doing anything else.
_____ your professors when you/they enter the classroom
_____ the store clerk on entering a small shop
_____ the waiter in a restaurant
_____ the person who answers the phone when you are calling for someone else.
_____ at the beginning of a letter or email message
_____ the person you stop on the street when you ask directions
_____ the host of a party as soon as you enter
_____ all other guests at a party
_____ the people in the waiting room of an office
_____ the others in the elevator
_____ the person you sit next to on the plane, train, metro or bus
_____ an acquaintance you pass on the street
_____ a taxi driver
_____ your Spanish profesor when s/he greets you

In an Intermediate Spanish class of twenty-eight students (to which this survey was delivered in Spanish), only "the host of a party" was marked by some students as an always-greet case. In terms of family-member greeting, students remarked 'I usually go straight to the refrigerator,' or 'I don't have to greet them—they're my family.' Whom would they almost never greet? Students marked professors ('they would think I'm brown-nosing'), store clerks ('I don't know them'), flight companions ('they'll think I want to talk'), person who answers the phone ('I just say, is so-and-so there, but I guess that's kind of rude'), and waiting-room strangers ('that would really be impolite, I think; they'd think I was strange'). The following student comments perhaps capture a sense of the meaning of greetings for youth in U.S. mainstream culture as residing in an individual choice that depends on factors of familiarity, desire to engage, and perceived "need."

I do not typically greet people I don't know.

If I greet someone, it may be perceived as an intrusion or invasion of their privacy.

If I greet someone it signals to them that I want to converse with them.

I do not need to greet my family because they're my family and I don't need to be polite.

When you see someone everyday, you don't need to greet them.

Why ask someone "How are you?" if I'm not really interested in their answer?

I only usually greet people who greet me first.

I only greet strangers I want to meet or get to know.

Having examined their own greeting habits and implicit meanings, students became alert to the possible, indeed probable, existence of other sets of behaviors and meanings in other cultures. They were then asked to use the Internet to gain some sense of norms for greeting in the Hispanic world. The following, excerpted from one such website students identified for Spain, reveals *saludos* embedded in a quite different meaning network—one of social obligation, "upbringing," and respect for hierarchy of authority in which *un saludo vale mucho más de lo que nos cuesta* [7]

> • *Quien ve primero debe saludar primero: Por ejemplo, si ves a un amigo tuyo que no te ha visto por ir despistado, eres tú quien debe saludar.*
>
> • *Quien llega a un sitio público debe saludar a quien está. Si entras en una tienda, debes saludar a la gente que está allí. En parte para que el dependiente note tu presencia y te atienda, en parte por educación. Esto no es aplicable si llegas a casa de alguien. En este caso seríais los dos quien deberíais saludaros primero. Tanto el invitado como el anfitrión.*
>
> • *Quien está en movimiento debe saludar a quien está parado. Si andando por la calle, pasas al lado de un bordillo en el cual está sentado un amigo tuyo, debes saludar tú.*
>
> • *La persona superior en el rango jerárquico es quién debe saludar primero a su subordinado, si lo considera oportuno. El jefe es quien suele saludar a su empleado, sobre todo cuando le acaba de conocer.*

Having glimpsed such fragments of different cultural-meaning frameworks, students were asked how they, themselves, might be perceived in the Hispanic world were they to follow their own culture's "rules" for greeting. An essay from the Canarias newspaper *El Día Digital*, excerpted here, lent a Spanish perspective to this discussion.[8]

> *Hace pocos días tomé un taxi. Al subirme al mismo, dije, como es normal en todo caballero que se estime un poco, «buenos días». Pero el «driver», o conductor, no se inmutó ... Debe ser de los «ensimismados», pensé para mis adentros. Y como no decía nada, le rogué me llevara a Correos y Telégrafos. Tampoco hizo el menor comentario a esta sugerencia o ruego mío. Seguía imperturbable. Como cada vez la sociedad, en una plausible iniciativa, busca una adecuada salida laboral para los disminuidos físicos, pensé si se trataría de un mudo que había logrado acceder a un puesto de conductor de taxi. Y juro que me quedé en la duda, pues, al llegar a destino, como vi en el taxímetro lo que valía la carrera, le di lo justo y bajé sin decir ni pío, para no violentarlo psíquicamente, si en verdad era un impedido del habla.*

Authentic voices such as these, now available in astounding array via the Internet, not only allow us to hear another perspective, but to join in on the intercultural dialog through a multitude of chat sites (see, for example, Katz; Lee). Use of these voices in the classroom, however, must be accompanied by some caveats: 1) Discrete practices vary greatly across cultures, even within the same country, so that what may be true in Madrid may not hold in Barcelona or Sevilla, for example, or may even be unheard of in a Spanish *aldea*; 2) just as students saw the variation amongst themselves in their greeting habits, many voices are required to express a "norm;" one voice may reflect merely one person's own interpretation or experience; 3) descriptions of norm, even out of the mouths of so-called "natives," do not tell the full story, as some notions or practices may be considered so assumed within the cultural community that they do not even merit attention; and 4) to whom the voice is speaking will also color the information, as when educating other groups to the ways of our own group, we will tend to represent ourselves more homogeneously.

> *Es obvio que a la hora de contarle a "otro" cómo somos "nosotros" utilizamos una serie de referencias que nos definen homogeneizándonos, pero no utilizaríamos estas mismas referencias para definirnos a nosotros mismos... cuando nos definimos como grupo frente a otro grupo no invocamos las diferencias que existen en el seno del "nosotros" y que generan la diversidad dentro de él, sino, por el contrario, invocamos las similitudes que nos aproximan.*(García Castaño, et al. 3)

Firth likens describing a culture to describing the (incredibly complex) 'grammar' of a language in that both are in essence mental realities. However, more than a mental reality, culture is constituted by social action; more than a grammar, a language is the process through which membership in a discourse community is mediated (Kramsch) and grammar is simply a map of this language's topography: "Like road signs, grammatical structures take on meaning only if they are situated in context in connected discourse" (Adaire Hauck & Cumo-Johanssen 37). While textbook offerings provide a quite ample array of such "linguistic maps," the cultural context of their use remains relatively uncharted. Yet, just as we cannot learn language from verb wheels and dictionaries, we cannot learn culture from capsules. In fact, contends Edward Hall, "there is no way to teach culture in the same way that language is taught" (48). We need, in Geertz' words, "thick" descriptions (6).

Charting the Course: The Need for Depth Perception

Certainly one of the aims of the *National Standards for Foreign Language Learning* was that of lending direction to the teaching of culture in our language classrooms in the belief that "whether the goal is Communication, Connections, Comparisons or Communities, Cultures are the recurring subtext" (Schwartz & Kavanaugh 99). The *Standards* are, in one sense, a type of map, in that they project the consensus of professional leadership regarding the perspectives and priorities of the FL teaching enterprise. However, like any map, the value of the *Standards* lies not in their existence, but in their interpretation and creative use. And, like any map, their "fiction" lies in literal translation and mechanical application.

The *Standards* define "communication" as "knowing how, when, and why to say what to whom" and, in their Executive Summary further state that students "cannot truly master the language until they have also mastered the cultural contexts in which the language occurs." Yet, as García (this volume) illustrates, language does not simply "occur"—it is purposefully and imperfectly used by people in what is largely a hit-and-miss effort to strike the chords of shared meaning. And in this undertaking, agreement and consensus are not pre-existent but must be repeatedly renegotiated. Indeed, language cannot be "mastered" in any real sense as, even in our own language, even amongst those of our own culture, and even within our very families we often "can't find the words;" we misspeak, misconstrue, misjudge actions, misread intentions and situations, mismatch discourse systems. Lest we interpret too literally the sense of the Standards then, the "contexts" of our language use —the how, when, why, what and to whom of it—are not identifiable 'givens' that can be inventoried, taught, and mimicked by our learners. As Geertz reminds us:

> We are not, or at least I am not, seeking either to become natives (a compromised word in any case) or to mimic them. Only romantics or spies would seem to find point in that. We are seeking, in the widened sense of the term in which it encompasses very much more than talk, to converse with them, a matter a great deal more difficult, and not only with strangers, than is commonly recognized. If speaking *for* someone else seems to be a mysterious process... that may be because speaking *to* someone does not seem mysterious enough (13-14).

"Communication" is much more than language; it is much more than tone of delivery, body movement, or territorial behavior; and it is much more than "knowing." Communication is about doing and, in doing, expanding one's vision of the world and enlarging the universe of human discourse. Indeed, as Scollon & Scollon remind us, cultures do not talk to each other, individuals do. And as García illustrates (this volume), the assumptions that each individual brings to an encounter, even to a supposedly intracultural encounter, come not only from different readings of shared cultural experiences but from unique personal experiences as well; thus, each context itself is quite singular. As Foucault puts it, "...a statement is always an event that neither the language... nor the meaning can quite exhaust...like every event, it is unique, yet subject to repetition, transformation, and reactivation... it is linked not only to the situations that provoke it, and the consequences it gives rise to, but...to the statements that precede and follow it (27). With this in mind, we might look at the how, when, why, what, and to whom of intercultural communication, not as a teachable set of contexts, but rather as the dimensions of an eternal process of way-finding. As we sail the Cs of the Standards, the big mistake that awaits a literal map-reading is that of viewing them as discrete plottings and in so doing, failing to see their depth, their vastness, their dynamic interdependence.

The "C" of Connections, for example, may be considered the mother of all five Cs. Far more than a "unit" on currency conversion that integrates math into language learning, interdisciplinary is what life is really all about—or was, before we "disciplined" it into study compartments. As everything we do in life is multidisciplinary, the FL classroom is, or should be, the place where real life is pondered and enacted. In fact, there is no way to explore a culture without "connecting" to what people do and how they communicate as they do it – in banks as they balance accounts or solicit loans; in jobs as they apply and interview, create and sell products and services, or predict the effect of weather conditions on the market of crops; in their homes as they plan healthy meals, make repairs, balance checkbooks, discuss the news, resolve conflicts; in their stores as they assess quality and negotiate purchases. Science, math, philosophy, psychology, ecology, history, economics—these are the things people talk about, participate in, every day of their lives throughout the world. Connecting to others in this world via the classroom means not simply practicing our own culture's version of these things through another culture's language, but seeing and hearing how others do them, why, when, how and with whom. Indeed, without connection, there is no communication. But "Connection" is not just interdisciplinary, it is also intradisciplinary—in our own classrooms it is connecting culture-learnings to expand and deepen the other-culture framework; it is connecting the grammar and vocabulary of the typical classroom menu to the discourses of shared meaning systems. And connection is both internal and external: We connect to other ways of perceiving and expressing the world by connecting to ourselves in heightened personal awareness.

Likewise, the meaning of "Community" is not captured merely "by getting out into it" through museum trips, native-speaker interviews, ethnographic projects and fieldwork data-collection—though these are enormously beneficial learning experiences. "Community" is not only a thing or a place; it is also a feeling of group, a sense of membership, an engagement in shared activity. In this regard, our classrooms, as learning communities, can present a powerful lesson. Through a process of open inquiry and collaboration, students build awareness not only of values and norms that join them in their own various communities of peers, but of the *range of variation* that exists within these communities as part of the dynamic nature of groups of individuals. The sharing of beliefs and points of view among classmates in regard to their own culture illustrates that no community is monolithic and that absolute consensus is not a requirement of membership. Outside the classroom, the Internet, via chat rooms and e-mail strings (Haas and Reardon; Katz; Lee) allows connection to other communities to form new cross-cultural "cyberlands" with unique discourse characteristics. Indeed, as Heusinkveld illustrates through song (this volume), one of the first culture lessons to be discovered is that of why and how people join in communities, how community is evoked and expressed, and how deeply felt is its need. As we will see in the sections that follow, deeply embedded in one's culture and personal experience is a notion of what community is, what it means to its members, and how it is achieved. While communities are our ties to others, their sense is also, cross-culturally, one of the greatest sources of our confusion, particularly in our quest to gain understanding of the Hispanic world.

Indeed, it is really only through communities of perspectives and values and belief systems that the C of "Comparisons" can be navigated at all. If we attempt to compare cultures at the level of discrete behaviors and observable customs, the only sense-making framework available to our learners will be that of their own culture, with the result that the other culture's behaviors will simply defy sense. After all, how does one reconcile a behavior substantially deviant from the only known norm without judging it as "weird," "wrong," "unethical," "uncultured," "corrupt" "antiquated" –in short, "un-American?" But cultures don't randomly select behaviors from a universal menu of options (let alone a U.S.-decreed menu); rather, we do what we do the way we learned to do it, the way it is logical to us to do it, the way we prefer to do it, and the way it fits our perspective of the world to do it. Our behaviors may reflect deep, unquestioned beliefs, or they may reflect our culture's compromise solution in the conflict between powerful values, but they will always make sense to us, within our own system. The U.S. "custom" of eating breakfast or lunch in the car (not to mention that that lunch is some type of *"comida chatarra"*) will undoubtedly strike others as "wrong," "uncultured," "silly," or even "barbaric," but it makes perfect sense to us —it represents our solution; it fits the reality we have constructed. As we will see in the final section of this chapter, guiding students to construct another view of the world and a different sense of sense-making to see behaviors as (mostly subconscious) expressions of a different but eminently logical reality is what the notion of "context" is all about.

Rather than interpret the *Standards* as goals or destinations, perhaps we might see them as the texture of our instructional terrain. The *Standards* can indeed guide us to see the dimensions of the culture-teaching mission we embrace as language teachers, as an internal map to aid us in widening our own perspective as teachers. In this sense, then, rather than start with the question of 'How can I get that Standard in?' we might start with the voice of a community and ask ourselves what we can do to help learners really hear this voice and connect to both its global and local message. To approach culture study through the realness of its community of members as they communicate among themselves is to approach learning as rich, connected and deeply felt experiences.

Products and Practices: The Signposts of the Territory

While "Culture" is thus implicit in the Cs of Communication, Communities, Connection and Comparison of the *Standards*, it also stands as a separate component, defined through the meaningful interdependence of three concepts: perspectives, practices and products. Of these, "products" best matches what Trompenaars and colleague refer to as the explicit or symbolic culture, the "first layer of the onion":

> What is your first impression of Burundi culture once you enter the airport? It is not "what a nice set of values these people have," or even "don't they have an interesting shared system of meaning." It is the concrete, observable things like language, food or dress. Culture

comes in layers, like an onion. To understand it you have to unpeel it layer by layer. On the outer layer are the products of the culture…These are expressions of deeper values and norms in a society that are not directly visible. (6)

Products are all that a culture conceives, creates or uses to mediate activity, and hence may be material (foods, transportation, fashion, technology, shrines, games, music, art, literature) or abstract (rules, laws, organizational structures). But, like the mother-product language, all products are codified; they arise from and are embedded in their culture's own distinctive "web of significance" (Geertz 5). Therefore, what we see on the surface will tell us little about its essence, its shared meaning within its own community of understanding. Products, in their constant social processes of construction, consumption and negotiation, serve to connect humans to each other within their culture's reality. Indeed, even though we may casually remark that a person is a "product" of his or her culture, we recognize that persons are not merely products of a culture, but also its constructive participants, "actively creating a world that is always in the process of creating them" (Gover & Conway). Foreign eyes on products, however, are quite apt to deceive in a number of ways, all attributable to a mismatch of some sort between the "other's" product and their own frame of reference: 1) misinterpreting the *unfamiliar* in what they see: "There is so much overcrowding here yet so much wasted space in these plazas" or "people are so poor, yet look at the gold on the walls of their churches;" 2) misinterpreting the *familiar* in what they see: "Mexicans can't get enough of our Wal-Marts—they're everywhere;" 3) misinterpreting what they *expect* to see but don't: "My host family must have been sort of poor—they didn't even have a car;" and 4) the most insidious trap of all: being *unable to see* what their own culture has not trained them to see.

Certainly our teaching cannot stop at the product layer of a culture without subjecting our learners to these perceptual traps and to the unfortunate judgments that will arise as they are forced to make sense using the only sense-making system they have. Moreover, learners must be sensitized to the observation/interpretation process itself, to become alert to the fact that they will—consciously or subconsciously—assign meaning to all that they witness or experience, and that "each opinion we voice regarding explicit culture usually says more about where we came from than about the community we are judging" (Trompenaars, et al. 21). In this regard, we can often learn a great deal about others through their impressions and interpretations of our own culture's products—a simple web search for the word *hamburguesa*, for example, in exposing how others see and attach meaning to this U.S. "delicacy," not only opens our eyes to ourselves but reveals much of the values and lifestyles of the outside observer.[9]

Food is, in fact, one of the most obvious and important of all cultural products, as it reaches into all aspects of human life. Indeed, Lévi-Strauss uses cooking as a metaphor for the way the 'raw' images of nature are 'cooked' in culture so that they may be used as part of a symbolic system. Weismantel figures food as the very core of our identity:

It is not only a physiological truism that we are what we eat; what we eat and how we eat it also defines us as social beings. To cook is to speak and to mean, as well as to make and to do. (6)

But if in our FL classes we leave the study of this valuable cultural product at the level of tasting and cooking demonstrations (or "food days," as Moore observes, this volume), we ignore its potential as an entrée into the complex web of significance in which it is embedded. Just at the level of product, "food" offers lessons in geography, economics, commerce, politics, religion, health and medicine, and so on; our foods reveal our culture's meanings of such notions as time, space, aging, gender, beauty, self-image, status, poverty and wealth, human relationships, individualness, nature; the aromas of certain foods evoke memories, images, faces, intense emotions; food is both social bond and ostracism, intimate words and political discourse. The foods we eat, in fact, say much about our norms of right and wrong and our values of good and bad, for what is "food" to us also raises the question of what is *not* food, what violates a culture's learned sensibilities or crosses the line of one's identity. The U.S. food industry, for example, invests huge sums in changing food images and disguising food origins, processing and packaging meat to make it look less like dead animals. Weismantel notes that foods may be highly charged symbols of ethnicity, citing among Ecuadorians the stigmatization of certain indigenous foods as "indian" and hence "unfit for consumption by non-indians" (9). So intimately tied to identity are the foods one eats that, as Mintz observes, "people who eat strikingly different foods or similar foods in strikingly different ways are thought to be strikingly different, perhaps even less than human" (3). Indeed, González points out (this volume) that U.S. students' own assumptions about food can often be a great source of cross-cultural conflict, not only in students' quest for a 'decent hamburger' overseas, but in terms of hosts' impressions of students' reaction toward table offerings. Yet, Moore (this volume) reveals that food may be a source of conflict in our FL classrooms as well—an increasingly delicate topic in a culture preoccupied with body image and in which fifty-five percent of the over-twenty population may be considered overweight or obese by "U.S. standards" (Schlosser).

How might we build both self- and other-awareness through analysis of what a culture consumes? The activity progression that follows was used with a class of Intermediate learners to begin examination of food as culture-product. Phase I was that of *self-awareness*—looking at our own patterns of consumption with an eye toward notions of taste, preference, health and lifestyle, to ultimately view the connectedness of products in practice within our own community of values. [All activities were conducted entirely in Spanish, with linguistic focus on 1) review of *gustar, encantar* and like verbs (*apetecer, volver loco, dar asco*, etc.) and 2) use of present subjunctive.]

Self awareness: *Dime qué comes y te diré quién eres.*

Step 1: Las preferencias. We began by brainstorming "favorite foods" as a class, with each student contributing at least two items to the chalkboard list [*a mí me gusta(n)/encanta(n)*]. Students were then called on to summarize class preferences [*Nos gusta(n) más... a dos les gusta(n)...*].

Step 2: La pirámide. To generate and expand vocabulary, students were shown the USDA food pyramid on transparency (available on www) and asked to brainstorm as many foods as they could in each category.

Step 3: El paladar. To explore the issue of 'taste' as very much a combination of cultural "programming" and individual experiences and preferences, students were asked to name (or describe through circumlocution) the "weirdest" food they had ever eaten and to explain the circumstances of its consumption a) what does it taste like (*Sabe a…*)/ smell like (*Huele a…*)/ look like, feel like, etc.? b) why did they eat it and how did trying it make them feel about themselves? c) would they recommend others try it and why (*[No] recomiendo que prueben…porque…*). Foods were recorded on transparency with whole class tallies of how many students had tried each. On a separate transparency, we then brainstormed foods students thought they would never try and on a grid checked the reason: 1) was the food unhealthy or dangerous, or 2) did it violate a law or a personal belief, or 3) did it evoke a stereotype, or 4) was it something that their culture does not associate with eating? Summary discussion focused on why we consider some foods "normal" and others "bastante raros"

Step 4: Los patrones. For homework, students listed (truthfully) the actual foods they'd consumed (meals and snacks) within the last 2 days, divided by day. For each dish or food item, they were to indicate how it was prepared (*frito, asado, en microondas,* etc.) and, whenever possible, list ingredients. They were told their assignments would be checked individually, but that they were not to put their names on the paper.

Step 5: Mil preguntas. Students used their food consumption inventories prepared as homework to find out what they had in common with other classmates: Working in pairs, they analyzed their inventories to come up with at least five good survey questions to interview classmates, using a closed-survey format. For example: In a typical week I… a) never; b) once; c) two or three times; d) four or more times. They were advised to keep their questions as global as possible, so as to generate cultural patterns rather than specific food-item inventories. Interviewers then rejoined their partners to compile their data and report back to class with survey responses expressed in percentages (e.g. *Un 50% dice que…*). As they reported, their survey questions were recorded on the board for subsequent use in whole class tallying. This procedure allowed students to create their own avenues of inquiry rather than be confined to an instructor-conceived list.

Step 6: Los perfiles. Students were then asked to circulate their (anonymous) food-consumption inventories (homework papers) by a continued-passing routine (one receives and passes to another who receives and passes to another until time is called) to ensure anonymity. With the USDA pyramid again posted on transparency, students were to create a pyramid-profile for the classmate whose inventory they received. As students reported back, we compiled the data for the class on transparency by tallying beside each pyramid section the number of student rankings. As they reported, students were also required to make healthier recommendations to their anonymous peers (*A esta persona le sugiero/aconsejo que… incluya /disminuya/ mejore/ tome más/ menos…*). [Since nutritionists relate food colors to balanced diet, this could also be done with colors: *Le aconsejo que tome más alimentos* *verdes y menos alimentos...*] We then devised a "food pyramid" that reflected the eating habits of the entire class. The class profile looked something like **Table 2**, with descending levels indicating more frequent consumption.

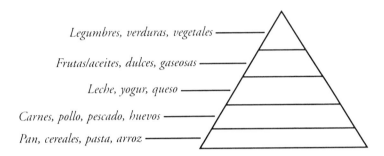

Approaching the collection of data in this way, from the (anonymous) individual outward, allowed students to maintain their own sense of uniqueness without having their "particulars" brought to full class attention; at the same time, it allowed the class to experience the variation that exists even within their own group, as each individual indirectly contributed to the class composite. Their first observation of the group profile was that it did not correspond to that of the USDA recommendations, being a diet especially slim in the areas of fruits and vegetables and heavily dependent on a mixture of grains and animal products. And the question posed to them was *¿por qué?* To show how products are only the tip of a culture's iceberg and that underneath the explicit product everything is connected and makes sense, students were asked to brainstorm clause contributions to a series of *"frases infinitas"* in which they could either expand on or explain a previous clause:

> **Comemos lo que comemos**... *porque no hay tiempo... y porque el horario es difícil... y porque no vivimos en casa ... y no hay tiempo porque algunos vivimos lejos y hay mucho tráfico... y hay mucho tráfico porque ...*

Class discussion revealed how our eating patterns are squeezed into a culture of cars, suburbs, independent lifestyle and hurried schedules. Students noted that what they consume depends primarily on *time* available in one's schedule, but also on other factors such as *distance* (traffic, being away from home), *cost* ("Cheap meals don't often include fruits and vegetables;" "McDonald's has salads—but they just call them salads") and *convenience/portability* ("It's easier to just pick up something and go somewhere to study—or watch TV"). All four factors combined to make fast food and quick foods (canned, packaged, frozen-microwaveable) the most popular options. Indeed, Schlosser estimates that in the year 2000 Americans spent more than 110 billion dollars on fast food; on any given day in the United States, about one-quarter of the adult population visits a fast-food restaurant; and every month, more than ninety percent of U.S. children eat at McDonald's. Schlosser indicates that Americans now spend more money on fast food than on higher education, personal computers, computer software, or new cars; they spend more on fast food than on movies, books, magazines, newspapers, videos, and recorded music combined. Indeed, Goldberg notes that the auto-only design of U.S. urban and suburban areas "locks even the most health-minded parent into a car culture that leans on fast-food meals and erases exercise from daily life" (3).

Students, for the most part, agreed that they did not think too much about what they ate ('I just eat what's there'), with some adding that they went where the portions were the biggest for the lowest price—the main ideas was to 'fill up' ("...*hasta que no pueda comer más*"). Most also conceded that they do not eat fixed meals at regular times ('I'm always hungry, but I don't eat lunch; I eat a snack in class;' 'sometimes I eat at 5:00 pm and sometimes at 11:00 pm—it depends'). Some remarked that hunger was not always the prime motivation—they ate when they were 'bored' or 'depressed.' According to a 1997 study conducted by *Prevention* magazine, these practices seem to abound in the U.S., where fifty-four percent of consumers say they "clean their plates" even when full; thirty-eight percent dine even if they do not feel hungry; nineteen percent report that they eat until they are "stuffed"; and approximately one-third of Americans eat out of sheer boredom.[11]

Having looked at the reasons behind our food products and at the web of practices and other products that seem to institutionalize them, we turned our attention to the results of our habits of consumption, using the same *frase infinita* technique, but this time with *por eso* instead of *porque*. In discussing the consequences of their tray-and-paper dining habits, students volunteered 'that's why we're so fat in this country,' 'that's why we spend so much on exercise machinery,' 'that's why we're always dieting,' and so on. Questioned as to why this culture obsesses about diets and thinness while seeming to promote the opposite through fast-food chains on every corner, students offered a number of theories from 'because you always want what you can't have' to 'thin is good because it shows discipline' to the rather intriguing 'thin is good because it shows you're too busy to eat.' The role of food in U.S. culture is indeed a rather conflicted one. To conclude this self-awareness phase of their analysis, a two-pronged reflective essay question was posed—in part directed to the individual and in part directed to the institutionalized culture level: 1) How can you, personally, improve your diet? and 2) If you could change one aspect of your society or U.S. lifestyle that would be most beneficial to you in this regard, what would it be?

Exposing and exploring their own concept of food-as-product—how what we eat is intrinsically connected to the how and why of it—opened the door to the idea that other cultures may have different concepts of food-as-product. Students were shown two other nutritional pyramids: 1) *la pirámide latinoamericana* and 2) *la pirámide mediterránea*,[11] both of which have been acknowledged by nutritionists to be not only healthier than that of the USDA, but more authentic: While the USDA pyramid is theoretical and, as some analysts note, possibly compromised by the politics of dairy and meat industries, both the Latin American and Mediterranean pyramids represent actual traditional diets from their respective regions and proven cultural models for healthy eating. As a class, we brainstormed healthy menu-planning that would use the Mediterranean pyramid, yet meet the U.S.-student-culture criteria of "fast, accessible, cheap and portable." Students observed that both menus limit consumption of meats to favor plant proteins, recommend lower intake of dairy products, and emphasize nuts, beans, legumes, fruits and vegetables as the bulk of the diet. There is a preference for locally grown products (olive oil figures prominently in the Mediterranean pyramid, for example), moderate wine consumption, and *daily preparation of meals in the home*—the latter, in contrast to U.S. fast-food preparation, according to Schlosser:

> The current methods for preparing fast food are less likely to be found in cookbooks than in trade journals such as *Food Technologist* and *Food Engineering*. Aside from the salad greens and tomatoes, most fast food is delivered to the restaurant already frozen, canned, dehydrated, or freeze-dried. Much of the taste and aroma of American fast food…is now manufactured at a series of large chemical plants off the New Jersey Turnpike. (6)

To begin our exploration of food-as-product in Hispanic cultures, we selected two of Pablo Neruda's *Odas elementales* for analysis: "*Oda a la papa*" and "*Oda al tomate*." Using a semantic-map approach to each poem, students extracted words and phrases to place under each of the associative branches of a *palabra clave*, thus revealing how the food item is embedded in its culture's web of significance. The two poems are quite different in this regard: "*Oda al tomate*" evokes the home, table, and synesthetic pleasures of simple foods; "*Oda a la papa*" evokes the land and people in its association with Chilean values and identity. [See **Appendix A** for more learner-accessible poetry that conveys the sense of a food's significance in Hispanic cultures.]

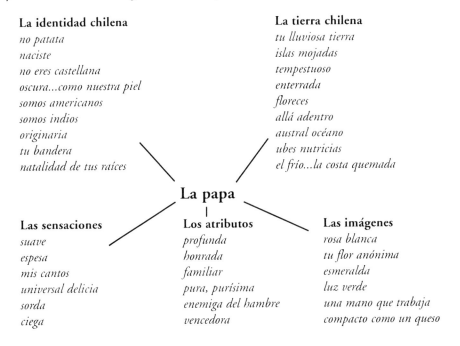

La identidad chilena
no patata
naciste
no eres castellana
oscura…como nuestra piel
somos americanos
somos indios
originaria
tu bandera
natalidad de tus raíces

La tierra chilena
tu lluviosa tierra
islas mojadas
tempestuoso
enterrada
floreces
allá adentro
austral océano
ubes nutricias
el frío…la costa quemada

La papa

Las sensaciones
suave
espesa
mis cantos
universal delicia
sorda
ciega

Los atributos
profunda
honrada
familiar
pura, purísima
enemiga del hambre
vencedora

Las imágenes
rosa blanca
tu flor anónima
esmeralda
luz verde
una mano que trabaja
compacto como un queso

While much the same physical "product," to students the potato had evoked "chips," "fries," and the stuffed-to-overflowing baked version of Wendy's fame; but the *papa*, symbol of the Andean world, captured different shared meanings, evoking the colors, sounds and tastes of the land and the values of honesty and hard work. To follow up this analysis, students working in pairs chose a food that had significance to them and their own culture and developed an "ode" to their food product that revealed its connectedness and meaning to important aspects of their lives.

Students then selected two regions of the Hispanic world—Spain and Peru—for their cross-cultural journey into food-as-product. The class of twenty-eight students was divided in half, with one half representing Spain and the other Peru. Within each country grouping, pairs of students selected one of the following (overlapping) Ps as a week-long research topic: ***Productos y...*** 1) *proverbios*; 2) *platos*; 3) *perfiles y preferencias;* 4) *pedidos;* 5) *precios, presupuestos y puntos de venta*; 6) *patrones emergentes*; 7) *el paladar peruano/español.* [*Preparación* could be substituted for any of these, to focus not only on combining ingredients, but on the cultural significance of the act of preparation.] Students were encouraged to do their own web searches; however, each pair of students was given a list of websites that constituted the minimal required reading for their topics (an abbreviated list of these is included in **Appendix B**). Each pair was given the task of "teaching" the class (not just presenting) how Peruvian and Spanish concepts of food-as-product differ from or resemble those generally manifested in the U.S. All pairs were required to meet with their country group at least once to discuss and coordinate their findings. In class, each pair of students had eight minutes to give its lesson (all were required to make well integrated use of visuals or props, as their aim was to teach) which was to conclude with some provocative question for the class as a whole that would lead to good discussion (in this particular class, students were also required to integrate correctly and appropriately the "passive *se*" and at least ten uses of subjunctive; however, any other structures could easily have been targeted for student practice). *Student as teachers* were required to keep their language as accessible as possible for the comprehension of their listeners and to refrain from citing whole phrases directly from the website texts. *Student listeners* were required to take notes on their classmates' presentations (in some cases, they would have to use these notes to prepare their own lessons) for use in follow-up activities; student listeners were also required to react to each presentation with at least one favorable comment about a learned point of cross-cultural comparison (*Me gusta/ encanta /intriga/ sorprende que los españoles/ peruanos...porque...*). The following is a description of the seven Ps of this product analysis, each of which was assigned to four people: two in Spain and two in Peru. For each, then, Task 1 would be done by one person for Peru and one person for Spain; likewise with Task 2, unless otherwise indicated. Student "lessons" took three (well spent) days of class time.

> ***1. Proverbios:*** What do proverbs tell us about the food preferences of a culture and about the beliefs and values a culture assigns to its food products? Study the list of *refranes* your instructor has provided and 1) choose 3 that reflect the food preferences of Spain or Peru, explain them and tell us something about the importance of these food items; 2) choose 3 that express a significance to food that seems different from that assigned in your own culture's practice; offer your best-researched explanation of these sayings; and teach the class one you consider most important for understanding the role of food in these cultures.

2. *Platos:* Every region of the world has what it considers its specialties—dishes for which the region is famous. In the websites your instructor has recommended, you see that Peru and Spain are noted for a number of dishes, according to their regions. 1) Teach the class about two dishes of your country of focus: give the ingredients and explain how these dishes correspond to the nutritional pyramid of the area (Mediterranean or Latin American); 2) teach the class about regional variation within a country by explaining how two dishes from your country (Spain or Peru) reflect the different geographies, histories, ethnicities or lifestyles of their regions of origin.

3. *Perfiles:* Many industries and government agencies conduct surveys of eating patterns, food preferences, household food expenditures and the like. Your instructor has provided you several websites for such surveys of *peruanos* and *españoles*. Notice that survey questions themselves often reveal a great deal about the culture. For example, from the question: "*De postre, ¿cuál es tu fruta preferida?*" one might assume that fruits are associated with "desserts" for the population being surveyed. 1) Share with the class the results of the surveys you find on the websites, using the data to illustrate a "typical" consumer profile and compare this profile to both the U.S. profile and the nutritional pyramid for the region under study. 2) Examine the *rubros* of each of these surveys to see how data are gathered in categories (*sexo, edad, clase socioeconómica*) and propose to the class a survey instrument that might gather categories of information in the U.S. in like fashion, on a food-as-product question of your choice.

4. *Pedidos y porciones:* Your task is to look at food as promoted and distributed by restaurants. As you know from experience in your own culture, menus often are quite challenging reading, as proprietors wish to "dress up" their language to present an image or to appeal to the senses of diners. Your instructor has provided you with some restaurant websites from Peru and Spain that present rather straightforward menus. Study these menus to: 1) teach the class the language of menu categories of your target country and describe a common dish associated with each category (research what the dishes are and what ingredients they include); 2) suggest to the class your own *menú del día* based on one of these menus, give its cost and explain how it incorporates the foods of that region's nutritional pyramid; explain how the concept of *porción* tends to differ from that of the US.

5. *Precios, presupuestos y puntos de venta:* How do people shop for groceries, where do they go, how often and how much do they spend? For Spain, you will 1) visit two on-line supermarkets and teach the class about the products they would find in each section; and 2) search for the ingredients of at least one dish identified as "typical" by your classmates in both supermarkets, compare the prices of these ingredients (use the same brand name), and present the total "bill" to the class, in *pesetas* (or *euros*) and dollars. For Peru, you will 1) teach the class about where families shop, what products comprise the *cesta familiar* and how much is typically spent on food per week; 2) you will make a "virtual visit" to the Peruvian marketplace of Pacasmayo and teach the class about the variety of sights, sounds and aromas of this experience.

6. Patrones tradicionales y emergentes: Your task is to look at traditional snacking and mealtime practices in your target country, including schedules. For Spain, 1) explain briefly how the daily meals are organized and of what they consist, then teach the custom of *tapear*: give examples of types of *tapas* and the "rules of the game" as given on the websites; 2) teach the class about emerging trends in Spain such as what is happening to the *siesta*, how/why "fast food" (including the *restaurante en casa* movement) is gaining popularity and what type of fast food is not as popular. For Peru, 1) explain how daily meals are organized and of what they consist, what/when are "snacks" consumed; then describe what changes seem to be occurring in eating habits, according to recent surveys—are there some traditional foods that are emerging as less popular? 2) teach the class about the role of food franchises (*franquicias*) in Peru (both foreign and national) and the reaction they have received from urban and rural markets. Explain what is meant by *tropicalización*.

7. El paladar peruano/español. We all have different tastes in foods as individuals; but our culture also, in a way, programs us to accept some foods and not others. Your task is to explore the idea of "taste" in Spain and Peru. 1) You will study typical dishes of your regions, focusing on those that are not at all typical in the U.S, or whose ingredients may strike those of your culture's programming as "odd" (e.g. *menudo (mondongo)*, *morcilla*, *pulpo, cuy, anticucho*). Research how people have described their taste. Devise a survey to see how many of your classmates would try these foods; propose to the class some types of food eaten in the U.S that might produce a similar reaction in populations from your target country. 2) Research how some U.S. food industries (e.g. McDonald's, Coca-Cola, Kentucky Fried Chicken) have adapted their menus to appeal more to the tastes of their consumers in Spain and Peru.

In follow-up to class discussions on the seven Ps of food-as-product analysis, students were given the following comment from Spanish chef Ferrán Adria: *Comer es uno de los mejores placeres, porque utilizamos los cinco sentidos; al excitarlos comiendo hace que podamos emocionarnos con varios sentidos a la vez.*[12] With this statement in mind, they were to choose one of the following summative tasks:

1. You work for a fast-food franchise operation in the U.S. that wishes to expand its market into Spain and/or Peru (if you presented on Spain, your target country will be Peru, and vice-versa). The company has solicited your ideas regarding a new menu offering that will appeal to the tastes and lifestyles of the market in either of these countries. You are aware that one U.S.-based fast-food chain, for example, offers *calamares* on its menu in Spain and *anticucho* on its menu in Peru. The new menu item you propose must meet the criteria of low cost, efficient preparation, and mass local appeal. To "sell" your new menu item to the international managers who will be present at the meeting, you will want to prepare an ad that will appeal to the culture and also evoke "*varios sentidos a la vez*": texture, taste, aroma, sound, eye-appeal. Reflect in your ad what you've learned from your classmates about food-as-product. Show your ability to use the subjunctive at least three different ways and include also at least three command forms.

2. In your analysis of what we eat in the U.S., you have seen that we can take a "food product" and, from it, derive a certain self –awareness of our own culture. Show how you have become more aware of the significance of food in Peru or Spain by creating an "ode" in the style of those of Pablo Neruda. Your topic may be a specific food item, a particular dish, or it may be any other related topic such as *el mercado* or *el tapeo*. Your poem must evoke at least four senses: texture, taste, aroma, sound, image and must reflect the culture's *own* associations and internal connections, as you are aware of them.

In this orientation to the *what* of foods in Spain and Peru, it was impossible to separate "product" from "practice" as the meaning of products resides in the practice or activity within which they are contextualized through functional, meaningful use. [See Bacon and Humbach; Humbach; Heusinkveld; Vidal; all this volume, for more discussion of products-in-practice.] However, just as there is no simple relationship between product and meaning, no observation of product-in-practice will inform solely about one aspect of culture; moreover, just as the notion of product is not confined to tangible objects, the notion of practice is not confined to physical or observable action. Nor again is it merely the observation of practices that differ obviously from one's own that triggers the judgment of "weirdness" in the observer. Our perception is shaped by many things we are not even aware of and feeling the full force and tenacity of our own perspectives will require experiencing them in dialogic interaction. Even then, our own culture's frame of reference sets, in a way, not only our interpretive parameters, but our very perceptual parameters and, ironically, leads us to experience *the most conflict in the most seemingly familiar situations.*

For example, we are living abroad with a host family. The things that are noticeably different from our own routines are relatively easy for us to adapt to, because we can focus on them and consciously adjust: mealtimes, for example, or different foods. But the rest seems so "familiar": the greeting we receive when we enter the home, the mother's indulgence, the conversation and laughter, the questions, the insistence on second and third helpings of dishes, the constant support, encouragement, patience, etc. It feels like "home"—it is a setting we know well in our own world, one for which we easily transfer our own culture's script and feel very comfortable. But, as Trompenaars and colleague point out, "culture is like gravity: you do not experience it until you jump six feet into the air" (p. 5). Through our own cultural upbringing we develop as individuals a sense of behavioral norm as well as a certain idiosyncratic-acceptance range, but the values in which these are rooted give them their weight; conflicting values find compromise. The result is a unique sense-making system that, while beckoning us to observe the differences amongst us, effectively limits our vision to those things we have considered, and in the way that we have considered them. Just as our students cannot define what they mean by 'competition' or 'pride,' let alone encase these meanings in foreign words, no simple English translation or culture-note description can convey the depth and breadth of *familia* in practice.

Data collected by González (this volume) indicate that it was precisely this *contexto familiar*, and especially mealtime etiquette, that left Spaniards misinterpreting their guest-students' behaviors. Indeed, since "*la mesa es uno de los lugares donde más clara y prontamente se revela el grado de edu-*

cación y de cultura de una persona" (Carreño), table etiquette may be one of the first clusters of food-in-practice learnings addressed in class. [See **Appendix B** for websites detailing table etiquette in different part of the Hispanic world.] The use of audio-motor units to teach culturally appropriate manners, as González suggests, could be conducted amidst the following "wraparound" activities.

List on transparency a series of table behaviors—some appropriate, some inappropriate—in Spanish infinitive form, such as in the example. In whole- or small-group fashion, have students indicate which of these they (or others they know) sometimes or always do at the table. For example: Sí, yo a veces me quito los zapatos. Write student names beside each, as they contribute.

Quitarse los zapatos **Juan**	*Servirse las porciones*
Peinarse **Julia, la tía de Andrea**	*Comer en silencio*
Estirarse **Andy**	*Hablar de la política*
Pasar el tenedor a la mano derecha **todos**	*Poner los codos en la mesa*
Cortar más de un trozo a la vez	*Mantener la mano izquierda sobre la rodilla*
Elogiar la comida	*Levantarse después de comer*

After teaching how table etiquette differs in the culture under study, use the same transparency and have students "correct" each others' behaviors in the most pragmatically appropriate form—formal or familiar commands or, in the case of *tía Julia* above, a polite and subtle suggestion.

—*Juan, estamos en...[país] No te quites los zapatos (Ponte los zapatos)*
—*Señorita Julia, yo también quisiera arreglarme (peinarme). ¿Por que no vamos al servicio?*
—*Compañeros, estamos en... [país] No pasen el tenedor a la mano derecha.*

Levi-Strauss has said that food is the soul of all cultures, as in all societies eating is the first form of initiating and maintaining human relations: Knowing the what, where, how, when and with whom of eating is knowing the nature of that society. In fact, in one brainstorming session, students developed the following list of associations with "food"—issues, questions they needed to answer in order to be aware of basic food practices in the other culture (**Table 3**).

Table 3. Food as Product and Practice

What

Geography, products
Mealtime characteristics
Snacks, treats
Tastes, preferences
Convenience
Taboos and prohibitions
Celebratory/festival foods
Religious foods
Ethnicity, race
Regional affiliation
Socioeconomic status
Gender
Age
Good and bad
Right and wrong (not food)
Trend foods
Rigid v. flexible patterns
Packaging/labeling/marketing
Import/export foods
Animals as food
Food as self-image
Concepts of nutrition
Fast foods
Courses and servings
Buying: markets/supermarkets
History/traditions
Act of choosing
"Healthy"/"unhealthy" foods
Food as "ugly" or "fat"
Leftovers, waste, recycling
Genetically altered foods
Food availability
Seasonings/condiments
Portion sizes
Food and laws (e.g. FDA)
Food as gift
Food as healing, "medicine" or remedy

When

Mealtime norms
What is hunger?
What is "full"?
Rigid/flexible scheduling
Order of courses
Celebrations/holidays
Denying/accepting offers
Non-mealtime eating patterns
Food events
Preparation periods
Meal duration
Table-stay duration
When is shopping?

Who

Dinner table authority
Server/serving order
Gender taboos
Food preparers
Men/women roles
Food sharing
Beauty/body image
Eater stereotypes
Home guest-diner behavior
Waiter/customer discourse
Host/guest discourse
Family roles/responsibilities
Praising/complaining
Assisting in kitchen
Eating disorders
Food as status
Who associated with foods

Where

Restaurant protocols
Food prep. spaces/places
Fast-food establishments
Home dining patterns
Where is eating prohibited?
Food eating spaces
Car dining/TV dining
Food purchasing/storing
Food gathering places
Guest/host behavior
Restaurant sanitation
Leftovers, food disposal
Treatment of waiters
Types of restaurants
Who sits where?

How

Table etiquette
Refusing/accepting servings
Self-serving protocol
What to leave on plate
Table talk, topics
Overeating/undereating
Weighing, measuring quantities
Menu ordering
Waiter/customer discourse
Using utensils
Finger foods?
Market bargaining
Tipping protocols
Politeness, courtesy
Requesting, passing food
Clearing plates
How foods are prepared
Food storage

To begin examination of food-as-practice, we may once again start with a self-awareness phase in which students in pairs or groups of three select one of the topics from the "product and practice" inventory (**Table 3**) and work together to devise brief surveys, open questionnaires or agree/disagree statements for use in interviewing classmates and others outside class. In addition, certain structures may be targeted for practice through format requirements such as the following (or, literally, any other):

1. The requirement that each question begin with a different question word, with no *yes/no* questions allowed.

2. The requirement that the survey instrument be phrased in terms of past time, using preterit/imperfect, or in terms of experience-summarizing, using present perfect.

3. The requirement that items be phrased in terms of present subjunctive (*Es mejor/ preciso/importante/imprescindible que...* or *Como ... a menos que.../con tal de que...*etc. or any other subjunctive use).

4. The requirement that questions be phrased in terms of passive se (*En casa, se cena...*)

In studying the ways of mealtimes in the Hispanic world, students will encounter practices that reflect quite different values systems from those of mainstream U.S. One of these practices that seems particularly difficult for students to understand is that of the importance of mealtime as reflected in the rhythm of a typical day. Whereas perhaps students' own notions of mealtime may be rather amorphous—shoved into a fixed schedule of projects, work or studies obligations, or even TV programming, they will see through such practices as the *sobremesa* or even the midday dinner and *siesta* period in some cultures, that mealtime tends to have a more prominent role in Hispanic cultures, even in some cases presenting itself as the core of daily scheduling (see Humbach, this volume, for discussion of "schedules" as products). The following is a sample activity progression that may be used to help students activate their own cultural framework while at the same time becoming sensitized to the possibility that other cultures may have other preferences and other ways, arising from other perspectives.

1. Practices and preferences. The purpose of this activity is to help students evoke a U.S. cultural framework for the notion of "dinner" that includes attention to intracultural variation and changing patterns. Through the "then/now" structure, students make comparisons between their past or childhood and their present, and assess their preferences. As students talk, write key words that come up on the board, in preparation for the following step. All questions and responses should be in Spanish, using vocabulary appropriate to the cultural region under study, and may be used in teacher-whole class interviewing or in student-student group interviewing and reporting.

¿Dónde y con quién(es)?	*Actualmente:* Where do you typically eat dinner? Lunch? Why? What days are different? *Antes, cuando eras pequeño(a)*: Where did you eat dinner? Lunch? Why? What days were different? *¿Cuál prefieres?*
¿A qué hora?	*Actualmente:* What time do you eat dinner? Lunch? Why? What days are different? *Antes, cuando eras pequeño(a)*: What time did you eat dinner? Lunch? Why? What days were different? *¿Cuál prefieres?*
¿Cuánto tiempo?	*Actualmente:* How much time do you spend eating dinner? Lunch? Why? What days are different? *Antes:* How much time did you spend eating dinner? Lunch? Why? What days were different? *¿Cuál prefieres?*
¿Qué?	*Actualmente:* What do you typically eat for dinner? Lunch? Why? What days are different? *Antes:* What did you typically eat for dinner? Lunch? Why? What days were different? *¿Cuál prefieres?*

2. *Practices and perspectives.* Follow up on these discussions to draw some conclusions regarding U.S. culture perspectives and values in preparation for learning about those of a different culture. Divide students into groups and give each group one of the following questions to analyze and report back to class. Take notes on the board as students report and, when the discussion has ended, transpose the board notes to a transparency for use in later activities. [Questions should be in Spanish. In a more advanced class, you may wish to give the topics/ questions in English for students to ask in Spanish.]

a. To what extent does schedule control meal habits? Why? Which meal habits does it control (*Dónde, con quién...* etc.)? How? Which is more important to you, the schedule or the meal? Why? Imagine you can control the schedule; will you change your meal habits in any way? How? Why?

b. To what extent does distance control meal habits? Why? Which meal habits does it control? How? Imagine you can control the distance; will you change your meal in any way? How?

c. Other than satisfying hunger, what role(s) do mealtime and dining play in your life?

How important is this role to you? Why? Are any of these roles more important, less important, or as important as satisfying hunger?

d. What do you like most about U.S. lifestyle regarding "lunch" or "dinner" as we have described it in our discussions? What do you like least? Imagine you can change one thing…what will it be, and how will you change it?

e. In our discussion, we have described U.S. "meals" in terms of both typical customs and variations—in other words, the "meal world" that we know. In which areas (*qué, dónde, con quién(es)*, etc.) might you expect to find differences in a culture that is not that of the U.S.? How do you think you will react to these differences? Which area of difference would probably most difficult for you to adapt to? Least difficult? Why?

f. Think about a time here in your own country that you observed someone do something at a meal that you found "strange." Prepare a description of the incident for the class. Why did you find it strange? What norm or "script" did the behavior violate, in your view? Do you think a foreigner might have made an assumption about the U.S. from seeing the same thing you did? [This question is included in order to provoke discussion of the consequences of facile generalization.]

Questions such as these ask students not only to call up eating patterns in their own culture, but to explore the why's of these patterns in terms of *schedule* (on what basis is a schedule formed and how does this reflect our sense of what is more important and what is less important?); *distance* (what does distance reflect about our living patterns and about what we value?); and the *role* of meals themselves (are meals to satisfy hunger or to commune with others?). Moreover, through these questions, students are asked to think about "difference" in several ways: First, they are asked to consider the differences that lie within our own culture and even within the group of the classroom. Second, they are asked to consider difference in terms of the time periods and changes that occur in the life of an individual. Third, they are asked to consider difference as a matter of preference—the students who responded to these questions, for example, almost unanimously expressed a longing for relaxed family dinnertime and relief from the pressure of schedules. Fourth, they are asked to consider difference in terms of their own reaction to it—how they or others might tend to judge it, and how they or others might tend to generalize on the basis of one observation of it. Perhaps exposed and unraveled in this way, "difference" is not so strange after all; in fact, it may be the greatest thing we all have in common.

Once students have activated the fullness of their own cultural framework and individual preferences on the notion of meals and mealtimes, receptivity to the exploration of another value system is greatly enhanced. For the purposes of examining in-culture meanings of products-in-practice in the cultures of the Hispanic world, input can come from any *authentic* source, such as other-country web pages, photos (including textbook photos), video clips, films, fine art, newspapers, literature and so on. For beginning students, restaurant menus such as those available on the Internet will often provide information about the norms for mealtime hours. For intermediate students who will likely already have some general knowledge of meal schedules, the first step will be to activate this information through the standard what, when, how, who, why categories. However, with both groups of learners, there is likely to be some misinterpretation of the *perspectives* underlying these observable practices, of the *variability* of norms across Hispanic cultures, and especially of the *changing nature* of the practices themselves and the circumstances from which these changes are arising. Around the Hispanic world, for example, the traditional extended mid-afternoon meal + *siesta* is undergoing many such changes. To exemplify this:

> Have students individually or in pairs conduct an Internet search of *la siesta* as a time of day in various countries (*siesta mexicana/española/peruana,* etc.) to explore and compare across cultures **a)** its hours and its purpose; **b)** its perceived health benefits; **c)** the extent to which its rhythms are institutionalized in shop/office closings; **d)** its variability between rural and urban areas; **e)** the why's of its changing nature or abandonment; **f)** the in-culture reactions to these changes. (See **Appendix B**, *Patrones emergentes,* for a few such websites on changing practices).

To explore meanings underlying particular practices and encourage reflection and divergent thinking, two columns may be written on the board, adjusted as to the national culture being observed, with students encouraged to contribute as many hypotheses as they can for each behavior. This very simple technique can be used to analyze virtually anything—from a sign, to a gesture, to an overheard phrase, to a conversation fragment, to a literature excerpt. Here, it is not "right or wrong" answers that are our focus (as students will hypothesize both and the most "authentic" explanation can usually be selected from the options students creatively propose); rather, the goal is to encourage thought "outside the box" of one's own culture, to equip students to consider multiple interpretations and explanations for any practice observed. It can also be used, as in the following example, to help students apply learnings to distinguish between the generalizable and idiosyncratic in their observations.

Observable behavior	Possible meanings
A Madrid store sign says "*cerrado*" but it's only 2:00 pm	??
A Madrid store sign says "*cerrado*" but it only 10:00 am	??

In Spain, you are invited to a home for a 10:00 *cena*
In Spain, you are invited to a home for a 6:00 *cena*

According to Scollon and Scollon, the goal of culture teaching is not merely to have students mimic behaviors, but rather to withhold the fast judgment or reaction of annoyance to see the interpretive possibilities of each situation, "to find ways to work together even when we know the other does not fully understand or appreciate our point of view or our values" (285).

While techniques such as these can help students develop the capacity for multiple interpretations of observed practices, often one of the most effective techniques for helping students grasp the point of view behind these practices is having them defend another point of view:

> Divide the class in half—one half represents the perspective of "U.S. culture;" the other represents the perspective of xx culture. Using a transparency of "differences" students have noted between U.S. practices and those of the other culture, have "nationality" groups alternate asking provocative questions of the other. Encourage active participation for all members of both groups; pose follow-up questions and mediate responses—not to defend either culture's practices, but simply to show how each makes sense within its own perspective. Whenever possible, bring in students' comments from the self-awareness phase of analysis to remind them of their own perspectives and their statements of preference or of what they might wish to change about U.S. lifestyle.

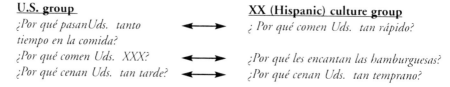

U.S. group		XX (Hispanic) culture group
¿Por qué pasan Uds. tanto tiempo en la comida?	⟷	*¿ Por qué comen Uds. tan rápido?*
¿Por qué comen Uds. XXX?	⟷	*¿Por qué les encantan las hamburguesas?*
¿Por qué cenan Uds. tan tarde?	⟷	*¿Por qué cenan Uds. tan temprano?*

In every culture there is some semblance of mealtime rules and rituals. While these may or may not be strictly adhered to by individuals, families, or groups, given the role of mealtime in Hispanic cultures, building sensitivity to the possibility (or probability) of cross-cultural difference in mealtime protocols is called for. Indeed, González (this volume) notes that some Spanish host families were, in fact, irritated by the mealtime behaviors of their U.S. student-visitors, whereas the students themselves seemed to be quite unaware that they had violated any cultural norms. The following is one such comment that relates to the appropriate protocols of accepting/declining meal invitations and food offerings in Spain.

> *...tienen que entender que cuando una madre de una casa les insiste mucho, no es que les quiere molestar, sino porque aquí en España se insiste, porque hasta que no haces tres veces una invitación, la otra persona no se siente autorizada para ir, ¿no? Aquí dices "ven a casa a comer" y tú "no, no, no," "que sí hombre, ven," "no, no, no" "por favor, ven." Entonces ya vas, o sea pocas veces aceptas a la primera invitación.* (González, this volume)

While in the U.S. students' culture, offerings of second or third helpings of food are taken literally as "Do you *want* more?" to which the individual, assessing his or her own desires, responds truthfully with 'yes, please' or 'no, thank you,' Vázquez & Bueso point out that Spanish host/guest protocol is typically composed of a series of insistences and refusals. Immediate acceptance of an offer to "*tomar algo*"—before the host has had the opportunity to insist—gives the impression of "*maleducados*" or "*jetas;*" outright rejection of such offers may cast the person as "*soso,*" "*ñoño,*" "*desagradable y brusco;*" moreover, to respond by saying *what* one would like is tantamount to treating the host as "*camarero*." Since in any visit to a Spanish home, perhaps even to pick up a friend, the offering of food and/or drink will be typical, the authors provide the following sample series of exchanges, noting that a guest's refusal of an offering must be accompanied by a reason and that, in this refusal, the intonation is, of course, crucial.

Te van a invitar a tomar algo. No se puede decir sí la primera vez. La persona de la casa va a insistir. Cuando se acepta hay que quitar importancia a la elección o dejar que elija el antiftrión. Si no quieres nada tienes que decir la razon, tienes que justificarte; en general no está socialmente bien visto no tomar nada por lo que hay que dar buenas razones para ello.

Host offers: *¿Quiere(s) tomar algo? / ¿Qué te/le pongo?*
Guest refuses: *No, no, gracias*
Host repeats offer: *¿Te(Le) pongo un café?*
Guest refuses: *No, de verdad, no quiero nada, muchas gracias.*
Host repeats offer: *Un té, o una coca-cola entonces.*

Guest refuses and offers excuse: **Guest accepts, leaving host option:**
Que no, que no, de verdad, es que...   *Bueno, vale, ponme (póngame) lo que quiera(s).*
Se(te) lo agradezco, pero lo que pasa es que...   *Bueno, pues venga, lo que usted/tú tome(s)*
                                                 De acuerdo, un cafecito, pero si no es mucha molestia,
                                                 si tienes, si no, cualquier cosa.

As language is the product of a culture, discourse is that language in practice within the cultural community and, as data collected by García (this volume) also illustrate, the discourses of real-life contexts are often quite different from those of our textbooks and classrooms. Exchanges such as the one provided here can be used to great advantage in the classroom, not only as illustrations of protocols but as practice of the linguistic gambits of communication (e.g., the intensifier "*que no;*" the softener "*lo que pasa es que...* ") and meanings conveyed by intonation. Likewise, such models can serve as the skeletal base for students to express what they have learned about the culture. In the case given here, for example, students might expand on the discourse sample provided by Vázquez and Bueso through the following types of activities.

1) **Focus on products.** Consider what you have learned about typical foods in Spain. With your partner, enact the dialog of host and dinner guest, offering some of these foods.

2) **Focus on practices.** From what you know about the role of food in Spain, in which of the following circumstances might an offer of food or drink be expected:
   a) you have gone to a classmate's residence to pick up class notes
   b) you have a meeting with a classmate; since you haven't had time for lunch, you take a sandwich to your meeting.

c) as a dinner guest in a home, you have had servings of each of the dishes and are now full.

3) Focus on perspectives. From what you know about your own culture and the culture of Spain, which of the following excuses for declining a food offer would or would not be perceived favorably:

    a) I'm sorry, I don't have time. I'm in a hurry.
    b) No, please, I really don't like…(X food).
    c) I've already eaten. Maybe next time.
    d) It's delicious, but I just can't eat any more.

In this section, we have only scratched the surface of exploring the meaning of products, practices, and products-in-practice; in fact, perhaps all we have done is show the depth of their cultural entanglement. Indeed, in assessing our treatment of this explicit layer of a culture, we might ask ourselves whether our classroom efforts are directed toward fostering a sense of the "thickness" of its internal significance and variability. Rather than give students pat mantras such as "*la comida/ familia es muy importante*" and rather than hand them answers and pre-compiled information about a culture, and we can provoke curiosity, promote inquiry and create opportunities for learners to discover the culture, build strategies for accessing other viewpoints through critical thinking so that, through their own mistakes and misinterpretations, learners begin to discover themselves. Our aim in teaching for intercultural communication should be to help students continually construct and evaluate their own maps, through an ever-refining awareness of place, through an ever-evolving sense of the complexities of their own identity, and through the ever-growing skills and strategies of way-finding.

The "logic" of one culture's products and practices is not accessed through another culture's values. While helping students expose their own mental maps sensitizes them to the probable existence of other mental maps, it does not avoid the proverbial question of "why?" Unfortunately *why* is, in essence, a logic-demanding question. And in typical catch-22 fashion, what is "logical" in terms of human behavior depends on one's cultural self. Products and practices alone are like the dots of a pointillist painting; capturing their scene is a matter of perspective.

Place-Knowing and Way-Finding: The Sense of Perspective

Thayer says that what we learn is not the world, but particular codes into which it has been structured so that we may share our experiences of it. Underneath the explicit layer of products and practices lie our ways of seeing and interpreting the world, our perspectives. It is *perspective*, a culture's core assumptions about existence, that propels the creation of behaviors and aligns them as a cohesive sense-making system. All cultures make sense. But their logic comes from their own vantage point, not from that of another. Thus, instead of debating whether to focus on "similarities or differences" in the foreign language classroom, perhaps we should be guiding students to understand the internal logic of a people's ways. Similarity/difference is not an either/or question. All cultures, being human, are similar in certain aspects. All cultures, being human, are also different. But it is the way we express this "difference" in the classroom that often makes it such a lighted fuse. To say 'Mexicans have a more relaxed view of time' or 'Hispanics are not as concerned about punctuality,' is to set up circumstances for immediate transfer and judgment from the U.S. learner perspective: "Relaxed" is a powerfully charged adjective in U.S. culture as, in the U.S. meaning framework it implies "not working" and to be not working is, of course, not good from the U.S. perspective. From the insider's perspective, moreover, such statements are also quite false, as we will see in this section.

Each of us, in other words, behaves in some ways like everyone else (universal behavior), in some ways like people from our own group and unlike people from other groups (cultural behavior), and in other ways like no one else at all, including people from our own group (personal or individual behavior). As Geertz says: "Certain sorts of patterns and certain sorts of relationships among patterns recur from society to society, for the simple reason that the orientational requirements they serve are generically human. The problems, being existential, are universal; their solutions, being human, are diverse" (363). Thus, while similarity most certainly exists, its assumption in any cross-cultural encounter may be dangerous. Understanding another culture will not come from comparing any discrete X-culture /Y-culture behaviors; it must come from exploring the *systemic* relationship of X-culture behavior to X-culture perspective and Y-culture behavior to Y-culture perspective. In other words, "cross-cultural comparison" can only fairly take place at the level of perspective.

According to Bennett's Intercultural Sensitivity Model, moving from the ethnocentric stage to the ethnorelative stage requires "examining dilemmas from different viewpoints." In their book, *Riding the Waves of Culture*, Trompenaars & Hampden-Turner look at cultures across the world first in terms of similarities; that is, these "dilemmas" or "existential problems" (as Geertz calls them) of humans living with others in the physical world. The authors target three broad areas of human dilemma: those that arise from our relationships with other people, those that come from the passage of time, and those that relate to humans in the natural world or environment. How we see these dilemmas, how we weight their elements, and how we prefer to approach them says something about how we view the world and what we value. While all manner of ways is always open to us, the impetus of our community of values may sway our choice in one direction or another. Based on their research in intercultural problem-solving in "conflict" situations, the authors identify seven interconnected values dimensions (**see Tables 4-5**) which, they contend, may help us as members of one culture not only see ourselves but the internal "logic" and cohesiveness of another's behaviors.

Before discussing these dimensions, it should be noted that what is presented is not the type of "map" on which a kind of cultural "mindset" can be plotted. The authors note that while a collection of voices from one culture may display a marked tendency or a sort of settling range in preference, the poles of the dimensions are not mutually exclusive; indeed, both extremes of each dimension ("individualism" and "communitarism," for example) are reflected in each and every culture to greater or lesser extent: "Generally speaking, what is strong in another culture will also be present in some form in our own culture" (203). Moreover, both extremes are, in a sense, always to be found in the same person: One may typically read and respond to situations quite subconsciously from a preferred perspective yet encounter an exceptional situation that pulls him quite consciously in another direction. The authors contend that peoples and cultures "dance" from one preferred end to the opposite and back. Indeed, as vibrant systems in constant flux, in constant discovery and surprise at their own internal diversity, cultures grow, as do individuals, through conflict—in the collision of points of view that unsettles complacency, in the encounter of the new that requires re-framing of the old, in the clash between one practice that can only be forwarded at the expense of another. In a culture's eternal movement, pressure points, like knots in fabric, are constantly emerging, tightening through increased tension, only to be loosened and re-aligned as the culture finds new ways to adapt to itself (Galloway 1999). As Trompenaars et al. put it: "We believe that one cultural category seeks to 'manage' its opposite and that value dimensions self-organize in systems to generate new meanings" (27).

Table 4 highlights the five dimensions of the dilemmas of "self in relationship to others." We will discuss three of these here, recognizing that the other two (Neutral-Affective and Achievement-Ascription) are certainly no less important. In each discussion, we will illustrate through the continued topic of "food" for the purpose of connecting perspectives to the products and practices of the previous section's discussion.

Table 4. Values Dimensions: Perspective of Self and Others

I. Universalist ⟷ **Particularist**

Problems solved through rules:

Problems solved through relationships:

Ideas and practices can be applied everywhere without modification.	Solutions depend on the "particulars" of the situation
Rules apply to whole "universe" of members; exceptions weaken rule	"Spirit of the law" deemed more important than "letter of the law"
Rules take precedence over particular needs and claims of friends/relatives	Exceptions must be made for friendships and intimate relationships
What is right is always right	"Right" depends on circumstances
Objectivity valued	Subjectivity expected

2. Individualism ⟷ **Communitarism**

Individual defined through "self":

Individual defined through "group":

Self-realization is paramount	Group and common good are paramount
"I" distinguished within the group	"We" are part of group
Individual is "end" and improvements to communal arrangement means to end	Group is "end" and improvements to individual capacities means to end
Each of us is born alone.	Each of us is born into a family
Task-oriented	Person-oriented
Autonomy valued	Solidarity cherished

---

3. Neutral ←——→ **Emotional (Affective)**
Display of emotion to be controlled: | *Display of emotion to be expected:*

3. Neutral	**Emotional (Affective)**
Display of emotion to be controlled:	*Display of emotion to be expected:*
Display of emotion matter of context	Display of emotion not matter of context
Interruption = rudeness, disruption	Interruption = interest, involvement
"Heart" separated from "Mind"	"Heart" joined to "mind"
"Space" is invaded	"Space" is shared
Words say it all; gestures can distract	Words tell part of story; gestures enhance
4. Specific	**Diffuse**
Self "joins" varied groups as part-time member:	*Group "accepts" individuals as lifelong member:*
Interactions compartmentalized	Interactions connected
Relationships specific theme/purpose oriented	Relationships non-thematic, diffuse
Public space segmented	Public space open
Doors between private, personal, professional	With "passport," movement between personal/prof.
Explicit (low context) communication	Implicit (high context) communication
Group membership ≠ commitment	Group membership = commitment
Start with elements of whole	Start with whole
Ideas ≠ person	Ideas = person
5. Achievement	**Ascription**
Status is "earned":	*Status is "born":*
Respect is derived from individual accomplishment	Respect derived from birth, age, gender, title, class
Status must be constantly proved and re-proved	Status is accorded
Respect-worthiness must be shown	Respect-worthiness is inherent
Personal identity negotiable	Personal identity non-negotiable
Horizontal, lateral organization	Vertical, hierarchical organization
Language negotiates relationship	Language affirms "given" relationship

   1. Universalism and particularism. Since every culture is composed of groups of persons who interact with each other and since the action of one person affects the group, this first dimension relates to how relationships are integrated with rules. The universalist perspective values the "universal" application of rules, codes, standards and laws, to the solution of problems or conflicts: Rules are applied equally to all members for advancement of the "collective good;" exceptions made for particular people, friends or families are seen as weakening the rule. It is not that relationships are viewed as unimportant; rather, there is a sense that once exceptions are made, the system will erode and eventually collapse. The more universalistic beliefs are shared within the culture, the greater the need for an institution to protect the "truth." Such perspectives may benefit societies characterized by diversity but striving for unity: Educational policies will favor assimilation, standardized measurement, and "zero tolerance;" business negotiations will rely on written legal contracts; conflicts between people or groups of people will be mediated through courts where the best fit of existing rules will be applied. Not surprisingly, the U.S., credited with being the most litigious society on earth, can be considered in mainstream highly universalistic.

The *particularist* perspective, on the other hand, views the ideal culture in terms of human relationships and the "particular" nature of situations. Rules of course exist, but may be more implicit; moreover, rather than their blanket application, the door is always open to their exception, as the spirit of the law is deemed more important than the letter of the law: One's commitment is to people—especially one's family, friends, and colleagues. The particularistic perspective, however, may distinguish between "in-group" and "out-group," with the former more entitled to exception than the latter.

What happens when the particularist and universalist come in contact? As Trompenaars et al. observe in business contexts: "Business people from both societies will tend to think each other corrupt. A universalist will say of particularists, "they cannot be trusted because they will always help their friends" and a particularist, conversely, will say of universalists, "you cannot trust them; they would not even help a friend" (32). Indeed, in Spanish-for-Business classes, for example, students accustomed to abiding by the U.S. EEOC policies typically leap to the conclusion that job-hiring practices in Hispanic countries are "invasive," "discriminatory," or "nepotistic" (yet in most cases they will be able to mention at least one case in which they, themselves, acquired a job or other opportunity through some type of *enchufe*—a family member or friend of a friend). Likewise, U.S. students accustomed to U.S. FDA regulations are typically shocked by what they consider lack of control or protection in some countries in the dispensing of pharmaceutical products. Moreover, students returning from travel-abroad experiences may comment on what their rule-based culture interprets as "disorganization" or "rudeness" as they witness people "cutting in" while they, themselves, stand patiently in line. On the other hand, the particularistic perspective may find it irritating or humorous that Americans will wait at a traffic light on a deserted road at 3:00 am with no other car in sight, simply because "the light is red."

Hegedus and Forrai note that universalism may lead to ethnocentrism in that highly universalistic countries tend to see their values as universal absolutes, an observation that seems to be supported by González' interviews with Spaniards (this volume). Indeed, since the days when World War II servicemen wrote home that they were 'fighting for the right to drink Coca-Cola' perhaps the greatest of all U.S. industries has been the marketing of the "American Way of Viewing the World" through global uniformity of franchises and chain enterprises. In this endeavor, the late Ray Kroc, one of the founders of McDonald's, believed there could be no room for particularistic behaviors if an absolute standard was to be adhered to.

We have found out...that we cannot trust some people who are nonconformists. We will make conformists out of them in a hurry...The organization cannot trust the individual; the individual must trust the organization. (Schlosser)

Yet, "selling America" through the food industry has been a global/local tightrope-walk. While U.S. students abroad seek out familiar fast-food franchises for a taste of "home cooking," well-publicized cases such as Pizza Hut's dismal failure in Argentina demonstrate that the one-size-fits-all philosophy does not always settle well in other cultures. Miranda, for example, notes that in Spain, McDonald's uniform dining environment clashes with the values of much of the adult population:

> *...la decoración está calculada para que el cliente no se apalanque, con luces potentes y colores vivos, además de mesas minúsculas y sillas poco cómodas...McDonalds se define como un restaurante familiar, con mucha clientela adolescente, en tanto que en muchas ciudades pequeñas todavía está mal visto que los adultos vayan al McDonalds.*

He observes, in fact, that even among Spanish adolescents, local fast-food franchises are beginning to eclipse U.S.-based ones in popularity:

> *...las cadenas españolas de reciente creación han frenado el avance del estilo de vida americano. Telepizza...se ha ganado un puesto de honor eclipsando al gigante Pizza Hut, al tiempo que Pans&Company y Bocatta siguen su progresión gracias a los bocadillos de siempre. Lógicamente los españoles no ofrecen tanta magia ni menús infantiles tan llamativos, pero captan un público más adulto.*

In Ecuador, Weismantel notes that the U.S. fast-food invasion has created not only conflicts in the family but in the nation as a whole. And this conflict has found reaction from those youth seeking to preserve their identity:

> "My children only want hamburgers and pizzas" the middle-aged women of Quito confess to one another, appalled. Like rock music and fast cars, such meals are signposts on the road to perdition as far as many parents are concerned. For other Ecuadorians, the threat implicit in fast-food cuisine is not to the family but to the nation. Kentucky Fried Chicken and Tina Turner are part of the cultural invasion from the north, attacking Ecuador's integrity as a nation and her people's self-identity as possessors of a unique culture. As a result, one finds young leftists conscientiously listening to *cumbia* and eating *ceviche* in an attempt to preserve some ideological and cultural purity. (122)

The universalist/particularist dimension—two ways of seeing the world—may help students understand the why of their own practices and attitudes as well as those of another people. But the fact that peoples may have different perspectives does not mean they cannot communicate—the secret to dialog lies in recognizing and compromising. For students to see how this is done—for better or for worse—on a global scale, they might visit the international websites for such companies as McDonald's and Coca-Cola, noting: 1) how menus of these companies are changed with "products" created to meet the tastes of the local culture (*glocalización* or *tropicalización*) or how the local outlets meet the needs of the culture (in Peru, for example, Domino's Pizza has now included seating areas); 2) how the different countries represent their cultural values and priorities through their own web pages of these companies; and 3) how products of these companies are marketed through the culture's own system of values. One case in point is the Peruvian top-selling Inca Kola, acquired a few years ago by Coca-Cola:

> *La campaña publicitaria de Inca Kola fue creada ...para conectar los valoresperuanos con este popular refresco. Los comerciales promueven un país rico en elementos que hacen que los peruanos se sientan orgullosos de sus costumbres, tradiciones, paisajes y comida.*[13]

2. Individualism and communitarism. Do people regard themselves primarily as individuals or primarily as part of a group? Many cross-cultural psychologists believe that the answer to this question may predict more in the way of cultural differences than any other dimension. A culture that fosters a predominantly individualistic perspective sees the individual as the core unit. Individual identity comes from self—not from relationships with others. From this perspective, happiness and fulfillment are matters of personal responsibility; success is a matter of the individual triumphing over others or against "all odds;" people are expected to decide matters largely on their own and to take care primarily of themselves and their immediate families; and self-actualization should be the central goal of each individual who has "dignity." Scollon and Scollon note that a society that focuses on the individual as the basic unit will adopt forms of education and socialization that focus on individual learning and advancement through meritocratic systems, even where those individuals become competitive with each other and destroy group harmony. Team effort is valued, but only if each teammate "carries his own weight;" only if, in the end, it results in improved individual performance; and only if, in the end, the individual's "product" is somehow distinguishable from that of the group and assessed accordingly. From the extreme individualistic perspective, the community is judged by the extent to which it serves the interest of individual members ("what's in it for me?"). Mainstream U.S. culture is, without doubt, the individualist par excellence; and, other than its language, perhaps no other products capture its perspective better than the car, the use of doors in our multi-roomed U.S. houses (Galloway 1998) or, as Humbach notes (this volume), the number of computers or TVs in our individual homes.

Whereas individualism is a prime orientation to the sovereignty of self, from the communitarian perspective, each one of us is born into a family, a neighborhood, a community that existed long before we did. Communitarism represents a prime orientation to common goals and objectives. This does not mean, as students are apt to put it, that such a perspective is a simple matter of "just being more friendly." Rather, it means that individual identity is defined not by self, but through one's group of family and friends. Nor, through this perspective, is personal independence "sacrificed," as students are also apt to conclude. On the contrary, opportunities for individual freedom and development may be very highly valued yet viewed not simply as realizing oneself but as impacting on the quality of life for all members of society. Whereas the individualistic culture sees the individual as the end and improvements to communal arrangements as the means to achieve it, the communitarian culture sees the group as its end and improvements to individual capacities as a means to that end. In contrast to the individualistic task orientation, the communitarian perspective would be more person-oriented, putting the who or whom over the what.

It is not that the individualistic perspective does not care for community, however; Americans, for example, are notorious "joiners" (in a class of twenty students, each student is, on average, a member of about eight different organizations). But from the individualist's perspective, these communities do not *define* the individual; rather, they are voluntary and often impermanent associations, to be stepped into and out of at will. In contrast to societies where the individual is "part-time joiner," predominantly communitarian societies generate and live highly cohesive groups, but in-group/out-group differences may often be much more pronounced. Scollon and Scollon contend that while individualistic societies cohere through rules, contracts and instrumental relationships, communitarian societies adhere through kinships, networks and an organic sense of social solidarity; thus, each culture approaches the communicative event through a quite different discourse system. Whereas the highly communitarian perspective will "tend to be more aware of the connections they have as members of their social groups [and] more conscious of the consequences of their actions on other members of their groups, the individualistic perspective will tend to emphasize autonomy and individual freedom of activity rather than connection to other members of the group" (146). However, what is important in studying cross-cultural differences, the authors contend, is "not whether a society is individualistic or collectivistic in itself, but what that society upholds as its ideal, even when we all recognize that we must all have some independence as well as some place in society" (146).

We can see these very different perspectives (*solitario* v. *solidario*) reflected in the discussion of food products and mealtime practices of the previous section. Students expressed a preference for fast foods that required no waiting, as food preparation robbed time from their schedules. In contrast, Laura Esquivel in *Como agua para chocolate*, offers a different, communitarian sense of the social nature of food preparation:

> *En el rancho de Mamá Elena la preparación del chorizo era todo un tiro. Con un día de anticipación se tenían que empezar a pelar ajos, limpiar chiles y a molder especias. Todas las mujeres de la familia tenían que participar... Se sentaban por las tardes en la mesa del comedor y entre plática y bromas el tiempo se iba volando hasta que empezaba a oscurecer. (16)*

Further, while mealtime is considered the ultimate bonding experience throughout Hispanic societies, it was defined by U.S. students as "when I want to eat." This was often the case even in their homes, as many commented that if there was a family meal, it was never obligatory—they could eat later if they wanted, or even "take a plate to their room" if they were working or if they didn't want to "miss a TV program." Indeed, asked to sketch their family home and place an X anywhere they might typically eat, the students marked every room in the house except the bath. Moreover, eating was not, in most cases, viewed as a "social event," but rather as personal enjoyment and satisfaction of hunger. Indeed, U.S. students have typically expressed a certain discomfort and/or impatience over the ritual of the *sobremesa* (Galloway 1999). On the other hand, the communitarian perspective will find it difficult to understand why, for example, someone would buy a cup of coffee at a drive-through window and drink it alone in the car when, as Labarca notes:

> ... in general, Hispanics derive energy mainly from the contact with other people... and from countless *cafés, cafés cubanos, cafecitos, tintos, tés, or yerba mates* (depending on the area), and

from one or two additional small meals or *meriendas* during the day, as indicated by the announcement of *hora de tomar té/onces/un café/una cosita para picar/ unas tapas/un taquito,* and so on.[14](112)

3. Specific and diffuse. This very important public-private dimension relates to the degree to which we get involved or engage others in our lives - either *specifically* and in single areas of personality, or *diffusely* and in multiple areas at the same time. From a highly specific-oriented perspective, relationships are discrete and segregated—one's self and family are "private," one's small circle of friends is "personal," and the much larger "public" sphere of one's personality is filled with an assortment of other friends, acquaintances, colleagues, neighbors, teammates and the like. The relationships of this "public" sphere, however, tend to be segmented or context-specific and typically insulated one from the other. One may have, for example, a variety of "public relationships," all of which are purpose-oriented and well defined: professional colleagues, with whom one "talks shop;" a tennis partner, with whom one talks sports; the members of one's church congregation, with whom one discusses community problems; fellow parents of the PTA, with whom one discusses school matters; fellow volunteers in a charitable organization, with whom one plans community projects. From this perspective, each area in which two people encounter each other is considered separate from the other, a specific case. People are easily accepted into the public sphere where they don't mix, but it is more difficult to get through the invisible doors into the more blended "personal" sphere, and the "private" sphere may be reserved for only one or two life-long bonds or even, in fact, be considered inviolable.

However, from a diffuse perspective, every life space and every level of personality tend to permeate all others. The "public" sphere is relatively small, while the "private" sphere is large and diffuse. Acceptance into the private *amistocracia* is not casually granted; however, once admitted, a friend gains entrance into all or nearly all layers of an individual's life—although within these layers hierarchies may construct themselves. While from a "specific" perspective the whole is the sum of its parts, from the "diffuse" perspective, the whole is more than just the sum of its elements: All relationships are related to each other; everything is connected through a multiplicity of bonds of loyalty, reciprocity, and mutual support.

Trompenaars et al. point out that one reason the American personality is so "friendly and accessible" is that from the specific perspective, being admitted into one public layer is not a very big commitment—"knowing" another for limited purposes neither requires long-term investment of self nor continual maintenance:

> When Americans let a colleague of a diffuse culture into one compartment of their public space and show their customary openness and friendliness, that person may assume that they have been admitted to diffuse private space. They may expect the American to show equivalent friendship in all life spaces and be offended if he or she comes to their town without contacting them. (87)

The perspective of relationships in terms of permanence, lasting bonds, and membership in one's *círculo* or *red* contrasts starkly with the more temporary and utilitarian perspective of "It doesn't matter; I'll never see him/her again" and, in fact, behaviors reflecting the more diffuse perspective may present some of the greatest sources of confusion to our students—either because they notice them and misinterpret them, or because they do not notice them at all. Students returning from visits abroad, for example, will frequently remark about the personal nature of questions they were asked (e.g., How much money do your parents make?) or will note a vague discomfort during home-stays: "I always felt there was something going on that was too subtle for my comprehension, some undercurrent to the communication that I didn't understand." Álvarez Evans & González note, for example, that U.S. students perceived the custom of reciprocating favors through *envíos* or *encargos* as an invasion of an individual's time and an unnecessary inconvenience. González likewise speculates (this volume) that had student-visitors in Spain even been aware of their hosts' expectations for more familial integration during their homestay program, they would likely have perceived this demand as an intrusion or loss of independence.

The notions of specific and diffuse can also be seen in the use of physical space—the design of cities, for example, or even that of homes (see Humbach, this volume). In 1950 the average size of a U.S. home was one thousand square feet; today, it is 2,265. Simonton notes that aside from the need to accommodate SUVs and big-screen TVs, the national trend toward taller ceilings and higher-pitched roofs satisfies the need to demonstrate wealth on a grand scale: "We feel like we deserve more space" (6). Yet, as the U.S. house grows bigger, it is also becoming more partitioned, as the two-storied vaulted "great room" of the 80s is being floored over to create a separate room in the airy space under the ceiling. Moreover, just as in past decades the formal living room spawned the casual "family room," the most recent trend in home building is that of the "keeping room," an area separate from the living room and separate from the "family room" that is just for family (really for family, this time). U.S. home trends seem to reflect much of the same characteristics of the old Westward Movement—when things get too "crowded," create more dedicated space for escape, privacy, and just getting away from it all (see Humbach, this volume).

Trompenaars et al. give the example of the house guest from a more "diffuse" culture in the home of a host from a more "specific" culture: Asked if he would like a beer, the house guest went to the refrigerator and helped himself, not realizing that, from the "specific" perspective, the refrigerator is considered private space, accessible only to family. Indeed, the kitchen in the U.S., a predominantly "specific" culture, may be viewed as the cook's domain: Guests may be expected to socialize in the living/family room until they are called to dinner and, although it is considered polite for guests to offer services in the kitchen, the offer is quite typically declined; a guest who then stays in the kitchen without invitation may be viewed as "meddling" or "nosy." In contrast, Weismantel describes the kitchen in the Quichua village of Zumbagua, Ecuador:

> The kitchen in Zumbagua is the locus of early socialization, not only through social interaction but through the sense experiences of taste, touch, and smell, the spatial orientations implicit in its architecture and the arrangement of objects, and the physical and temporal rhythms found in the work performed there (25-26)…kitchen in itself implies much more than a room in which food is pre-

pared. It is there that meals are made and eaten, male and female heads of the household sleep and live, baths are taken, decisions made, wakes held, babies born and the sick nursed back to health. Other buildings are storage rooms and sleeping places; only the kitchen is a home. (169)

In describing the *"cultura de la comida familiar,"* Padre Clemente Sobrado of Perú refers to the *cocina-comedor* as having a *"función socializante, creadora de relaciones familiares, amicales de la comida."* This is a common space for family, friends, guests *"donde nos sentimos como hermanados y unidos, compartiendo nuestras vidas, nuestros sentimientos, nuestras inquietudes..."* Mealtime is not merely for filling the stomach but also *"...espíritus y corazones gozosos de compartir el mismo cariño hecho sopa, arroz o cualquier otra cosa."* Yet, he mourns the changes occurring in this feeling of family belonging:

> *...eso que llamamos carencia de "sentido de pertenencia a la familia" y que hoy observamos en los jóvenes, no se debe tanto a que sean mejores o peores que los de antes, sino a que son hijos de estos cambios culturales, carecen de espacios y de tiempos vinculantes familiares.*

Of utmost importance in the discussion of this dimension, however, is that the perspectives of specific and diffuse go far deeper than the level of behaviors and use of space. Trompenaars et al. note that in highly diffuse cultures, one's ideas are not separated from one's person which, in turn, is not separated from the views of one's compatriots. To criticize one's idea, or one's country, is to profoundly affect one's whole system of personal honor: "Pleasure and pain, acceptance and rejection, ramify more widely in the diffuse system" (87). While the words "Don't take this personally, but..." allow the specific-culture bearer a great deal of freedom to react to a particular segment without crossing into another compartmentalized one, for those from more diffuse preferences, such a feat would be quite impossible. The authors also contend that this perspective explains why some conversations seem to "take so long to get to the point... things must be broached delicately as so much is at stake." It is also one of the reasons, conclude the authors, that Americans have so much difficulty understanding the abstract notion of "losing face" (see García's discussion of "face," this volume).

From the diffuse perspective, as one's ideas are not separate from one's person, one's cuisine may not be easily separated from valued national or cultural or ethnic identities either. As a handmade product, constructed through labor and artistry, imbued with pride, a dish prepared reflects not only the individual preparer, but the group as well. As Weismantel notes, to proffer a prepared dish may be an act laden with social significance: "the product of work transformed into the satisfaction of desire; and the proof of the household's ability to survive and to reproduce itself " (29). Thus, offers of second and third helpings, so common at Hispanic tables, may carry with them the implicit obligation to accept; moreover, the act of tasting a prepared dish will not be complete until its praise has been uttered. Refusal even to try a food offered, on the other hand, may be viewed as a refusal to "know" the people and the person who offer it.

Table 5 highlights two other dimensions proposed by Trompenaars & Hampden-Turner—those that relate to the passage of time and those that relate to the environment; that is, the relationship between humans and the physical and temporal world. We will discuss each of these briefly, with attention to their value in helping learners not only understand the perspectives behind behaviors, but in seeing how intercultural communication lies in the ways these perspectives can be made to work together.

Table 5. Relationships with the Natural World: Perspectives of Time and Nature

Time as sequential ←——→ **Time as synchronic**

Time as sequential	Time as synchronic
Time as linear, sequence of disparate events	Time as circular, past & present synchronized
Tasks completed one by one	Activities juggled in parallel
Schedules give order, tardiness disrupts plan	People vie with punctuality
A->B is direct for minimal effort/maximum effect	A->B has spontaneously occurring detours
Time is tangible and divisible	Time is flexible and intangible
There is never enough time	There's always more time

Internalistic view of Nature ←——→ **Externalistic view of Nature**

Internalistic view of Nature	Externalistic view of Nature
Inner directed	Outer-directed
Man can/should control Nature	Man is part/ product of Nature
Nature as machine to be operated	Nature as force in which to operate
Nature is resource to be used	Nature is to be maintained
Free will	Destiny

Sequential and synchronic perspectives of time.   What do the words past, present and future mean? Is an event that has passed "the past," or does it live within us as part of our present or future? When does our past end and our future begin? Macera notes that in the ancient Inca world, a key concept was *Kai*, which meant both "here" (in space) and "now" (in time). In relation to *Kai*, were *quipa* (signifying both "behind" and "future") and *ñaupa* (both "ahead" and "past"). While the idea of past being ahead and future being behind is disconcerting to the European perspective, in the Tawantinsuyo view of the world, the past is ahead of us and can be seen, but the future is coming up behind us, about to enter our *Kai*, the world of the here and now.

How do we perceive the passage of time—is it viewed as progressive? Destructive? Restorative? Repetitive? Do we value more what is "old" as the vault of our wisdom and the reflection of our histories and traditions? Or do we value more what is "new" as the expression of our movement, change, and innovation? As Geertz says:

> There are many ways in which men are made aware, or rather make themselves aware, of the passage of time… but surely among the most important is by the recognition in oneself and in one's fellowmen of the process of biological aging, the appearance, maturation, decay, and disappearance of concrete individuals. How one views this process affects, therefore, and affects profoundly, how one experiences time. Between a people's conception of what it is to be a person and their conception of the structure of history there is an unbreakable internal link. (389)

Indeed, the way we perceive time is at the core of our basic assumptions, both in terms of our consciousness of it and our experience in it. While different individuals and different cultures may be more or less attracted to past, present or future orientations, obviously, no one locates his or her time-consciousness exclusively in either, but rather may accentuate one over the other. In U.S. mainstream culture, where "time" is concrete, animate, divisible, consumable as a precious and limited commodity, there is a predominantly sequential or lineal view of time and a decidedly "present + future over past" values orientation. Pat phrases such as "that's history" or "today is the first day of the rest of your life" capture a temporal orientation that tends to discard the past in favor of focus on the present as prelude, preparation or approach to the immediate future. While a future orientation implies such things as goal setting, diagnosis, risk assessment and planning, combined with a present orientation, it poses conflict in the need for instant gratification, and the assessment of progress-by-the-moment. "Time is of the essence" in U.S. culture where it is managed and manipulated, measured and meted, courted and caressed, saved and squandered. U.S. culture grabs moments from a concept of "time" that moves independently forward at a consistent rate—to look backward is to lose gathered momentum and thus to obstruct or deter "progress." Yet, there are tensions within this racing view of time that produce a certain schizophrenia — the longings for old values and "simpler times" (as in recent re-definitions of "conservative" politics) conflict with the need to "keep moving forward."

We might compare this orientation to what Octavio Paz views as the Mexican orientation: "*El presente es ese momento en que el pasado se lanza hacia el futuro.*" Indeed, rather than a lineal representation, many cultures view time as circular of cyclical: The past and present are synchronized with future possibilities. Rather than now-abandoned points on a line, the past nourishes and gives vital energy to the future, serving as compass to guide people through change. Castañeda contends that the notion of time itself divides U.S. and Hispanic cultures as much as any other single factor, for inside some Hispanic cultures, the passage of time is not very noticeable; it is flat and the sense of its going by is absent. In nations where the past looms large and where time orientations overlap, status is more likely to be legitimized by ascription based on durable characteristics such as age, class, gender, ethnicity and professional qualification (Trompenaars, et al.).

Among people who tend to value what is young and new and modern over what is old or "used," the terms "past" and "traditional" may have negative connotations that cast a net of immediate stereotype over entire cultures. Such is the case, Weismantel observes, in both popular and scholarly representations of the *indigena* in Latin America:

> The identification of indigenous practice as "the past" and "white culture" as "the future" is part of the process by which indigenous culture is denied validity as a choice for living. In both popular and scholarly representations, indigenous people are thus denied a history: their culture is "timeless," except insofar as they have slowly over the centuries taken on a few trappings of modernity, borrowed from the outside. They are a "traditional" people. (154)

Yet, among the Quichua of Ecuador, Weismantel notes the past and present in constant conflict as younger people want things their mothers never cooked, foods that are store-bought, not "home-grown"—foods that represent the urban "Hispanic" lifestyle. Interestingly, the same type of conflict, though with poles reversed, can be seen in the U.S. where speed, schedules, preservatives, and microwaveable dining provoke longing for the "real thing." Advertising abounds with phrases such as "tastes like homemade" as our palate for the past is packaged into the reality of our present.

In a class of (very future-oriented) Intermediate learners, we explored the past within us and how vivid sensory memories are evoked through the aromas of food (see also Bacon & Humbach; Heusinkveld; Vidal; all this volume, for use of music and literature to evoke memory). Students were given the following passage from Isabel Allende's *Afrodita* that beautifully captures the connectedness not only of past and present, but of the senses—polychromatic images, vivid fragrances, and powerful emotions mix when evoked by the perfume of violets:

> *Mi tía Teresa…está ligada para siempre al olor de las pastillas de violeta. Cuando esa dama encantadora aparecía de visita, con su vestido gris discretamente iluminado por un cuello de encaje y su cabeza de reina coronada de nieve, los niños corríamos a su encuentro y ella abría con gestos rituales su vieja cartera, siempre la misma, extraía una pequeña caja de lata pintada y nos daba un caramelo de color malva. Y desde entonces, cada vez que el aroma inconfundible de violetas se insinúa en el aire, la imagen de esa tía santa, que robaba flores de los jardines ajenos para llevar a los moribundos del hospicio, vuelve intacta a mi alma. (10)*

In this class, students unanimously agreed that certain smells have the power to evoke the flood of memory; they had all experienced it. They were then asked to imagine a pleasant food aroma from their childhood—perhaps bacon frying on a Saturday morning, the barbecue grill on a hot summer night, cookies baking in their grandmother's house. Their task was then to capture a particular or typical childhood scene evoked by this aroma, as completely as possible, opening themselves up to the full sensory experience '*que vuelve intacta al alma.*' They began by simply recording memories evoked in sensory categories:

Aromas/fragancias Sonidos/ruidos Imágenes Texturas Sabores Emociones/sentimientos

For this particular class, instead of having them then convert their notes into a vivid description (as had been done in previous classes), students were asked to explore the use of synesthesia in writing; that is, mixing the senses to evoke a more powerful and total experience in the reader, just as our sense of smell invokes taste, for example. Their writings thus began to show a deeper texture, with the *sound of smells*, the *emotions of images*, the *flavors of sounds*. Equally important, however, was that they were beginning to see a different way of viewing the world—that their "past" had not gone, but was and always would be a vital part if their present, their future, and indeed, their very identity.

Individuals who perceive time as sequential—moving forward, second by second, minute by minute in a straight line—will tend to structure it and "use" it sequentially, by doing one thing at a time. Staying on schedule is a must; since time is lineal, any outside interruption of the task at hand will cause a loss of time that cannot be recovered. On the other hand, those who perceive time synchronically—moving round in cycles of minutes, hours, days, years—will tend to structure time synchronically, usually doing several things simultaneously, juggling activities in parallel. From this perspective, time is fluid and flexible; there is always enough of it and plans can be easily changed—what is important is not how much time is spent on the task, but how the time is spent in interaction. Synchronic cultures may be less insistent on punctuality in certain contexts; however, where relationships are seen as emergent, developing, and worthy of long-term investment, "… it is not that the passage of time is unimportant, but that several other cultural values vie with punctuality. It is often necessary to 'give time' to people with whom you have a particular relation" (Trompenaars, et al. 128).

With the immediate future as destination, the sequential perspective finds it "logical" to get there fast; and moving directly from point A to point B with minimal effort and maximum effect, is the most efficient route. From the synchronic perspective, however, movement from point A to point B will rarely be a straight line. Instead of the efficiency of getting from A to B in the shortest possible time, there is the effectiveness of developing closer relationships along the way. In fact, in comparing written rhetorical styles across cultures, Kaplan contrasts the straight arrow ("get to the point") of English style, to the detouring rhetorical style most noted among Spanish-writers.

As Trompenaars et al. note, synchronic styles are extraordinary for those unused to them: People who do more than one thing at a time can, without meaning to, insult those who are used to doing only one thing. Likewise, people who do only one thing at a time can, without meaning to, insult those who are used to doing several things. As I write this, my daughter has just entered the room. I hold up a finger to her to signal "wait one minute while I finish this thought." She had important news to tell me, but she waited. From a synchronic perspective, however, not being greeted spontaneously and immediately, even while still doing something else, could be considered a serious slight. Moreover, while from a sequential perspective, it is considered very impolite to pay unexpected visits, or to "drop in" on someone, among individuals who share a more synchronic view of time, the spontaneous visit would likely be quite welcome. Likewise, while the sequential perspective may interpret synchronic behavior as slow, disorganized, or uncooperative, the synchronic perspective may interpret sequential schedule-following behavior as rigid, compartmentalized and cold.

To help Intermediate students perceive the rhythms of daily life in other than clock terms and to see the difference between the notion of "food as schedule" contrasted to the U.S. "food in schedule," we began with the following passage from Laura Esquivel's *Como agua para chocolate*. Students were then asked to recount in like fashion the passage of time and schedule of a typical day from their childhood (since our grammatical focus was past-time description) as evoked only through *only* one of their senses: sound or smell.

> *Sus habitos alimenticios estaban condicionados al horario de la cocina: cuando en la mañana Tita olía que los frijoles ya estaban cocidos, o cuando a mediodía sentía que el agua ya estaba lista para desplumar a las gallinas o cuando en la tarde se horneaba el pan para la cena, ella sabía que habia llegado la hora de pedir sus alimentos (14)*

Internal and external control: How we relate to Nature. In broad terms, individuals may view mankind as being apart from or a part of the physical world of Nature. Each view carries enormous consequences for human behavior, both in terms of the natural environment and in terms of individual action. To the extent that one or the other views is shared within a culture, institutions or rituals or "customs" will arise to promulgate or protect them, to save or salve them. The perspective of "mankind apart from Nature" sees the physical world as a machine on which human will may be imposed for the benefit of its human operators, a resource to be used for their benefit. This orientation has been labeled *inner-directed*, in that the locus of control is perceived as being "inside" the perceiver. The other, *outer-directed* perspective is that which views man as part of nature, owing his development to the nutrients of the environment and obliged to go along with its laws, directions, and forces.

Trompenaars et al. note that some cultures, such as mainstream U.S., appear almost completely internalized: One's personal resolution is the starting point for every action; man can dominate nature—if he makes the effort. Indeed, phrases such as "you are the master of your fate" and "create your own future" echo the view that life is a series of choices: You can live the life you want if you take advantage of and give shape to life's opportunities. Yet, labels such as "control freak," the modern-day plethora of stress-related diseases induced by need-to-control/can't-control conflicts, and the resultant "victimization" movement ('It's not me, it's a disease') portray a culture caught in the throes of its own (quite institutionalized) belief system. Observers of mainstream U.S. note behaviors corresponding to the belief that through the dynamic of one's society, any change is possible: One can change socioeconomic class, given the opportunity-ladder of education; one can "own" an idea, even granting that ideas may not arise from a vacuum; one can change individual appearance through plastic surgery, given the financial resources; one can use natural resources inexhaustibly, given the innovation of the human mind to discover more; and one can use and dispose of items, given that there are more of the same always readily available. From this perspective, the key to controlling all is having the right expertise. Indeed, the way we relate to our environment is linked to the way we seek to have control over our own lives and over our destiny or fate.

The *externalistic* perspective, however, presents a more "organic" view of humans as part of Nature and subject to her mysterious forces. From this perspective, people are outer-directed—accepting that they cannot entirely shape their own destiny. A more outer-directed attitude will tend to result in behavior that adapts to shifts and circumstances, that recognizes arbitrariness and unpredictability as natural elements of life, and that may be able to ride the waves without assignation of blame. The externalistic perspective, further, may see life as controlled by fate and hierarchies and station as natural and unchangeable parts of life.

We may view cooking as symbolizing the nexus between the external and internal, a manifestation of the interaction of nature and culture. Weismantel, for example, observes the close relationship of the Quichua to the land through food:

> *The landscape is filled with it, all activities have to do with it; the place, Zumbagua, is colored*

and formed by the foods it produces just as the bodies of its people are made out of the food the land gives them (117).

Peoples who view mankind as living in harmony with nature will perhaps favor different lifestyles than those who view mankind as controlling nature. Of no minor significance, for example, would be the issue of "waste" to both groups. González, for example, notes that Spaniards commented on what was perceived as wasteful behavior on the part of U.S. students — "*el despilfarro de los servicios de la luz, del agua, del teléfono, de todo...*" Indeed, water, a resource so taken-for-granted in the U.S., is liquid gold in those areas of the world prone to drought (such as Spain), or in which both the quality and quantity of water are of unequal distribution (such as the Andean region). In a "land of plenty," where industry and marketing tend to disconnect people from the environment, the complexity of sustainable development (ecological, economic and cultural) is not readily fathomed by learners; yet, in many respects, an awareness of the key issues of sustainability is vital not only to understanding the societies of Latin America and the connectedness of land, industry, social structure and government policy, but to understanding both the nature and impact of globalization in its present and potential forms. The following is a quite simple, but rather stimulating activity for exploring, via the junk generated by our food habits, just one aspect of ecological sustainability—the consequences of what O'Neill calls "affluenza."

1. Bring to class an assortment of throwaway food-related items, such as the following (or have students go through their trash and bring in 2-3 items from it).

plastic soft-drink or water bottle	a paper or foil hamburger wrapper
a six-pack plastic ring	a plastic spoon
an egg carton	a paper cup
a Styrofoam cup	a plastic bag from the supermarket

2. Have students in pairs **a)** describe the item (composition, function, etc.); **b)** suggest a more ecologically friendly way that that same function could be performed; and **c)** then speculate as to the changes in U.S. lifestyle that this substitute would require for implementation and that this substitute would trigger as consequence (positive and negative).

3. Follow up as a group by speculating as to whether U.S. society could/would adapt to such lifestyle changes as those students suggest, and why or why not? How many other areas of life would the change impact? You might also wish to bring in an old toaster or some other kitchen appliance and ask students **a)** how long we might use such an appliance; **b)** what do we do with it when it no longer works? **c)** for what reasons other than malfunction might it be discarded?

4. Compare some of these practices to those of an area of the Hispanic world you are familiar with. For example, in their travels to Hispanic countries students will no doubt find that **a)** many stores (and especially markets) will not provide bags for purchases; if available, show students the type of shopping bag that women typically carry into the mar-

kets; and **b)** Styrofoam cups and plastic glasses are very much less common. Why? How is this explained by what they know about practices and perspectives of this particular culture? c) the tendency to repair items rather than discard and buy new ones.

5. Finally, have students reunite with their partners to invent a new use for their trash item—one that will "keep it off the street" by turning it into a different and equally functional product.

Conclusion

It is said that *cada cabeza es un mundo*. Indeed, our human minds are simply incapable of not assigning meaning to the words we hear and the actions and objects we observe. The challenge to us as teachers of culture is to guide students to explore their own cultural "mindset" as they go beyond it to experience other systems of sensical behavior and to understand that a culture's language harkens not the meanings of our own culture, but those given it by the people who constantly create and recreate it through interaction. Good human relations require both common ground for understanding and respect for differences. Understanding that difference exists should not paralyze us or tongue-tie us; rather, difference is also a matter of perspective—the deeper we go, the more evident it becomes that most cultural differences probably lie in ourselves. Indeed, there is only one human state in which "difference" is not present: *alone*.

In our classrooms, we must plunge deeper into these realities. Under the level of products and typical or institutionalized practices lie other perspectives, other patterns of thought, other ways of configuring experiences and other ways of constructing and structuring the world. This itself is a valuable, mind-opening lesson for our learners. But even more liberating is the notion that different ways of seeing, both "poles" of every dilemma-solving continuum, are to some extent in all of us—that we all have the potential and, in some form, the experience, to relate to the perspective of another. Yet, perhaps the most powerful message we can send learners is this: Effective cross-cultural interaction is not a matter of just "knowing" that the other person behaves differently or has a perspective that is different from yours or mine; it is being able, through mutual involvement, to negotiate a "place" between the two of us where both perspectives maintain their integrity, where both are respected and neither is sacrificed, and where both values work together to achieve more than either could achieve on their own (Trompenaars, et al. 43)—it is, in essence, the fervent desire to communicate.

He had brought a large map representing the sea,
Without the least vestige of land:
And the crews were much pleased when they found it
to be a map they could all understand.
"What's the good of Mercator's North Poles and
Equators, Tropics, Zones and Meridian lines?"

So the Bellman would cry; and the crew would reply,
'They are merely conventional signs!
'Other maps are such shapes, with their islands and capes
But we've got our brave captain to thank'
(So the crew would protest) 'that he's brought as the best-
A perfect and absolute blank!'

"The Bellman's Speech"
Lewis Carroll (xxx)

Notes

[1] Throughout this chapter, an attempt has been made to reproduce student responses as authentically as possible, complete with actual errors. Minor corrections have been made to such things as agreement, simply to avoid repeated reader irritation.

[2] To offer students a quite different worldview, teachers may wish to consult the following website for viewing or ordering the "upside down map" in which North-South poles are reversed: http://www.flourish.org/upsidedownmap. To view a wide selection of many other types of world maps (in Spanish and English), visit the Great Globe Gallery at: http://hum.amu.edu.pl/~zbzw/glob/glob1.htm.

[3] Peters' projection website: http://www.petersmap.com/table.html

[4] Website of the OECD (Organization for Economic Cooperation and Development): http://www.oecd.org/dac/

[5] From: http://www.css.edu/users/dswenson/web/CULTURE/CULTMAPS.HTM#MEXICO

[6] Jorge Parra, Bilbao, en Argentina; from website visited on July 31, 2001: http://www.salvador.edu.ar/sv8-ede1200.htm

[7] From: Samuel Sánchez, webmaster. *"Cuando no sabemos si saludar."* http://adepoju.tripod.com/sa/sa-es/articulos/sa-saludar_es.htm#normas

[8] From: *"Ni una cosa ni la otra."* El día digital, 13-7-2000: http://www.eldia.es/2000-07-13/criterios/criterios1.htm

[9] See, for example, "Jaime y Angela go to America," the journal of two Spaniards in the U.S. at: http://members.fortunecity.es/netcine/index3.html

[10] A summary of the findings of this study may be found at foodchannel.com Vol. 9 #13, July 15, 1997.

[11] For comparison of both pyramids with that of USDA, see: http://www.oldwayspt.org/html/pyramid.htm

[12] Ferrán Adria, cited from *"El ángel de la gastronomía in serie titulada."* El pais.es, 29 julio 2001.

[13] See: http://www.rtpnet.org/~felipe/estampas/costumbres.htm

[14] The following website offers a rich source of literary fragments all dealing with the role of coffee (*tomar un café*) in Hispanic cultures: http://www.nodo50.org/espanica/litera.html

Works Cited

Adaire Hauck, Bonnie and Philomena Cumo-Johanssen. "Communication Goal: Meaning Making through a Whole Language Approach." *Collaborations: Meeting New Goals, New Realities.* June K. Phillips, ed. Lincolnwood IL: National Textbook Co., 1997. 35-95.

Allende, Isabel. *Afrodita: cuentos, recetas y otros afrodisíacos.* NY: Harper Collins, 1998.

Álvarez Evans, Gilda and Olgalucía G. González. "Reading 'Inside' the Lines: An Adventure in Developing Cultural Understanding. *Foreign Language Annals* 26 (1993): 39-48.

Bennett, Milton J. "Towards Ethnorelativism: A Developmental Model of Intercultural Sensitivity." R.M. Paige, ed. *Education for the Intercultural Experience.* Yarmouth, ME: Intercultural Press, 1993.

Borges, Jorge Luis. "*Del rigor de las ciencias.*" *Collected Fictions.* New York: Viking, 1998.

Carreño, Manuel A. "*Conducta en Sociedad: 30 Reglas para comer.*" *Manual de Urbanidad y Buenas Maneras*, 4ª edición. Panamá: Editorial América, 1985.

Carroll, Lewis. "The Bellman's Speech." *Lewis Carroll—The Complete Illustrated Works.* New York: Gramercy Books, 1982.

Castañeda, Jorge G. "Ferocious Differences." *The Atlantic Monthly* 7 (1995): 68-76.

Chazarra Montiel, Antonio and Gema María Cilleruelo López. "*El asociacionismo juvenil: crítica a la legislación vigente.*" *Edicions 2* (1985). Madrid: Consejería de Educación de la C.A. de Madrid, 1985. [http://www.2000jove.org/85/chazarra.htm]

Clemente Sobrado, P. "*Recuperar la 'cultura de la comida.*'" *Misión sin fronteras: Boletín* 217, n.d. [http://www.consamu.com/Misiones/]

Esquivel, Laura. *Como agua para chocolate.* New York: Doubleday, 1989.

Firth Alan. "Language and Culture: An Introduction." Intercultural & International Communication. 2000. http://www.sprog.auc.dk~firth/Teaching/culture/def.html

Foucault, Michel. *The Archaeology of Knowledge and the Discourse on Language.* New York: Pantheon Books, 1972.

Galloway, Vicki. "Bridges and Boundaries: Growing the Cross-Cultural Mind." *Language Learners of Tomorrow: Process and Promise.* Margaret A. Kassen, ed. Lincolnwood, IL: National Textbook Company, 1999. 151-87.

Galloway, Vicki. "Constructing Cultural Realities: Facts and Frameworks of Association." Jane Harper, Madeleine Lively and Mary Williams, eds. *The Coming of Age of the Profession: Issues and Emerging Ideas for the Teaching of Foreign Languages.* Boston: Heinle & Heinle, 1998.

Galloway, Vicki. "Toward a Cultural Reading of Authentic Texts." *Languages for a Multicultural World in Transition.* Heidi Byrnes, ed. Lincolnwood, IL: National Textbook Company, 1992. 86-121.

García Castaño, F. Javier, Rafael A. Pulido Moyano and Angel Montes del Castillo. "*La educación multicultural y el concepto de cultura.*" *Revista iberoamericana de educación* 13 (1997). Madrid: Organización de Estados Iberoamericanos para la Educación de la Ciencia y la Cultura.

Geertz, Clifford. *The Interpretation of Cultures.* New York: Basic Books, 1973.

Goldberg, David. "Super-sized Kids." *The Atlanta Journal and Constitution*, Section F. August 26, 2001.

Gover, M. and P. Conway. "To Borrow and Bestow: Identification as the Acquisition of Value." Paper presented at the Association of Moral Education Conference, Atlanta GA, November, 1997.

Haas, Mari and Margaret Reardon. "Communities of Learners: From New York to Chile." *Collaborations: Meeting New Goals*, New Realities. June K. Phillips, ed. Lincolnwood, IL: National Textbook Company, 1997. 213-41.

Hall, Edward T. The Silent Language. Garden City, NY: Doubleday and Company, Inc., 1959.

Hegedus, András T. and Katalin Forrai. "Particularism, Universalism and Teaching Someone to Be Different." *The Roma Education Resource Book* 1 (1999). [http://www.osi.hu/iep/ minorities/ResBook1/ResBookAll.htm]

Kaiser, Ward and Denis Wood. *Seeing Through Maps: The Power of Images to Shape Our World View.* Amherst, MA: ODT, Inc., 2001.

Kaplan, Robert B. "Contrastive Rhetoric and the Teaching of Composition." *TESOL Quarterly* 1 (1967): 10-16.

Karliner Joshua. *The Corporate Planet: Ecology and Politics in the Age of Globalization.* San Francisco: Sierra Club Books, 1997.

Katz, Stacey L. "Videoconferencing with the French-Speaking World: A User's Guide." *Foreign Language Annals* 34 (2001): 152-57.

Kramsch, Claire. "The Cultural Component of Language Teaching." *Language, Culture and Curriculum*, 8 (1995): 83-92.

Labarca, Angela. "Hispanic Technical and Cultural Content." *Spanish and Portuguese for Business and the Professions.* T. Bruce Fryer and Gail Guntermann, eds. Lincolnwood, IL: National Textbook Company, 1998. 93-113.

Lee, Lina. "Student Perspectives on the Internet: The Promise and Process of Online Newspapers and Chats." *Language Learners of Tomorrow: Process and Promise.*

Margaret Ann Kassen, ed. *Language Learners of Tomorrow: Process and Promise* Lincolnwood, IL: National Textbook Company, 1999. 125-50.

Lessard-Clouston, Michael. "Towards an Understanding of Culture in L2/FL Education." *The Internet TESL Journal* 3 (1997): No. 5. [http://www.aitech.ac.jp/~iteslj/Articles/ Lessard-Clouston-Culture.html]

Lévi-Strauss, Claude. *The Raw and the Cooked.* John & Doreen Weightman, translators. London: Jonathan Cape, 1970.

Macera, Pablo. *Historia del Perú.* Lima: Editorial Bruño, 1993.

Mintz, Sidney. *Sweetness and Power: The Place of Sugar in Modern History.* New York: Viking Press, 1985.

Miranda Azurmendi, Francisco. *"Aprender de McDonalds (El secreto de su éxito)." Calidad Total en Hostelería.* [http://www.iespana.es/calidadtotal/menu.htm]

National Standards in Foreign Language Education Project. *Standards for Foreign Language Learning: Preparing for the 21st Century.* Yonkers, NY: ACTFL, 1996.

Neruda, Pablo. *"Oda a la papa," "Oda al tomate." Full Woman, Fleshly Apple, Hot Moon*: *Selected Poems of Pablo Neruda.* Stephen Mitchell, ed. New York: HarperCollins, 1997.

O'Neill, Jessie H. *The Golden Ghetto*: *The Psychology of Affluence.* Milwaukee: The Affluenza Project, 1996.

Paz, Octavio. *"Mesa Redonda, Mexico: Presente y Futuro." Revista Plural* 2 (1971). [http://www.excelsior.com.mx/archivo/personajes/octaviopaz/plural2.html.]

Schlosser, Eric. *Fast Food Nation: The Dark Side of the All-American Meal.* Boston: Houghton Mifflin, 2001.

Scollon, Ron and Suzanne Wong Scollon. *Intercultural Communication: A Discourse Approach*, 2nd ed. Malden, MA: Blackwell Publishers, 2001.

Simonton, Stell. "Living Rooms Losing Their Prominence." *The Atlanta Journal and Constitution*, Section F. August 27, 2001. 1-6.

Smith, Richard J. "Maps, Myths, and Multiple Realities: Chinese Representations of the 'Other' in Late Imperial Times." Madison: Paper delivered at University of Wisconsin, June 5, 1997. [http://polyglot.lss.wisc.edu/east/maps.html]

Thayer, Lee. "Human Nature: Of Communication, of Structuralism, of Semiotics." *Semiotica* 41 (1982): 25-40.

Trompenaars, Fons and Charles Hampden-Turner. *Riding the Waves of Culture: Understanding Diversity in Global Business*, 2nd ed. New York: McGraw Hill, 1998.

Vázquez, Ruth and Isabel Bueso. "*El ingrediente pragmático, parte indispensable de la cocina de E/LE.*" Madrid: Centro de Estudios Internacionales Enforex, Marzo 1999.

Weismantel, Mary J. *Food, Gender and Poverty in the Ecuadorian Andes.* Prospect Heights IL: Waveland Press, 1988.

Appendix A. Food in Poetry

México
"*La sandía.*" José Juan Tablada (mexicano).
"*Soneto de la granada.*" Xavier Villaurrutia (mexicano).

La América Central
"*Padre nuestro maíz.*" Werner Ovalle López (guatemalteco)
"*El naranjo.*" Mercedes Durand Flores (salvadoreña)
"*La poesía es como el pan.*" Roque Dalton (salvadoreño)
"*La vendedora de mangos.*" Francisco Valle (nicaragüense)
"*Quiero un poema sencillo y bueno.*" Michele Najlis (nicaragüense)
"*Canción de Juan.*" Marco Aguilar (costarricense)
"*Sobremesa.*" Claudio Gutiérrez (costarricense)

El Caribe
"*Mulata-Antilla.*" Luis Pale Matos (puertorriqueño)
"*Nancy.*" De Pan Caníbal. Noel Jardines (cubano)

La América del Sur
"*Coles.*" Campo Ricardo Burgos López (colombiano)
"*El festín.*" Germán Pardo García (colombiano)
"*Alheña y azúmbar.*" Jaime Jaramillo Escobar (colombiano)
"*Uva.*" Angela García (colombiana)
"*Una forma de ser.*" Edmundo Perry (colombiano)
"*El maíz.*" Manuel Felipe Rugeles (venezolano)
"*Hambre.*" Virginia Martínez (venezolana)
"*I. Que la vida amanezca.*" Edmundo Aray (venezolano)
"*Nuez.*" Jorge Carrera Andrade (ecuatoriano)
"*El maíz.*" José Santos Chocano (peruano)
"*El pan nuestro.*" César Vallejo (peruano)
"*El camión con letras naranja.*" Federico Torres (peruano)
"*Loa del panadero.*" Alfredo José Delgado Bravo (peruano)
"*Salsa de ají.*" Receituario amazónico. Nicomedes Suárez Araúz (boliviano)
"*El pan.*" Vicente Barbieri (argentino)
"*La mujer de Albahaca.*" Canto Popular de las Comidas. Armando Tejada Gomez (argentino)
"*Tregua del día.*" Armando Tejada Gómez (argentino)

"*Poema IX.*" El libro de Lucía. Glauce Baldovin (argentina)
"*Uvas Rosadas.*" Joaquín Giannuzzi (argentino)
"*Ana, mujer de Nicolás y el puñado de arroz.*" José Pedroni (argentino)
"*La sartén.*" Edgard Bayley (argentino)
"*Una canción*," "*Lo cotidiano.*" Martín Prieto (argentino)
"*Citrus.*" Ing. Teodoro R. Freitman (argentino)
"*El trigo.*" De El cántaro fresco. Juana de Ibarbourou (uruguaya)
"*Pimiento.*" Victor Jara (chileno)
"*La casa.*" Gabriela Mistral (chilena)
"*Sociedad de consumo.*" Oscar Hahn (chileno)
"*Oda a la cebolla*,""*Oda al limón*," "*Oda al maíz*," "*Oda al aceite*," etc. *Odas elementales.* Pablo
     Neruda (chileno)
España
"*Poema 86*," "*Nanas de la cebolla.*" Miguel Hernández (español)
"*Higo-desconocido*," "*Higo-sazón y hojas*," "*Limón.*" Miguel Hernández (español)
"*La sandía.*" Salvador Rueda (español).

Appendix B. Web Resources*
Food as Product, Practice, and Perspective
A. Proverbios

1. *Por qué decimos lo que decimos*:
http://www.arcom.net/belca/del_dicho/indice%20dichos.html
2. *Refranes de mi abuela*: http://home.earthlink.net/~vanders/refran.html
3. *La salud en 80 refranes*:
http://www.revistanatural.com/primavera299/refranes.htm
4. *Piropos clásicos* http://www.geocities.com/SouthBeach/Lights/1011/index_piro
pos.html

B. Platos

1. Central American and Carribean recipes, histories, legends, significance.
Includes both Spanish and English links: http://www.cs.yale.edu/homes
/hupfer/global/regions/cam.html
2. Spain: http://www.algoasi.com/menun.htm
3. Regional dishes of Spain, by comunidad autónoma: http://www.terra.es/per
sonal6/jimpvc/cocina.htm
4. Spain: *Un poco de todo:* http://www.bongust.com/links/
5. Spain, *productos y cocina*:
http://www.ontheline.org.uk/spanish/paseo/espana/food.htm
6. Spain: *platos y prácticas*:
http://www.ontheline.org.uk/spanish/paseo/espana/print.htm
7. Spain: *Tapas*; recetas: http://www.arrakis.es/~jols/tapas/recetases.html
8. Spain: *Panaderías* (great photos): http://www.sergiokohn.com/catalogo/panade

ria/pan.htm; http://rt0032ud.eresmas.net/; http://www.comsv.com/asociados/0106/Default.htm; http://www.rusticpa.com/; http://www.galeon.com/mariasenora/productos28715.html

9. *Cocina vasca*: http://www.avepa.es/grupos/gevo/jornadas01/gastronomia.htm

10. Peru: *Comida peruana*:
    http://www.consuladoperuguayaquil.org.ec/cultura_comida.htm

11. Peru: *Platos*: http://www.geocities.com/TheTropics/Breakers/4162/food.htm

12. Peru: *La papa*: http://www.caretas.com.pe/2001/1675/articulos/papa.phtml

13. Peru: *Ceviche/cebiche*:
    http://www.bongust.com/noticias/63/firmas/ruth/2508/;
    http://www.geocities.com/TheTropics/4100/index2.html

14. Peru: *Recetas peruanas*: http://www.chiclayo.dynip.com/

15. Peru: *Cocina peruana*: http://www.cultura.com.pe/gastronomia/recetas/cocina/index.htm

16. Peru: *Platos principales, cocina peruana*:
    http://www.exceso.net/cocina_y_vino/cocdic25/p046s1.htm

17. Peru: *Cocina peruana*: http://www.uninet.com.py/GUITEL/anuarios/gourmetel/cocina_peruana.htm

18. Peru: *Productos, recetas*: http://www.comidaperuana.com/Bienvenida.htm

C. Perfiles y preferencias

1. Changes in food consumption/purchasing habits, Latin America:
   http://www.waba.org.br/wbw97/esp3.htm

2. Peru, encuestas: *¿Cuál es la fruta preferida de los limeños? ¿Qué plato de la comida peruana usted cree que se está dejando de consumir?* (Enero 2000):
   http://cultura.rcp.net.pe/gastronomia/aldia/index.shtml

3. Spain: *Estudio nacional de nutrición y alimentación*: http://www.fuentestadisticas.com/numero7/paginas/indice-pub.html#publ1

4. Spain: *¿Qué comemos y a qué precio?*
   http://www.patagon.es/NotDet.asp?ID=3801&Op=2

5. Surveys of bread consumption in Spain; favorite ways of enjoying bread:
   http://www.panaderia.com/informes/consumo.html#1

6. Spain: surveys of bread consumption; bread and health: http://www.panaderia.com/informe_consumidor.html

7. Spain: *Ir de tapas*, Spain: http://sevillahoy.net/ciudad/tapas.htm

D. Pedidos y porciones

1. El Peregrino restaurant menu, Miraflores, Peru:
   http://www.ascinsa.com/ELPEREGRINO/

2. Casa Botin restaurant menu, Madrid, Spain:
   http://www.gomadrid.com/rest/botin.html

3. La Chacra restaurant menu, B.A., Argentina:
   http://www.lachacra.com.ar/index.htm

4. Los Cochinitos restaurant menu, Mexico, D. F. :

http://www.loscochinitos.com.mx/

5. Antigua Hacienda de Tlalpan, Mexico, D.F. http://www.antiguahaciendatlal pan.com.mx/ant/barra.htm

6. Restaurante Las Margaritas, Bogotá, Colombia: http://members.tripod.com/latin_sites/margaritas/

7. El dilema norteamericano (article on portion size): http://www.uole.com.ve/estampas/2001/02/18/salud.htm

E. Precios, presupuestos y puntos de venta

1. Peruvian marketplace, *Estampas pacasmayinas*: http://www.rtpnet.org/~felipe/estampas/costumbres.htm

2. *El mercado peruano*: http://perso.wanadoo.fr/lepever/cuzco-es.htm

3. Peru: contains video of meat section, supermarket: http://www.ukans.edu/~latamst/ecuador/food/

4. Spain: online supermarket: http://portal.lacaixa.es:8008/Shopping/Shopping_Home/0,1185,1,00.html

5. Spain: online supermarket: http://www.condisline.com/

6. Spain: online supermarket: http://hiper.alcampo.es/

7. Spain: online supermarket: http://www.secretariaplus.com/tienda/v2/view.asp?section=market

8. Spain: online supermarket: http://supermercado.elcorteingles.es/frameset.asp

9. Argentina: online supermarket: http://www.coto.com.ar/ENTRETENIM/ZONAe.htm

10. Venezuela: online supermarket: http://www.globalasist.com/supermercado/

11. Costa Rica: online supermarket: http://www.milventas.com/rubro.php?categoria=56

12. Guatemala: online supermarket: http://www.misuper.com/

13. Dominican Republic: online supermarket: http://www.detodonet.com/detodonet/supermercado/departamentos.asp?dept=1

14. Mexico: online supermarket: http://www.mexgrocer.com/spmex/index.asp?BannerID=0905

15. Colombia: online supermarket: http://www.mercomas.com/

F. Patrones emergentes

1. Spain: Telepizza: http://www.telepizza.es/flash.htm

2. Spain: *A tu gusto, del restaurante a casa*: www.restauranteencasa.com

3. Spain: *Appétit, tu restaurante en casa*, Las Palmas de Gran Canaria: http://appetit.idecnet.com/

4. Fast food in Spain: http://www.iespana.es/calidadtotal/mac.htm

5. Peru fast food: http://www.mcdonalds.com.pe/mccombos.asp

6. Peru: fast-food franchises: http://www.pyeasociados.com/panorama.htm

7. Peru: fast-food franchises and *tropicalización*: http://www.pyeasociados.com/franquiciaenperu.htm

8. Peru: franchise market, including local fast-food franchises, in English: http://www.tradeport.org/ts/countries/peru/isa/isar0008.html

9. Frozen foods and the Latin American market:
http://www.enlacelatino.com/importadoralatina/Actual/ html/contenido/peru.html
10. Coca-cola en el mundo: http://www.coca-cola.com.co/coca_col_mundo.php
11. KFC in Mexico: http://www.afrpm.com.mx/historia.htm
12. Chilean site for reading comments, complaints about fast-food establish
ments: http://www.meenoje.com/guiacons.asp
13. Changes in siesta, Spain (English): http://www.bol.ucla.edu/~dbacich/siesta.htm
14. Argentina: Changes in food consumption patterns
http://usa.clarin.com/suplementos/zona/2000-07-02/i-00301e.htm

G. El paladar

1. Spain: *Jamón serrano, chorizo, tintos Rioja y la empresa alimentaria española.*
http://www.ac-nantes.fr/peda/disc/lv/espagnol/textes/btsci/ecrit97.htm
2. Peru: *el paladar peruano*: http://www.redperuana.net/
3. Peru: *influencia china*: http://www.tercera.cl/diario/2000/06/29/t-
29.16.3a.CRO.S_CHIFA.html
4. Peru: *paladar peruano*: http://www.bongust.com/noticias/53/firmas/kari
na/2191/
5. Peru, Ecuador: instructional unit with Ecuador focus from U. Kansas,
includes videos of supermarkets; video of cooking cuy (quite graphic):
http://www.ukans.edu/~latamst/ecuador/food/
6. Peru: *comidas típicas*: http://www.geocities.com/Athens/Crete/7763/
7. Peru: *fusión de sabores* (history, tradition, influences):
http://www.terra.com.pe/cocina/historia.shtml

H. La etiqueta

1. Mexico: table etiquette (including treatment of waiters; detailed):
http://www.dobleu.com/bin/ir.du?ID=38478;
http://www.restauramex.com/interes/etiqueta.html
2. Mexico: rules for eating tacos (humorous and informative):
http://www.webtelmex.net.mx/paloma17/
3. Peru: table etiquette:
http://data.terra.com.pe/comidaperu/stilo/etiqueta1.asp#SENTADOS
4. Venezuela: table etiquette: http://www.rena.e12.ve/naturales/etiqueta.html
5. Spain: *¿Cómo reclamar en un restaurante?*:
http://www.patagon.es/NotDet.asp?ID=3801&Op=2
6. Comparison of European and American: http://www.accua.com/cocina/con
ten/COC613.asp

* Note: As Internet users are aware, the lifespan of URLs is unpredictable. Although every effort has been made here to provide stable websites, it is impossible to guarantee their continued existence to readers. At this writing, the websites listed have been "up and running" for at least the past 4-5 months.

Chapter 2

Deepening Cross-Cultural Learning in the Classroom

Olgalucía G. González
Washington and Jefferson College

"This already has been an absolutely amazing experience ... One of the things that has made it so great though, is the fact that while learning, accepting and loving a new culture, I have also found a new appreciation for my own."

Third-year Spanish student studying in Seville

As the profession entered the 1980s with a clear idea of what type of curriculum was needed in the foreign language classroom, an area of intense discussion was (and continues to be) that of the importance of integrating the teaching of culture into the teaching of language. In 1981, Loew stated that foreign languages could be strengthened through a global or world-centered orientation. In 1983, Morain concurred with Loew that the foreign language classroom is the place to promote harmony among the peoples of the world: "There is no area of education with a greater potential –or a greater responsibility— than that of foreign language education [because] in our classroom we have the opportunity to help students become open, accepting, caring citizens of the world community"(410). On the other hand, Kramsch's major concern was that students continued to be exposed to the target culture in a passive manner. She believed that in order to avoid the development of a "tourist perspective" on the foreign language culture, teachers should pay attention to "patterns of interpretation or personal constructs" that are used by individuals to look at their own and other people's cultures (437-8). [See González for an historical overview of the teaching of culture in the United States in the 1970s and 1980s.]

Today, foreign language teachers around the country proudly profess to teach culture. But in spite of our commitment, the difficulty we have had in the last four decades persists: "culture still remains a superficial aspect of language learning…It has been talked about, talked around, and has been the subject of workshops, conference presentations, books…" (Lange 58). Perhaps culture remains a superficial aspect of language-learning programs because there is no consensus about what aspects of the culture should be taught and how exactly practitioners are to integrate language and culture in the classroom.

According to Lange, The National Standards Project is providing us with some guidance about the teaching of culture. *The National Standards for Foreign Language Learning* emphasize that all the linguistic and social knowledge required for effective human-to-human interaction is reflected in its goal: "Knowing how, when, and why, to say what to whom"(11). However, a superficial interpretation of this statement might lead to a likewise superficial view of culture teaching. Very often, cultural conflicts do not arise from what our students say, since it is easy for them to memorize what to say and when and to assimilate surface customs and facts. Rather, as will be illustrated in this chapter, serious misunderstandings may arise from what is not said, what is not heard, or what is not even seen, and these misunderstandings are as much the result of a lack of self-awareness as a lack of other-culture knowledge.

Our culture teaching must go much deeper. We must take culture out of the box of textbook *notas culturales* and, as we make a commitment to nurture the cross-cultural mind, be willing to shift our teaching focus from the basic instructional mechanics to the educational outcomes that require deep learning processes and complex thinking. In this way, as students learn about other people's perspectives, practices and products and compare them with those of their own, they will also be able to discover "the boundaries, the defining edges of separate realities" (Galloway 1999, 153) that they must understand to appreciate other cultures as well as their own.

Although only goal area 2 (2.1, 2.2) and goal area 4 (4.2) of the *Standards* deal directly with "culture," it must be understood that all goals are interconnected, since the study of another language and culture enables communication with the people who speak it, builds community, and facilitates connections with other disciplines. The final result of this interconnectedness goes beyond the school boundaries, as the ability to communicate in other languages and to understand cultural patterns different from their own prepares students to function effectively in a global context, increasing opportunities of employment, community service, travel and pursuit of personal interests. Fantini notes that including "Comparisons" as one of the goal areas of the Standards is a significant development in its implications for the education and growth of every learner. Throughout the language-learning process, students go beyond the surface to discover similarities and differences in the perspectives, practices, and products of their native and second cultures and are able to see how language affects and reflects culture.

An ideal way for students to apply the "how, when, and why to say what, to whom" is in interaction with members of other cultures while living/studying abroad. The experience abroad provides learners the opportunity to commune with native speakers in informal contexts and to immerse themselves in the culture. However, when students study abroad for short periods of time, during a summer or a four-week period for, example, their attitude toward the target culture and language (the cultural and linguistic assumptions they bring to the foreign country) is crucial to a successful experience.

These attitudes and assumptions are acquired in a variety of ways, but perhaps mainly through the foreign language classroom. Therefore, culture teaching should be integrated regularly with language instruction so that students understand the perspectives of the culture (traditional ideas, attitudes, meanings, and values) from which products and practices are derived. Since we use language to express cultural perspectives and to participate in social practices, studying languages provides students with opportunities to discover cultural insights that are unique. It is only through the language that students interact meaningfully and directly with members of the culture, and it is this "insider's perspective [that] is the true catalyst for cross-cultural understanding"(*Standards* 48-49).

The Need for Authentic Cultural Information

My many journeys to Spanish-speaking and other-language-speaking countries in the world has made me realize that any attempt to have successful communication must be based on proficiency in both the language and the cultural system of the country one visits. Given the increasing number of American students traveling abroad and the large Spanish-speaking population in the United States (35 million), it is imperative that students develop a cultural context for communication. When language teachers' cultural experiences are Latin American, it is natural to emphasize cultural patterns from those cultures with which they are familiar. However, because cultural patterns cannot be generalized, especially when dealing with a world as politically, economically, geographically, racially and ethnically varied as the Hispanic world, it is important for students to learn that people who speak the same language do not necessarily share the same culture. Equally important for students to recognize is that members of one culture usually make assumptions about other cultures based on the perspectives of their own culture (Standards 48). The erroneous conclusions that result from these assumptions may produce negative reactions to the foreign culture and lead to the formation of stereotypes. It is the responsibility of foreign language teachers, therefore, to foster learning that will help students counteract inappropriate assumptions and prejudices. The culminating experience will provide students the opportunity to interact with members of the other culture beyond the classroom, either in the community or abroad.

In order to prepare appropriate activities based on comparisons of similarities and differences of U.S. and Hispanic cultures and to help students of Spanish anticipate sources of miscommunication, the author traveled to Spain to interview Spaniards who interact with U.S. students on a regular basis, either as their language instructors or as members of host families. Fifteen Spaniards of different ages and professions were interviewed (see **Appendix A**). In addition, a cultural survey was constructed and administered to sixty U.S. students studying at three different institutions in Spain. The survey was divided into four sections with a total of sixty questions and allowed students the option of writing additional comments in the fifth section (see **Appendix B**). Answers to three of the questions asked of Spaniards during the interviews were especially important because they provided the author with critical cultural insights that were useful in planning classroom activities: (a) *¿Qué diferencias culturales has observado entre los españoles y estadounidenses?* (b) *¿Qué es lo que más te molesta de ellos? (c) Según tu opinión, ¿qué deberían saber los estudiantes antes de venir a España para estar mejor preparados a adaptarse y aprovechar la experiencia?*

The following are sample responses of Spaniards to these three interview questions. Because these voices are authentic, they serve to create a "cross-cultural mindset" that Spanish teachers can use as the basis for classroom activities that will help learners embark on an active process of cross-cultural discovery. Responses revealed important opinions shared by most of the interviewees; however, it is necessary to remind our students and ourselves that in expressing their views, Spanish respondents were not necessarily criticizing U.S. culture; rather, they were reflecting the perspectives and practices of their own culture.

Question A: *¿Qué diferencias culturales has observado entre los españoles y estadounidenses?*

Respondent #1
Una diferencia cultural es que los jóvenes estadounidenses se emborrachan porque se asombran con la libertad aquí (aunque hoy los jóvenes españoles también se emborrachan). Otra, las niñas son tontorronas (silly) en el trato con los chicos, las españolas son diferentes. Tienen un doble estándar como cuando desaprueban las expresiones de cariño en público...

Respondent #2
Pues, de entrada, por ejemplo, que en España lo bueno que tenemos es el sol y el ambiente, la fiesta, entonces los estudiantes o los turistas americanos, digamos, cuando llegan a España llegan a divertirse y a tomar el sol, parecen como cangrejos y es una cosa que llama la atención...

Using these comments as a point of departure, teachers may ask students to work in groups to share their ideas about the topics of friendships, having a good time, drinking. For example: *¿Por qué muchos estudiantes estadounidenses quieren emborracharse cuando van a otros países donde la edad para beber es menos de 21 años? ¿Por qué buscan las chicas establecer más que una simple amistad cuando conocen chicos en otros países? ¿Hacen lo mismo en los Estados Unidos o actúan de una manera diferente?*

Respondent #3
Un tema muy importante es la gran independencia... El chico no ha querido integrarse con nuestros hijos ni con nosotros y todo para evitar control y poder vivir a tope, o sea, se va con un conocimiento completo de la calle, de lo español... El debe decir: "yo en la familia, en cuanto menos mejor para que no me controlen."... Me parece que él vive, que éstos viven, su vida más con sus amigos que con la familia...

Respondent #4
Pues no sé, quizás que están menos con la familia, o sea, están más con los amigos que con la familia, creo yo, al menos eso vi.

Respondent #5
En las relaciones interpersonales que quizás ellos, pues les gusta ser más independientes y aquí las familias son más protectoras y cuando ellos llegan son todavía más.

These remarks reach to the core of cross-cultural differences in that underneath behaviors are ways of seeing self and the world. The fact that U.S. students were so "independent" bothered some of the interviewees whose concept of *familia* is quite different from the U.S. individualist perspective of "family." Yet, it is doubtful that U.S. students saw anything "wrong" with their behaviors, or that they were even aware that they were offending their hosts. While in the earliest stages of their Spanish learning our students learn to recite "*la familia es muy importante en la cultura hispana,*" comments of these respondents indicate that our teaching of *familia* must go much deeper than simply alerting students to its importance. Indeed, we must reach into the very meaning of the word within its own cultural framework.

Respondent #6

Bueno, en el estadounidense lo primero que notas es la gorra, la gorra vuelta hacia atrás, le identifica de entrada. Después en su forma de actuar, siempre actúan muy exageradamente, se notan llamando la atención...se ven porque se expresan mucho, brazos, no sé, hablan muy alto.

Respondent #7

Yo veo que la diferencia más grande es la extroversión del americano con respecto a la introversión, a la vergüenza del español a decir ciertas cosas o a actuar en cierta forma, ¿no? El americano no tiene mucha vergüenza, puede expresarse libremente y se expresa, de hecho, libremente, hablan, hablan alto...

A possible explanation for this perception is that Americans abroad very often tend to speak louder to make themselves understood. Elliott et al., however, observe that U.S. speech volume is typically not only greater than that of "Spanish speakers," but also tends to be broader and more varied (perhaps the English use of intonation for emphasis contributes to this). Spanish speakers, they note, typically employ a narrower range, reserving volume for situations of anger or excitement. U.S. tourists in groups are extremely noticeable in Spain when they react enthusiastically to the sights around them because Spaniards tend to be more solemn and quiet in these situations. Spaniards (who, by the way, were also perceived as "loud" by U.S. students) resent what they interpret as Americans' overconfidence and display of power outside their own country.

Respondent #8

Normalmente el estudiante norteamericano es muy concreto. Tiene la mente cuadriculada. Ellos quieren saber exactamente lo que significa cada cosa. Quieren codificarlo todo. No soportan lo ambiguo.

Respondent #9

En tema de exámenes, me parece como si cada uno fuera enemigo, hay una competencia muy grande; el otro no le va a copiar, tiene que sacar mejor nota. Hay una necesidad muy grande de superación, que aquí en España se está viendo ahora, no sé si será un efecto americano o español.

The behaviors observed by these respondents once again reflect the clash between two different systems of preferences in seeing the world. Edward Hall has referred to cultures as "low context" or "high context" communicative systems. High-context communication relies heavily on shared cultural meanings and on how things are said rather than what is said. This mode tends to be preferred in collectivist societies where backgrounds are common and shared and where the individual assumes identity through relationships. High-context cultures have a high tolerance for ambiguity, as the relationship and the context—not necessarily explicit words—invoke the meaning. U.S. students, however, come from a very "low context" culture (reinforced through a low-context preference in the

U.S. educational system) where information is transmitted via explicit code ("say what you mean"). If information is not explicit and detailed, meaning is distorted. The low-context mode is preferred in cultures where backgrounds and experiences are diverse, and where an individual's identity lies in sense of self, rather than in others. Likewise, in the individualistic U.S. mainstream, the achievements of a person are valued above the harmony of the group. Competitiveness is viewed as a positive trait and it is often quite difficult for U.S. students to understand that "competition" between friends or directly between two classmates in a school setting is not a "natural" phenomenon in Hispanic cultures (see Galloway, this volume).

Question B: *¿Qué es lo que más te molesta de ellos?*

Respondent #1
El patriotismo cerril (blind patriotism). *Deben entender que América no es todo. Les duelen las críticas afectivamente, pero deben aceptar las críticas. Si se toca a América, todos se tornan muy defensivos, aún los liberales. En cambio los españoles son muy críticos del gobierno y la política. Solo un 5% respeta a los políticos en España.*

Respondent #2
Molesta que todo lo vean a través del cristal americano, todo lo comparan con lo americano. Su ignorancia en cuanto a eventos mundiales y aún de su propio país. Esto contrasta con los estudiantes españoles de su edad.

Respondent #3
Pues está el tema también de que llegan aquí con un poquitín de ego de superioridad. Allí se nota, ¿no? Cuando hay una exaltación y tal, "pues soy americano" y tal, ellos hacen énfasis que son americanos.

Respondent #4
A veces si que les gusta criticar cosas pequeñas, como bueno, "qué desorganización," cuando realmente en su país ocurriría lo mismo, porque yo también he viajado y he tenido que soportar cosas de ésas.

Respondent #5
Lo que más me puede molestar a veces es la incapacidad, parece, de comprensión de la forma que tenemos de ser aquí en algunos aspectos, cosa que es natural. Me puede molestar en el caso de la forma en que lo digan, algunos alumnos no entienden y no quieren entender que están en otro [país]. ... Pero es que ellos mismos se encargan de poner obstáculos porque no quieren permitir que les entren.

Ranking first place in irritations are those behaviors perceived to reflect an attitude of U.S. superiority. While explicit student behaviors are not revealed through these comments, the nature of the conflict once again seems to lie at the level of beliefs and values, with U.S. students, as members of a markedly "universalistic" mainstream culture, tending to judge another culture in terms of the "things" of the American way of life and the extent to which they satisfy the individual. Indeed,

Gómez Dacal, reporting on his experience as a Spaniard teaching in the U.S., makes a similar observation that "*uno de los principios no escritos que regulan la vida escolar es el que postula que el alumno se sienta a gusto, feliz*" and interprets an operant personality "*...que disemina a diestro y siniestro sus insatisfacciones y frustraciones, y sus a veces sesgadas percepciones, muy frecuentemente trasladando las responsabilidades propias a los 'otros'.*"   Indeed, in our classrooms we must begin to open minds as well as eyes: If we compare cultures at the level of "what they have and what I have," the logical consequence is perceived superiority of "I and mine." Comparisons can be made only at a deeper level— the level of beliefs, values and other systems of logic.

Respondent #6
A nivel de clase, la exigencia que tienen con respecto al profesor. Se ven como "clientes." Es una relación causa-efecto. Los alumnos españoles se quejan cuando han suspendido, los norteamericanos, [aún] cuando tienen una buena nota. Es una competitividad malsana. Esto no sucede en España con un 1%. Trasciende el compañerismo. Los españoles hacen trampa, los norteamericanos no, posiblemente debido a la competitividad. Los dos extremos son tremendos.

Respondent #7
Más que molestar me ha dado pena que no hayan aprovechado el tiempo lo suficiente porque creo que muchos han desperdiciado una oportunidad fantástica, lo que pasa es que también sé que tienen una edad en la que no eres consciente de eso, porque todos hemos tenido esa edad...

Respondent #8
Pues a mí lo que más me molesta, digamos es que salgan todas las noches. Pero, ¿por qué? Porque tienen cinco horas de clase, salen a las seis de la tarde es tener mucho tiempo para poder hacer otras cosas ... para decir "me pongo a estudiar una hora o dos horas todos los días, por ejemplo, pues se llega a las diez de la noche y todavía se puede salir a tomar una café, a tomar una copa," pero ellos están de salir todos los días ... el ritmo de verano para una persona que salga todos los días es insostenible porque hay que tener un aguante increíble.

For better or worse, the client-server relationship is one that has grown in U.S. classrooms through the last few decades—indeed, it has been promoted in demands for "accountability" and the blurring of boundaries between business and academia. It is also a relationship that has startled many foreign visitors (and foreign students) in U.S. classrooms who interpret both the free inquiry and frequent outspokenness of student - "clients" as signifying a lack of respect. While this relationship may correspond logically to a system that fosters egalitarian relationships, it will be perceived differently through the eyes of a culture accustomed to seeing a more established framework of authority in this context. By the same token, the Spaniards, expecting to see certain study behaviors as indication of the seriousness of U.S. learners, may have perceived their nightly outings as neglect of learning and concern only for having fun. In truth, they may have been right; or they may have misread what for students was seen as an opportunity to interact with others in the effort to use their language skills and learn through the practical, "hands on" approach that is, once again, fostered through the U.S. school system. On the other hand, students could simply have been behaving the way they believed was appropriate: It is quite possible that, using their own culture's framework, this was the type of behavior they associated with a culture that values "working to live" instead of "living to work."

Respondent #9

El comportamiento en la mesa. Hay cosas que a nosotros nos chocan mucho[pero] para ellos no es ninguna falta de educación, cuando para nosotros es lo primordial. Por ejemplo, comer y eructar, que nosotros no lo consideramos buenas costumbres. Estirarse en la mesa es otra cosa que no es normal para nosotros...

Respondent #10

El despilfarro de los servicios, de la luz, del agua, del teléfono, de todo... Los modales en la mesa, pero más que modales es falta de uso de, pues, los cubiertos en este caso...

In a society where meal times and table behaviors are flexible and varied, the importance and complexity of dining etiquette across cultures is an area of behavior that simply cannot be overlooked in our classrooms. Stretching, yawning, burping or taking off one's shoes are, of course, unacceptable behaviors in U.S. society as well, and students should be guided to understand the importance of their role as ambassadors when they are abroad, and how easily their idiosyncratic behaviors can lead to generalized impressions about the "American way of life" that they so pride. Likewise, coming from a society of taken-for-granted abundance where nature is viewed as a resource to be used, it is especially important that learners become attuned to the existence throughout the world of very different values of sustainability and conservation, very different views of the relationship between Man and Nature and very different attitudes toward use, waste and disposability (see Galloway, this volume).

Question C: *Según tu opinión, ¿qué deberían saber los estudiantes antes de venir a España para estar mejor preparados a adaptarse y aprovechar la experiencia?*

Respondent #1

No sé, yo les diría que se organicen el plan de estudios que quieren realizar, porque el plan de estudios no es solamente las clases, sino decir, "bueno, lo voy a realizar para decir una vez que salga de clase voy a estudiar una hora u hora y media, después pues dedicarme al tema, por ejemplo de los intercambios (conversation partners)." *Luego que vengan mentalizados, que hay tiempo para todo. El salir no quiere decir que sea a diario, ... si decides salir la semana entera, ya es un problema.*

Respondent #2

La comida es otro tema, desde luego. Yo entiendo que las comidas no son las mismas, ni los hábitos tampoco, ni los horarios, entonces, pues estás en otro país, sabes que no vas a ir la vida entera. ... Pero en los hábitos alimenticios ya es el tema de si la cultura española se basa en el aceite famoso, ¿no? Pues oye, aquí se va a cocinar con aceite... Yo nunca he probado la crema de cacahuate, o sea que a lo mejor me gusta, pero sé que si voy a Estados Unidos probaré la crema de cacahuate, es que es así. ¿Hamburguesas? Pues comeré hamburguesas y de todo, ¿no? Pero vamos, que ya está.

Respondent #3

Bueno, pues yo creo que deberían saber más de nuestras costumbres, los horarios no suelen ser problema porque se acostumbran en seguida, pero el trato familiar sí que tienen que entender que cuando una madre de una casa les insiste mucho, no es que les quiere molestar, sino porque aquí en España se insiste, porque hasta que no haces tres veces una invitación, la otra persona no se siente autorizada para ir, ¿no? Aquí dices "ven a casa a comer" y tú "no, no, no," "que sí hombre, ven," "no, no, no" "por favor, ven." Entonces ya vas, o seas pocas veces aceptas a la primera invitación.

Respondent #4

No sé, luego también pues que sepan en qué consiste aquí la comida, pues aquí se cocina con aceite, que es diferente y bueno... la dieta mediterránea. Por ejemplo, no les gusta nada comer pescado, pues yo creo que deberían saber las vitaminas que tiene el pescado y que se puede comer de muchas maneras muy ricas, ¿no? Y que hay que estar abierto a todo eso... y no sé bueno también conviene siempre que sepan un poco de la historia del país, del gobierno, de las costumbres, de la economía, de la ciudad donde van a estar, ¿no?

Spanish cuisine is quite varied. Spaniards enjoy their food and, for the most part, prefer to eat fresh products rather than canned or fast food. Mealtime is almost sacred, as it represents those moments when the whole family gathers to enjoy the company of others without hurry. Perhaps one of the most frequent observations made of U.S. students abroad is their reluctance to try new foods. Yet, food is very much a window to the culture. Students need to understand these are special products of the culture, created by its members, and that their value derives from their sharing not just as a meal but as an expression of community spirit. There are, indeed, often certain "rituals" associated with this food sharing (such as accepting/declining food offerings) that, if unknown and therefore unpracticed, can lend the impression of a guest as "uncultured," "uninterested" or just plain rude (see Galloway, this volume). Our culture teaching must go deep into the values associated with food and family, must also educate as to proper behaviors in the context of mealtime gatherings, but at the very least must equip students with knowledge about the country they will be visiting to awaken an interest in getting to know the people who share a history, a geography, a government and some common way of viewing the world.

Respondent #5

Pues para la convivencia y para las comidas sobre todo. Qué es lo típico en España, qué clase de comidas se hacen, que horarios las hacemos, las costumbres españolas, aunque nos solemos adaptar un poco al horario de ellos, sobre todo a la hora de las cenas que acostumbramos hacerlas a las 10 de la noche y cuando los tenemos a ellos nos limitamos a que sean a entre 8:30 o 9:00.

Respondent #6

Sí, creo que es importante que conocieran nuestras costumbres mínimas de convivencia, de esto de gastos, de comida, de estar unidos a la familia, de higiene mas que de limpieza, de costumbres. Yo creo también que es importante, que cuando vengan, no venir con el sentido de superioridad con que vienen los críos (kids) *y entonces eso duele a la familia, y cuanto más pobres son las familias, más les duele porque ellos unen a España. Yo creo que también sí que sería bueno [que supieran] que somos muy susceptibles a las comparaciones.*

Respondent #7

Yo creo que [ese estudiante] debía haberse portado mucho mejor y que España era diferente de allí y que quizás por eso es que no nos llevamos tan bien porque estaba todo el día que hacía lo que quería, se estaba todo el día afuera, no decía ni "hola" ni "adiós," ni hablaba y debería haber sabido que España es diferente de allí, que las costumbres son diferentes y que la familia está más unida.

An area that perhaps students don't think too much about is that of the *saludo*; indeed the rules for its use in U.S. culture are quite loose—one may greet or not greet according to one's preference at the moment. In fact, I have had to train my students to greet me when I enter the classroom, or even to respond when I greet them! In Hispanic cultures, however, the greeting is extremely important—one is expected, for example, to greet others when entering a room and also to say good-by to others when leaving, regardless of the whom or what of one's visit. As we teach our students how to greet (handshakes, hugs, kiss on one or both cheeks), we need to guide them also to understand the why of their practice (see Galloway, this volume).

Students were also given a survey in which they were asked to reflect on their experience in Spain (**Appendix B**). Their responses reflect observations made by Americans as "outsiders" who also judged Spaniards through their own cultural lenses. Question #44, for example, provided students with a list of areas of cultural difference between Spaniards and Americans and asked them to mark those they had noticed while abroad:

The following are some cultural differences between Spaniards and Americans. Check all of those you have noticed.

a) Concept of time	h) Social class distinctions
b) Close-knit family structure	i) Table manners
c) Formality of clothes	j) Speech volume
d) Formality of greetings	k) Use and amount of leisure time
e) Greeting strangers	l) Working to live vs. living to work
f) Male-female interactions	m) Sex roles
g) Picking up the tab	n) Others that you have noticed

From this list, the concept of time, formality of clothes, formality of greetings, male-female interactions, use and amount of leisure time, and working-to-live versus living-to-work were noticed (checked) by most of the respondents. However, differences in table manners were noticed only by

30% of the Americans whereas the Spaniards had observed significant differences in the way the Americans conducted themselves at the table, leading us to believe that the students may have been unable to adapt to Spanish etiquette because they were oblivious to the differences.

Answers to question #45 ("Of those items listed above, which has been the easiest for you to adapt to?") indicated that the customs easiest to adapt to were the close-knit family structure—which most students really liked—and the formality of greetings with handshakes, hugs and kisses. Some also enjoyed the amount of leisure time Spaniards have and the idea of working-to-live versus living-to-work. At the same time, Spaniards commented on students' lack of diligence and observed that they were always partying. It seems that what Spaniards criticized was not that students would enjoy themselves on the weekends but the fact that they did it every day, to the probable neglect of their learning. On the other hand, most students found it very difficult to adapt to the difference in male-female interactions and sex roles. Both male and female students noticed a great deal of *machismo* reflected, for example, in the *piropos*—suggestive remarks made by men to passing women on the street—or by the 'traditional woman' role many women over forty still embrace. Other items that were problematic for some students were the concepts of time and minimal personal space, the formality of clothes, and voice volume. As we see, a typical comment Spaniards and Americans make about each other is that "they are loud." U.S. students were probably reacting to the way Spaniards act in social situations and celebrations and also to the fact that when they get excited they raise their voices to the point that outsiders think they are about to hit each other. Expression of emotion is indeed another dimension on which cultures may vary.

Most students reported having experienced some vague, difficult-to-describe cultural conflict or frustration due to the fact that they "are Americans" and "not used to the culture" or lacked knowledge about "the cultural differences between the United States and Spain" and "differences between the way men and women act in the United States and in Spain" that made them feel out of their "comfort zone." Still others decried the Spaniards' "ignorance about Americans" or simply gave the assessment that "people are weird here" without offering specific explanation.

Interviewing Spaniards was an eye opener. It provided me with a deeper understanding of their traditions, ideas and values and helped me discover why Spaniards are so sensitive when people break the rules of social practices. Many noted, for example, that American students were very independent and did not value the close-knit family structure in Spain. However, it is interesting to remember that while American students did notice a difference in the family structure, they stated that it was easy for them to adjust to it and, furthermore, that they really enjoyed it. The concept of *la familia hispana* is one of the first things taught in Spanish classes from the very beginning when students learn the appropriate vocabulary for the nuclear as well as the extended family. However, while both teachers and students think that students understand, it may well be that they do not. We can only "see" what exists in our own framework of reality and, as a result, what students may be seeing from our lessons is not that *familia* is a different, deeply tentacled concept but rather that *familia* is the same as "family" only it's more important in Hispanic cultures'. Students enjoyed the Spanish family perhaps as they do their own U.S. family —as a source of support and comfort there for them, as autonomous beings, when they needed it. But the U.S. sense of "family" is not typically rooted in the same network of responsibility and connection and mutuality as *familia*—it does not take from them as much as it gives. Further, had the Spanish families expressed their observations to students at the time, such comments would likely have represented a tremendous source of conflict to the students, who would interpret family attention as the sacrifice of independence. As Wattley-Ames states, perhaps "the fundamental difference between Spanish and American individualism is that for an American, personal individuality or independence is a state of mind and source of identity." However, Spaniards do not see family loyalty and closeness as a loss of personal identity.

Other student-survey responses corroborated the notion that we usually interpret behaviors in a foreign culture in terms of our native culture, as students' own notions of time, order and efficiency colored their observations. Through the *cristal americano*, food should always be fast, and "at times Spaniards are lazy and forgetful; e.g., restaurants, sometimes their pace of doing things is too slow;" likewise, food should be similar, and one frustration was that of "not being able to get a 'real' hamburger." Accustomed to certain material goods and the U.S. "order" of things, students complained about "the lack of things that make life easier in the United States," about "most of the stores being closed at lunch time," and about the general "lack of order." Their own notion of privacy and its value in their culture explains why students felt such distaste for "public displays of affection." As Galloway notes, "things that don't fit are different, and therefore either illogical, immoral, nonsensical, or the result of a naive and inferior stage of development of 'human nature' (1992, 88).

Applying These Insights to the Classroom

How can the insights gained through the analysis of the interviews and surveys described here help us as teachers in the Spanish classroom? Of paramount importance is encouraging students to engage in interaction with native speakers and preparing them for this type of experience, teaching them to go deeper into the culture and below the surface of "how, when, and why, to say what to whom" (*Standards* 11) and "what to do when and where, and how to interact within a Hispanic cultural context" (*Standards* 445).

I had the opportunity to apply what I had learned from this fieldwork in Spain when I prepared activities for a second-year Spanish class the following year. Several students in the class were considering the possibility of studying in Spain for a month and living with local families. In planning classroom activities then, it was necessary to provide experiences that represent the diverse cultures that constitute the Hispanic world (with an emphasis on Spain, in this case) while being relevant to their own lives while studying in Spain. Culture learning in this class was organized around the cross-cultural themes that surfaced during the interviews with the Spaniards and in students' answers to the post-visit survey. Some of the themes included were: family structure, male-female interactions and sex roles, greetings, leisure time, and meals (with all the related aspects of mealtimes, importance and length of time spent at the table, etiquette and types of food). These themes are rather common in first- and second-year courses and are easily integrated with grammar instruction.

The broad goals were for students to understand the perspectives underlying the products and practices of the Spanish culture (Standard 2.1 and 2.2) and also to demonstrate understanding of the concept of culture through comparisons of the Spanish culture and their own (Standard 4.2). Before designing activities, it was necessary to decide what students should do to demonstrate that they had met these goals. Lange believes that in the case of culture standards, "the specific learner perform-ances related to the understanding of the relationship between practices and perspectives, products and perspectives, and the understanding of the concept of culture through comparisons" between the learner's C1 [in this case U.S. culture] and the C2 [in this case, Spanish culture] should be deter-mined (87). By engaging in this intercultural comparison, students were expected to go beyond the surface of both cultures to develop their own self-awareness, without which understanding of another culture is not possible. Asking some of the questions proposed by Lange and focusing on the results of the interviews and surveys were useful in designing the course curriculum(87).

- What practices in this culture should students learn? What perspectives do they reflect?
- What judgment might they initially have of these practices? What cultural perspective does such a judgment reflect?
- Upon learning more about these practices, how will these perspectives change?
- What products should students learn about? What perspectives do they reflect?
- What judgment might students initially have of these products? What cultural perspective does this judgment reflect?
- Upon learning more about these products, how will these perspectives change?
- How are the practices, products, and perspectives related? (Lange 87)

Having decided on the content (themes that emerged in the interviews and surveys), it was also necessary to consider the process. There are several models that teachers can draw upon when think-ing about how to address the culture (2.1 and 2.2) and culture comparison (4.2) goals in their cur-riculum (Fantini; Hadley). Throughout the semester, Hanvey's four stages of cross-cultural awareness (moving from a tourist perspective, to the ideal level of empathy) reminded the author that cultural proficiency does not happen overnight, that learners can move back and forth between levels, and that experiencing conflict is part of the learning process (Galloway 1999, 96).

Hanvey's Levels of Cultural Awareness			
Level	Data	Mode	Interpretation
I	Superficial stereotypes	Tourism, text	Exotic, bizarre
II	Significant and subtle contrasts	Culture conflicts	Unbelievable, irrational
III	Significant and subtle contrasts	Intellectual analysis	Believable
IV	Awareness as insider	Cultural immersion	Believable from subjective familiarity

Hanvey's four stages were also helpful in deciphering and explaining comments made by students in the surveys when trying to express the conflicts or frustrations they experienced while studying in Spain. Such comments ranged from "people are weird here" to "I'm used to another culture" to "One has to get used to the way Spaniards [act]."

Sample Classroom Activities

The Process Approach developed by Fantini and Dant is helpful for guiding teachers in developing lesson plans because it integrates the teaching of culture with the teaching of language. The model is composed of seven stages (Fantini 194-96):

1. Presentation of new material

2. Practice of new material within a limited and controlled context

3. Explanation or elucidation of the grammar rules behind the material, where necessary or useful

4. Transposition and use of new material (cumulatively with other materials previously learned) into freer contexts and more spontaneous conversation

5. Sociolinguistic exploration of the effect of social context on language use, emphasizing the appropriateness of specific language styles (as opposed to grammaticality)

6. Culture exploration for determining appropriate interactional strategies and behaviors, while also learning about values, beliefs, customs, etc., of the target culture

7. Intercultural exploration, i.e., comparing and contrasting the target culture with the student's native culture

The approach is cyclical and flexible, allowing teachers to begin either with Stage One and continue sequentially, or to start at another point, depending on the content, level and learning styles of the participants. I prefer to focus on a cultural event so as to frame language within the cultural context.

Cultural events can be presented through authentic readings, videos, audiotaped or videotaped interviews with native speakers, demonstrations, slides, pictures, culture capsules and role-plays (see Humbach, this volume). Fantini provides an array of sample activities that can be incorporated within the Process Approach (197-207); Hadley includes a number of activities designed in keeping with the *Standards for Foreign Language Learning* (360-71); and the Education Department of the Spanish Embassy also provides useful activities that can be accessed via its web page (www.spainembedu.org/materials). The following are some of the activities I used with my second-year Spanish class, but they can be adapted for beginning and more advanced levels of language proficiency via pre-listening or pre-reading activities. I have chosen to focus on *la comida*, since it was one of the primary sources of cross-cultural conflict in Spaniards' interviews. All phases of this activity would, of course, be conducted in Spanish.

Las comidas y su importancia

Standards: Communication, Cultures, Comparisons
Procedure:
1. Have students in groups come up with ideas of what "lunch" is in their culture. Then ask groups to share their ideas with the class in order to compare them with those of other groups.
2. As a class, brainstorm U.S. associations with "lunch" by means of a semantic map; start students off with the category *¿Cómo?*

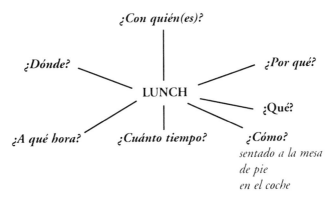

3. Show photos, slides or a short video clip of people having lunch in Spain or Latin America. Such videos are available commercially and typically accompany basal Spanish textbooks.

4. Ask students to take notes as they watch, recording as many observations as possible. Use these observations to build a semantic map for the Spanish *comida* in the same fashion as was done with the US "lunch".

5. Have students compare the two semantic maps to note the similarities and differences they have identified. As a class, hypothesize as to the possible reasons for some of these differences.

6. As homework, have each pair of students choose one area of difference, form a hypothesis, and independently explore the Internet for evidence that confirms or rejects their hypothesis.

7. In class, provide time for each pair of students to unite and discuss/compare their independent research findings. They should also identify at least two questions that arise from the data they have gathered. Then, have pairs of students report to class on the composite of their findings as well as their questions for further research.

Student research will undoubtedly trigger a great deal of curiosity, particularly about the taste of certain unknown foods. While there is no substitute for firsthand experience, teachers may supplement student presentations with pictures from the web or descriptions, to acquaint students with some of the *platos típicos* (see Galloway, this volume). But students may also appreciate the art of Spanish cuisine through the experience of preparing a *gazpacho* or such deceptively "simple-looking" Spanish dishes as a *tortilla de patatas*. Each student question should be viewed not as requiring a direct teacher-answer, but as an avenue of exploration, the opportunity to ask another question. We must keep in mind, however, that student research is fallible. It is quite natural for misreadings, overgeneralizations or "wrong" information reporting to occur when learners are conducting their own research. These misunderstandings, however, are extremely informative to us as teachers, as they tell us where learners are in their thinking and thus serve to direct us down certain avenues of further inquiry. Indeed, considering Spaniards' interview responses, the type of activity progression illustrated here sets the groundwork for many areas of exploration, such as those offered in the following examples.

Follow-up direction #1: Table etiquette.

1. Show slides, pictures or videos (or perhaps take a closer look at the video used in Step 3) in which table manners can be observed clearly (left hand is not in the lap, there is no switching of hands between cutting and eating food, fruit is typically peeled, etc.). Have students take notes on their observations.

2. Show on transparency selected comments offered by Spaniards concerning U.S. students' table manners and adaptation to Spanish foods and dining customs. Have students play the role of unbiased observers and explain the perspectives underlying the behaviors of both cultures: Why did the U.S. students behave this way? Why did the Spaniards react to their behavior?

3. To acquaint students with appropriate "rules" of etiquette (including body language, use of utensils, placement of hands, and so on), an audio-motor unit (Elkins, et al.) may be used. In

this technique, students follow the teacher's commands as they enact typical mealtime table manners: Follow this by having students summarize differences and then by doing their own role-plays in varied mealtime contexts.

Follow-up direction #2: *El tapeo.*

1. Brainstorm with students about common snacks in their culture. As a class, have students contribute thoughts to the right column of the grid that follows.

2. Activate background knowledge about the traditional *tapeo* in Spain (have pictures ready in case students are not familiar with the custom).

3. Present a short reading on *tapas* or have students visit some of the very friendly, colorful and imaginative Spanish websites on tapas.

4. As a class, have students share what they learned in their research on *tapas* to complete the left column of the grid.

5. Begin cross-cultural discussion by focusing on the when and where questions: do we have scheduled snacking times and snacking places in the U.S.? Why or why not? Would we like to have such scheduled times? Snacking places?

6. Proceed to the what and where questions of the grid: Ask students to imagine their reactions if they were in Spain and were served different types of *tapas,* such as whole shrimp with eyes, snails, squid, octopus, and so on. Would they be open to trying these foods that are very popular in Spanish culture, or would they opt for those with ingredients already familiar to them as Americans? Ask students to weigh the pros and cons of both options.

7. Discuss the importance of social interaction in both cultures in relation to having tapas or "snacks" through the questions ¿por qué? and con quién(es)? In the U.S. do we "snack" alone or with others, generally? What are our reasons for snacking in the U.S.? Are these different from Spaniards' reasons? If they could choose a "snacking system," which one would they select and why?

	Tapas en España	Snacks in U.S.
¿Qué?		
¿A qué hora?		
¿Dónde?		
¿Con quién(es)?		
¿Por qué?		

Such activities can be adapted to focus on any aspect of dining customs in any Hispanic country. For example, another tradition closely related to the importance of food is that of having coffee after meals and chatting at the table with family and friends for hours (*la sobremesa*). It is also a social reason to get together with friends at other times of the day. Coffee in the U.S. is a product of a culture on the move and the practice associated with it does not involve social interaction. In contrast, having a cup of coffee for Hispanics is a reason to relax and enjoy the company of friends. The practice of *tomar un café*, in fact, is as important, if not more important than the coffee product itself.

While the *product* of American coffee has been the subject of a great deal of other-culture jesting, the fact is that the *practice* of preparing coffee is usually quite different across cultures, as one of my methodology students illustrated in her microteachings: After demonstrating and priming the necessary vocabulary, she proceeded to prepare coffee the American way with an electric coffee maker; she then prepared coffee the Costa Rican way using a rustic-looking artifact that consisted of a beautifully decorated wood stand and a cloth filter. She discussed the importance of coffee in la *cultura costarricense*, not only socially but also economically, integrating the teaching of command forms into her culture lesson. Everyday tasks using products-in-practice are invaluable not only for intercultural exploration, but for provoking and maintaining student cross-cultural interest (see Humbach, this volume).

Authentic Performances: Understanding the Perspectives behind Practices and Products

According to Lange, an important question to be asked when designing a curriculum and determining standards is "What authentic performance will give evidence that learners meet the standards?" (87). Students who were exposed to cross-cultural teaching before their visit to Spain tended to have more successful and satisfying travel-abroad experiences than those of the two-year-old surveys reported here. Their post-travel journals and classroom presentations provide clear evidence that cross-cultural learning took place in the classroom and that the preparation they received made a positive impact. When they arrived in Spain, although scared, they were able to approach the culture in the right frame of mind because they had already gone beyond the tourist and textbook stereotypes stage in the classroom. They recognized cultural similarities and differences, but for them, Spanish culture had become "believable" (in Hanvey's definition). Many plan to return to Spain or to another Spanish-speaking country; and for most, as the following comments illustrate, the experience abroad was a life-changing one:

My journey to Spain has been one of the most amazing experiences of my life. It's very difficult to put into words exactly what I saw and how I felt, but I can definitely say that both the people and the country of Spain have taught me more than I can ever have imagined. This trip made me better. Yes, my Spanish is better, my ability to write, to listen and to communicate, but also my character is better because now I can really appreciate another culture. Even more importantly, however, I learned a lot about myself.

I cannot believe that we have spent three weeks in Spain! The worst is that I don't want to leave. I believe that the most important thing I learned is the way in which Spaniards communicate. My Spanish sister taught me a lot about young people's culture. It's interesting; although there are big and small differences between the two cultures, all of us are human beings, we are similar. This is one of the most important things that I learned during this trip. And also, I realize that American culture is not the only one in the world. This trip has made me a better person.

This trip has made me change some of the decisions I made in the past. The life I had in Spain is the one I want. I feel a need to explore new places and have new experiences. This trip has been important because it has made me realize that I don't want to stay in Pittsburgh. Now, in the plane, I am sad and afraid because I don't want to go back. Thank you for this opportunity and for what you did for us because all of that has had a great impact on my life.

I only know that I have a family in Spain and that I love them very much. Right now, I am not sad even though it hurts to say good-bye. I know I will return to Seville to live, to work and to enjoy this special city. There will always be a place in my heart for the memories, the experiences, and the people. Thank you for a fantastic opportunity.

Before leaving, you said we would change. Well, I have changed. This trip has changed my life for the better. I hope you know how my life has changed for the better. I hope to be able to return some day.

I must say that in the days leading up to my departure I started to feel a little apprehensive about leaving. I was a little nervous about going to a different country for the first time, living with a strange family, but as soon as I arrived I knew this was going to be an experience I would never forget. I quickly began to love my family, the culture I was immersed in, and the beauty of the country. I will never forget this experience, and all the things I've seen and done while here in Spain will forever make an impact on my life.

The trip to Spain seems like a dream now. Before leaving the U.S., you told us we would not be the same persons after the trip. Although one doesn't realize when changes happen, I am sure every individual has learned a great deal about himself/ herself, about the Spanish language, and about the Spanish culture. This month has meant a lot to me. My Spanish family, the teachers, the Sevillanos and, of course you, everybody has taught me a lot and I am thankful for that. I hope to return to Spain again.

Conclusion

This chapter has described the results of data collection on perceptions of Spanish hosts and U.S. students during the travel-abroad experience and has presented some implications and samples of classroom application of these findings. The interviews with Spaniards focused on very key topics that will help us in choosing *what* to teach. The situations in which Spaniards most quickly noticed inappropriate behavior should also direct us as to *how*, in giving us a message that we need to go deeper in our culture teaching—to develop deeper self-awareness, stronger skills of observation (including self-observation), more varied strategies of analysis and synthesis. Both the host- and visitor-voices recorded here tell us that there are things students are not seeing, points of conflict that they are not recognizing and hence not able to reconcile. And these voices of students and foreign hosts tell us that we cannot simply go on dispensing culture in the form of quick notes; rather, we must face the fact that preparing students to experience another perspective is a long-term project that will always be incomplete and that will require both care in classroom planning and patience in classroom practice. It has also shown the importance of authentic materials as input in developing cross-cultural awareness prior to students' study-abroad experiences. Since culture occupies a central place, a core place, in the *National Standards for Foreign Language Learning,* there is hope that the FL classroom may become the place where students move away from tourist-corner behaviors not only to explore and recharge their own sense of identity but to become more open to the perspectives of other world communities. As has been demonstrated in students' testimonies quoted here, good cultural preparation can result in an attitude that welcomes newness and difference as adventures in a continual process of personal transformation and enrichment.

Acknowledgements

I express my sincere thanks to Dr. Vicki Galloway for her invaluable suggestions. Special thanks are also due my Spanish students who, after receiving cross-cultural instruction, immersed themselves in the culture of Spain with an open mind and allowed me to use their voices as testimony of their experiences.

Works Cited

Elkins, Robert J., Theordore Kalivoda and Gennelle Morain. "Teaching Culture Through the Audio-motor Unit." *Foreign Language Annals* 6 (1972): 61-67.

Elliott, Candia, R. Jerry Adams, and Suganya Sockalingam. "Communication Patterns and Assumptions of Differing Cultural Groups in the United States." Oregon: Office of Multicultural Health, Department of Human Resources, September 31, 1999.

Fantini, Alvino. "Comparisons: Towards the Development of Intercultural Competence." *Foreign Language Standards: Linking Research, Theories, and Practices.* June K. Phillips and Robert M.

Terry, eds. Lincolnwood, IL: National Textbook Company, 1999. 165-217.

Galloway, Vicki. "Bridges and Boundaries: Growing the Cross-Cultural Mind." *Language Learners of Tomorrow: Process and Promise.* Margaret A. Kassen, ed. Lincolnwood, IL: National TextbookCompany, 1999. 151-87.

Galloway, Vicki. "Toward a Cultural Reading of Authentic Texts." *Languages for a Multicultural World in Transition.* Heidi Byrnes, ed. Lincolnwood, IL: National Textbook Co., 1992. 86-121.

Gómez Dacal, Gonzalo. *"Ser maestro en Estados Unidos."* Washington, D.C.: Embajada de España. www.spainembedu.org/apoyo/pdf/gonzalo1.pdf

González, Olgalucía G. *Teaching Language and Culture with Authentic Materials.* Unpublished Doctoral Dissertation. Morgantown: West Virginia University, 1990. 13-73.

Hadley, Alice Omaggio. *Teaching Language in Context*, 3rd ed. Boston: Heinle & Heinle Publishers, 2001.

Hall, Edward T. *The Silent Language.* Garden City, NY: Doubleday and Co., Inc., 1959.

Hanvey, Robert. "Cross-Cultural Awareness." *Toward Internationalism: Readings in Cross-Cultural Communication.* E. C. Smith and L.F. Luce, eds. Rowley, MA: Newbury House, 1979.

Kramsch, Claire J. "Culture and Constructs: Communicative Attitudes and Values in the Foreign Language Classroom." *Foreign Language Annals* 16 (1983): 437-448.

Lange, Dale L. "Planning for and Using the New National Culture Standards." *Foreign Language Standards: Linking Research, Theories, and Practices.* June K. Phillips and Robert M. Terry, eds. Lincolnwood, IL: National Textbook Company, 1999. 57-135.

Loew, Helen Z. "A Global Orientation to Culture Content." *Proceedings of the National Conference on Professional Priorities.* D. L .Lange and C. Linder, eds. Hastings-on-Hudson, NY: ACTFL Materials Center, 1981. 31.

Morain, Genelle. "Commitment to the Teaching of Foreign Cultures." *Modern Language Journal* 67 (1983): 403-412.

National Standards in Foreign Language Education Project. *Standards for Foreign Language Learning in the 21st Century.* Lawrence, KS: Allen Press, 1999.

Watley-Ames, Helen. *Spain is Different*, 2nd ed. Yarmouth, Maine: Intercultural Press, 1992.

Additional Readings

In addition to the different activities provided in class as part of the second-year Spanish curriculum, students who decided to travel to Spain were asked to read chapters from several books as part of the preparation for their journey. Since students agreed that the readings were beneficial and often referred to them in their journals, a list is offered here for reference.

Graff, Marie L. *Culture Shock! Spain.* Portland, OR: Graphic Arts Center Publishing Co., 1997.
Hess, J. Daniel. *Studying Abroad/ Learning Abroad.* Yarmouth, ME: Intercultural Press, 1997.
Storti, Craig. *The Art of Crossing Cultures.* Yarmouth, ME: Intercultural Press, 1990.

Appendix A. Interview Questions

The following questions were used as general guidelines to interview Spaniards. Questions varied slightly depending on the previous answers and to keep the conversation flowing in an informal manner.

1. *¿Cuántos años hace que tienes contacto con estudiantes de los Estados Unidos?*
2. *¿Corresponde el comportamiento de los alumnos estadounidenses a lo que esperas de ellos, generalmente?*
3. *¿Qué diferencias culturales grandes has observado entre los españoles y estadounidenses?*
4. *¿Qué críticas tienes de ellos, o sea, qué es lo que más te molesta de su comportamiento?*
5. *Por otro lado, ¿qué es lo que más te agrada de ellos?*
6. *Al final, ¿qué cambios positivos resaltan?*
7. *En tu opinión, ¿qué deben saber los estudiantes estadounidenses antes de venir a España para que se puedan adaptar mejor? ¿Qué deberíamos enseñarles para prepararlos mejor para esta experiencia?*
8. *¿Qué más puedes añadir?*

Appendix B. Cultural Survey

When traveling abroad one realizes that very often words and actions of a person from one culture may motivate, frustrate, or embarrass someone from another culture. The purpose of this questionnaire is to find out about cross-cultural communication between you and those Spaniards with whom you have contact during your stay in Spain. Your answers will be useful in determining points of potential conflict to prepare some guidelines to help people understand and approach the Spanish culture. The information you supply will be kept confidential.

Thank you for your cooperation.

Section I. Background Information

1. Age _____   2. Gender: Female _____ Male _____

3. Rank at school: Fr. _____   Soph. _____   Jr. _____   Sr. _____Other _____

4. Semesters of College Spanish before this trip _____

5. Have you been in Spain before? _____ 6. When? _____ 7. How long? _____

8. Reasons for spending this period of time in Spain

_____

_____

Section II. Host Family

9. Host Family _____

10. Number of family members living at home and their approximate ages

_____

_____

11. Occupation of head of the family _____

Using the scale from Excellent to Poor, please indicate your answer to each of the following questions. Also, please explain your answers when requested.

    5=Excellent   4=Very good   3=Good   2=Fair   1=Poor

12. How would you describe your host family? 1____ 2____ 3____ 4____ 5____

13. Please explain your previous answer.

_____

_____

14. How would you describe your relationship with your host family?
    1__ 2__ 3__ 4__ 5__

15. Please explain your previous answer.

_____

_____

16. How would you describe your living accommodations?
    1____ 2____ 3____ 4____ 5____

17. Please explain your previous answer.

_____

_____

18. How would you describe your meals with the family?
    1____ 2____ 3____ 4____ 5____

19. Do you feel as a member of the family or as a guest? _____

20. Do you participate in daily family activities?

    Eating with the family _____

    Watching TV with the family _____

    Chatting with the family at the table or at other times _____

    Shopping with the family _____

    Visiting with their relatives _____

    Attending church with the family _____

    Attending a special celebration (birthday, Día del Santo, etc.) at a relative's home

    Other_____

21. Has your host family imposed any restrictions regarding:

    Telephone use _____

    Use of shower / hot water ____

    Having same sex visitors _____

    Having different sex visitors _____

    Rearranging your room _____

    Time to come home during the week _____

    Time to come home on weekends _____

    Other_____

22. Overall, how reasonable do you feel these restrictions are?

    5 Very reasonable_____ 4_____ 3_____ 2_____ 1 Very unreasonable_____

23. Is your host family tolerant and helpful when you have difficulties with the language?

    Yes _____   No _____

24. Have you had any misunderstandings with your host family?

    Yes _____   No _____

24a. Please give examples:

    _____
    _____
    _____

25. What do you believe caused the misunderstanding?

    Language_____

    Culture_____

    Other (Please explain)   _____
    _____

Section III. Teachers and School Personnel

26. How would you describe your relationship with your teachers and other school personnel?

    5=Excellent   4=Very good   3=Good   2=Fair   1=Poor

26a. Teachers   5____ 4____ 3____ 2____ 1____

26b. Administrators   5____ 4____ 3____ 2____ 1____

26c. Staff   5____ 4____ 3____ 2____ 1____

27. Please explain your answers to 26
    _____
    _____
    _____
    _____

28. Do you have informal contact with teachers and school personnel in non-academic settings?

    Yes_____ (Answer next question)   No_____ (Skip next question)

29. Has this informal contact helped you understand the Spanish culture better?

5 Extremely helpful_____ 4____ 3_____ 2_____ 1 Not helpful

30. Have you had any misunderstandings with your teachers or other school personnel?

Yes _____   No _____

30a. Please give examples:

_____

_____

_____

_____

31. What do you believe caused the misunderstanding?

Language_____

Culture_____

Other (Please explain)

_____

_____

Section IV. Spanish Society

32. Have you met Spaniards other than your host family or teachers and school personnel?

Yes_____ (Answer next two questions)   No_____ (Skip next two questions)

33. How pleasant has your contact with these Spaniards been?

5 Very pleasant_____ 4_____ 3_____ 2_____ 1 Very unpleasant_____

34. Please explain your previous answer

_____

_____

_____

35. Where have you spoken to Spaniards who provide services?

Airport_____

Bus or train station_____

Bars_____

Restaurants____

Stores____

Travel agency____

Other   (Please specify)_____

36. How helpful have these people been?

    5 Extremely helpful____   4____   3____   2____   1 Not helpful____

37. How successful do you believe you have been in dealing/communicating with Spaniards?

    5 Very successful____   4____   3____   2____   1 Unsuccessful

38. What do you think your success or lack of it in dealing with Spaniards is due to?

    Speaking the language____   Not speaking the language well ____

    Understanding the culture____   Not understanding the culture well ____

    Other (Please be specific)_____

    _____

39. In your contacts with all Spaniards have you encountered any hostility or resentment toward the United States or the American people?

    Yes____ (Answer next question)   No____ (Skip next question)

40. What do you think these feelings are due to?

    US international politics____

    US domestic politics____

    US economic policies toward other countries ____

    An image of Americans being uncultured and rude (the "ugly American") ____

    Other (Please be specific)

    _____

    _____

41. During your stay in Spain, have you experienced any cultural conflicts or frustrations?

    Yes____ (Answer next two questions)   No____ (Skip next two questions)

42. Please explain the conflict or frustration you experienced _____

    _____

43. What do you think was the cause of the conflict or frustration? _____

    _____

44. The following are some cultural differences between Spaniards and Americans. Check all of those you have noticed.

    _____ Concept of time

    _____ Close-knit family structure

    _____ Formality of clothes

    _____ Formality of greetings (handshake, hugs, kisses)

    _____ Greeting strangers in stores, restaurants, etc. (Buenos días, Adiós, Hasta luego)

    _____ Male-female interactions

    _____ Picking up the tab

    _____ Sex roles

    _____ Social class distinctions

    _____ Table manners

    _____ Talking loudly

    _____ Use and amount of leisure time

    _____ Working to live vs. living to work

    _____ Others that you have noticed (Be specific)

    _____
    _____
    _____

45. Of those items listed above, which has been the easiest for you to adapt to?

_____

46. Which has been the hardest for you to adapt to?

_____

Section IV. Personal Growth

47. Has this trip enriched your life?

Yes _____   No _____

48. Please rate the value of the following experiences during your study trip

5=Extremely enriching   4=Very enriching   3=Enriching   2=Little enriching
1=Not at all enriching

48a. Improving my knowledge of Spanish   5____ 4____ 3____ 2____ 1____

48b. Being immersed in the culture   5____ 4____ 3____ 2____ 1____

48c. Living with a Spanish family   5____ 4____ 3____ 2____ 1____

48d. Meeting Spaniards my age   5____ 4____ 3____ 2____ 1____

48e. Visiting cultural and historical sites   5____ 4____ 3____ 2____ 1____

48f. Sampling typical dishes   5____ 4____ 3____ 2____ 1____

48g. Finding out how Spaniards view my culture 5____ 4____ 3____ 2____ 1____

48h. Sharing my culture with people from cultures other than my own
                                                 5____ 4____ 3____ 2____ 1____

48i. Other (Please be specific)
_____5____ 4____ 3____ 2____ 1____
_____5____ 4____ 3____ 2____ 1____
_____5____ 4____ 3____ 2____ 1____

49. Please indicate the extent of your personal growth that you can attribute to this study trip.

5=Very much   4=Much   3=Moderate   2=Little   1=None

49a. Interacting well with people from cultures other than my own
                                                 5____ 4____ 3____ 2____ 1____

49b. Learning to be tolerant, and willing to negotiate

5_____   4_____   3_____   2_____   1_____

49c. Becoming more aware of global and nternational issues and events

5_____   4_____   3_____   2_____   1_____

49d. Becoming a more effective member in multicultural society

5_____   4_____   3_____   2_____   1_____

Section V. Comments and Suggestions

Please use the space provided below for additional comments and suggestions.

_____

_____

_____

_____

_____

_____

_____

_____

Chapter 3

Perspectives in Practices:
Teaching Culture Through Speech Acts

Carmen García, Arizona State University

Empleado	*1 Buenos días Sr. Gutiérrez, ¿me llamaba?*
Jefe	*2 Sí. He venido notando una conducta diferente de la que usted normalmente*
	3 muestra, y quería saber si tiene algún problema, si en este momento está
	4 atravesando por alguna situación difícil. ¿Qué me puede decir al respecto?
Empleado	*5 Mire, este... el problema es que algunas veces llego tarde pero no siempre y*
	6 encima este... yo siempre cumplo con mi trabajo y...
Jefe	*7 Usted está llegando con retraso a las horas de trabajo y sabe que nosotros*
	8 tenemos aquí un horario estricto, de entrada, y un problema más grave aun es
	9 que usted se está retirando antes de la hora estipulada por la empresa, o sea,
	10 pues 'tonces como usted puede notar, es una...una situación que no podemos
	11 tolerar.
Empleado	*12 Bueno, sí, perdóneme pero es que he tenido problemas familiares y no he*
	13 podido llegar exactamente a la hora, pero...
Jefe	*14 Usted tiene que participar el problema que tiene y darle la solución.*
Empleado	*15 Sí sí sí, yo comprendo, pero es que...*
Jefe	*16 Cumpla con su horario y su trabajo.*
Empleado	*17 Sí, sí, supuesto, pero como le decía...*
Jefe	*18 Si no, esta situación vamos a tener que discutirla con su supervisor. De todas*
	19 maneras esto va a pasar a su hoja de servicios y si se repite, queda despedido.
Empleado	*20 Pero señor, si le dije que...*
Jefe	*21 Ni una palabra más. Puede retirarse.*

What happened in this conversation? Why was the employee not allowed to finish his explanation in response to the boss' request for justification? Why did the boss threaten the employee with termination? Was the boss so upset that he could not listen, or was it that the employee was not assertive enough and failed to present his case in a clear and straightforward manner? The fact is that we simply don't know, and although this impasse might occur when communicating in one's native language with people who belong to one's own speech community—that is, people who share our same rules for the production and interpretation of speech (Hymes)—or among people who have frequent social interaction (Gumperz), it is more prone to occur when communicating with people outside our speech community, as when communicating in a foreign language. To understand this conversation and its outcome, it is helpful to consider the following: the frames of participation, the stylistic devices, and the politeness strategies used. We will now look at these three different aspects.

According to Bateson, speakers' utterances can be interpreted in terms of their understanding of how the communication is intended; that is, the hearer must understand the activity the speaker is engaged in and the frame within which he is participating (business, friendly, ironic, etc.). Along these lines, reprimanding within a 'this is business' frame is not a personal confrontation. The metamessage 'this is business' signals the context within which the reprimand does not represent personal hostility. It might then be interpreted that the Boss was participating within a 'this is business' frame (mentioning the negative effects of the Employee's behavior on the company, for example) and the Employee was participating within a 'this is friendly' frame (giving the personal, family reasons and problems). This different type of frame of participation is one of the factors that might have influenced the negative outcome of the conversation, since it might also have triggered different types of stylistic devices.

Tannen (8) defines stylistic devices as the linguistic choices speakers make in different situations to convey a given message. These choices are considered in terms of all the other devices with which they co-occur and in terms of the possibilities from which they are chosen. According to Tannen, stylistic devices determine the effect of an utterance in the interaction and influence judgments made both about what is said and the speaker who says it. In the previous dialogue, the Boss' stylistic devices are clear, direct and complete, showing a well considered objective. The Employee, on the other hand, hesitates, does not finish his statements and, consequently, does not state his case effectively. Speakers' linguistic choices might vary according to the situation they are in, their own personalities, their interlocutors, and so on, but it is also true that a speaker's individual behavior might be influenced by his or her culture. Brown & Levinson's theoretical framework suggests that, in the course of interaction, speakers have the need to be liked and/or approved of (to maintain their positive face) and to be respected and not imposed upon (to maintain their negative face). When we pay a compliment, for example, we are respecting the interlocutor's positive face, but when we criticize that person, we threaten or go against that person's positive face. Along the same lines, when we give a person freedom to do or not to do something, we are respecting her negative face; but when we threaten someone or give him an order we are threatening his negative face. In the dialogue above, the Boss threatens the Employee's positive face when he expresses disapproval of his behavior (*Ud. está llegando con retraso a las horas de trabajo*) and threatens his negative face when he forces him to stop talking (*Ni una palabra más*), asks him to leave (*Puede retirarse*) and threatens to fire him (*...y si se repite, queda despedido*). The employee, however, saves his own positive face when he defends his performance (*...algunas veces llego tarde pero no siempre y encima yo siempre cumplo con mi trabajo y...*) and saves the boss' positive face by expressing agreement (*Sí, sí, sí, yo comprendo... Sí, sí, por supuesto*), but does not threaten his own negative face or his Boss' positive or negative face at all.

Brown & Levinson categorize politeness strategies as: 'bald-on-record,' 'positive politeness,' 'negative politeness,' 'off-record,' and 'do-nothing.' *Bald-on-record* are those strategies speakers use either when they want to be rude or when they are more powerful than their interlocutor and there is very little risk in threatening his or her face. Insults, commands and threats are examples of bald-on-record strategies. *Positive politeness* strategies express interest and approval of the interlocutor's personality, possessions, likes and dislikes. Their effect is the creation and maintenance of closeness and camaraderie. Compliments, agreement, use of slang and in-group language are examples of positive politeness strategies. *Negative politeness* strategies, on the other hand, are used to express respect and non-imposition. Their effect is the creation of deference and/or distance. Use of hedging, apology, and expression of pessimism are examples of negative politeness strategies. *Off-record* strategies are those used when speakers prefer to be vague or indirect. Giving hints, understating, making rhetorical questions are all off-record strategies. Finally, *do-nothing* strategies are characterized by the speaker's silence. Scollon and Scollon (156-179) collapse Brown and Levinson's politeness strategies into two groups: deference and solidarity. *Deference politeness strategies* (DPS) are those that imply formality and respect and include negative politeness, off-record, and do-nothing. *Solidarity politeness strategies* (SPS), on the other hand, imply camaraderie and in-group membership between speakers and include bald-on-record and positive politeness. According to Brown and Levinson, speakers use different types of strategies according to their culturally based perceptions of Power (P)—that is, their degree of authority over the hearer—and in terms of social distance (D) between speaker and interlocutor—that is, the closeness of their relationship, the frequency of their interaction. However, in this distinction a caveat is in order: In some cultures, SPS are used when the power (P) and social distance (D) between interlocutors is the same (two friends/colleagues/siblings, for example) or when the speaker is talking to someone with less power (-P) and with whom there is less distance (-D)—a boss to an employee or a professor to a student, for example. By the same token, in some cultures, deference politeness strategies are used when talking up (-P →+P), as in the introductory dialogue between the Employee (-P) and the Boss (+P), or when talking to someone with the same power and with whom there is no social distance (P = P; D = D)—for example, two CEOs or two presidents talking to each other or, in some countries, husband and wife.

According to Lakoff, "every culture adopts [different politeness strategies] as its dominant mode ...These strategies are distance, deference and camaraderie ... Formality, the avoidance of individual or personal references, is characteristic of distance politeness ... Deference politeness [on the other hand] is indecisive: it uses questions and hedges in profusion ... [and camaraderie assumes] that interaction and connection are good in themselves, that openness is the greatest sign of courtesy [and] since signs of trust and intimacy indicate that the user means no harm, their presence signifies that confrontation need not be feared" (1990, 35-38). It can then be inferred that the Employee, with his indecisiveness, came from a deference politeness system, while the Boss, with his abruptness and directness, came from a camaraderie politeness system.

As has been noted, speaking the same language or even belonging to the same country does not imply preference for the same politeness system. If it did, there would be no differences, for example, in the way New Yorkers and Californians communicate and relate to each other. In a language like Spanish, this problem is multiplied by the differences existing between one cultural group and another—that is, views of what is appropriate and effective from the sociocultural perspective in Cuba, Puerto Rico, the Dominican Republic or Venezuela might not be shared in Peru, Ecuador or Bolivia.

The following sections first present summarized results from analyses of the communicative practices of male and female speakers of two different national-culture groups, Venezuelan and Peruvian Spanish speakers, in four situations: 1) making a request for a service and 2) responding to a request for a service; 3) reprimanding and 4) responding to a reprimand (García 1993, 2001) to illustrate how perspectives govern the relationships among individuals and influence their choice and sequence of stylistic strategies and communicative practices. Following this discussion, suggestions for applying these findings to the Spanish classroom are provided.

Collection and Analysis of Data

To study the communicative practices of Venezuelans and Peruvians, data were collected in both Caracas and Lima using adult male and female subjects in role-play scenarios. Twenty Venezuelan subjects and twenty Peruvian subjects, ranging in age from eighteen to sixty-five, participated in each situation. Although social class was not controlled, most participants came from the middle-middle class. Before engaging in the role-play interactions, both the subjects whose speech was being analyzed and their interlocutors (whose speech was not being analyzed) were told to engage in a regular conversation and that the conversation would be videotaped. Instructions described the following situations:

a. **Making a request and responding to a request**
   Usted necesita contratar a alguien para que le dé clases de inglés a su hijo que tiene 11 años. Usted habla con su vecina. Ella está preparada para hacerlo. (You need to hire a person to teach English to your eleven-year old son. You talk to your neighbor and ask her to do it. She is qualified to do it).

b. **Reprimanding and responding to a reprimand**
   Su empleado(a) ha estado llegando tarde al trabajo, saliendo temprano y no ha estado cumpliendo con su labor. Esta mañana Ud. lo(a) llama a su oficina y le habla. El/ella noestá de acuerdo con Ud. (Your employee has been coming late to work, leaving early and not doing his/her work. This morning you call him/her and talk to him/her. He/she does not agree with you).

The role-played interactions were transcribed and classified using both the Blum-Kulka et al. model and the Brown & Levinson framework. Blum-Kulka et al. differentiate between the main strategies used to make the request/reprimand per se ('head acts') and those that modify the impact of the request/reprimand, making it either more mitigating or more imposing ('supporting moves'). We apply the same differentiation scheme to responding to a request, reprimanding, and responding to a reprimand. The following boss' reprimand of an employee will help illustrate this difference:

> *No estoy muy satisfecha con su trabajo, y eso no -- no exactamente con su trabajo pero usted ha estado llegando tarde muy a ... quisiera saber la razón de esta situación.*

In this fragment, the boss reprimands the employee by expressing her dissatisfaction with the employee's performance, saying: "*No estoy muy satisfecha con su trabajo.*" Now, the strength of this 'head act' is mitigated by "*...y eso no -- no exactamente con su trabajo,*" but aggravated by her request for a justification or explanation: "*quisiera saber la razón de esta situación.*" Obviously, the strength of the head act is affected by its accompanying mitigators and aggravators.

How Did Venezuelans' and Peruvians' Perspectives Impact Their Linguistic Practices?

Venezuelan Spanish speakers, at least those who participated in the studies reported here, tended to exhibit a preference for SPS as head acts and mitigators as supporting moves in requesting, responding to a request, reprimanding and responding to a reprimand. Thus, in all cases, regardless of the role- relationship between the interlocutors, they preferred the creation of solidarity to the creation of distance. This is particularly interesting in the case of responding to a reprimand, where Venezuelans' preference for SPS, rather than the expected DPS, reflects an egalitarian attitude that, as Lakoff (1990, 18) points out, "is rapidly taking over as the preferred form of politeness for both sexes in many parts of the United States and appears to be making in roads in Europe as well."

Along the same lines, Venezuelans also expressed marked preference for imposing on the interlocutor's freedom of action (threatening his or her negative face) over expressing their disapproval (threatening his or her positive face). The exception to this was the case of reprimanding, where they preferred to threaten the interlocutor's need to be liked and approved of rather than his or her need not to be imposed on—that is, Venezuelans were imposing, but mitigated their imposition; they created camaraderie, but also showed respect. The following excerpt of Venezuelan participation in 'reprimanding' illustrates this pattern. [See **Appendix A** for an explanation of the symbols used in the transcript.]

Boss	1	*Bueno mira Orlando, quería conversar contigo porque me ha llegado una*
	2	*situación, me está explicando el superintendente que el trabajo no se está*
	3	*cumpliendo el trabajo, estás saliendo temprano y como podrás comprender, tu*
	4	*trabajo (está perjudicando a) la empresa y quisiera aclarar esta situación*
	5	*porque tú sabes ( ) situación ( ) y ver a qué acuerdo llegamos ( )*
Employee	6	*Mira pero qué tipo de queja te ha llegado? porque si es cierto que estoy*
	7	*llegando tarde no:: no*
Boss	8	*=yo esperaba*
Employee	9	*=no sé de - yo en ningún momento momento he dejado de realizar mi trabajo.*
	10	*Yo cumplo con mi trabajo diariamente inclusive a mediodía me quedo en mi*
	11	*casa, me quedo acá, no voy a mi casa y bueno y y realizo el trabajo. sí estoy*
	12	*llegando un poco más tarde [( )*
Boss	13	*[pero bueno esa es precisamente la queja, la queja es que el trabajo no se está*
	14	*dando.*
Employee	15	*Ah mira discúlpame [si si el trabajo no se está dando.*
Boss	16	*[si entras a las siete y sales a las cinco verdad?,*
	17	*a mí no me importa porque el trabajo se cumple.*
Employee	18	*=[a no*
Boss	19	*[pero si no se está cumpliendo y estás entrando a las siete y saliendo a las*
	20	*cinco entonces ya me preocupa.*

Here we see that in lines 1-4 the boss reprimands the employee with presentation of facts about his unsatisfactory performance at work, reiterates his complaint in lines 13-14, 16, and 19-20. However, in line 17 he mitigates his stance (*a mí no me importa porque el trabajo se cumple*). Earlier, he claims common ground in line 3 (*como podrás comprender*) and expresses willingness to solve the impasse in lines 4 and 5 (*quisiera aclarar esta situación and y ver a qué acuerdo llegamos*). In other words, there is a smooth combination of imposing head acts and mitigating supporting moves.

As pointed out in García (2001), it may be that within Venezuelan society, to be imposing is not a bad trait. On the contrary, it may be considered fundamental to the maintenance of a healthy relationship in all type of situations. Along these lines, what came through in this interaction was participants' camaraderie, congeniality, closeness and generosity along with preferred rules of rapport consisting of: 1) Be (Un-)Friendly; and 2) Impose, in that order. This is a complete opposition to U.S. Americans' preferred rules of rapport: 1) Don't Impose; 2) Give Options; and 3) Be friendly (Lakoff 1973, 298), and it is this opposition that might create miscommunication as U.S. Americans interact, specifically, with Venezuelans in this type of context.

The studies of Peruvian discourse, however, showed a completely different pattern of behavior, the product of different perspectives. The Peruvian participants showed deference when making a request and when responding to a reprimand but solidarity when responding to a request for a service and when reprimanding; that is, when requesting, they preferred to express deference and respect towards their interlocutor and their desire not to impose (García 1993), but when responding to a reprimand, they preferred to express respect and deference towards the interlocutor—the boss. The following is an example of Peruvian subjects responding to a reprimand:

Employee   1 *Gracias por brindarme la oportunidad de conversar con usted y así poder hacerle*
            2 *llegar algunas de las razones porque he llegado tarde sin que esto signifique*
            3 *justificación a una falta que ya lo considero yo mi asistencia al trabajo con falta*
            4 *de puntualidad pero yo ofrezco e e e reemplazar las horas perdidas no? con*
            5 *horas de: trabajo adicional, e hágale llegar usted al jefe, al señor gerente, mis*
            6 *excusas, espero que esto no se repita. Son muchas las razones que ya es de tipo*
            7 *estrictamente personal, de tipo familiar por lo cual por esta vez he podido, e*
            8 *incurrir en esta reinteradas inasistencias y faltas al trabajo*
Boss   9 *Ok*

As can be observed, the Employee admits responsibility in lines 2-4 (*sin que esto signifique justificación a una falta que ya lo considero yo mi asistencia al trabajo con falta de puntualidad*), promises to repair in lines 4-5 (*yo ofrezco e e e reemplazar las horas perdidas no? con horas de: trabajo adicional*), apologizes in lines 5-6 (*e hágale llegar usted al jefe, al señor gerente, mis excusas*), promises forbearance in line 6 (*espero que esto no se repita*), provides reasons/justifications in lines 6-8 (*Son muchas las razones que ya es de tipo estrictamente personal, de tipo familiar por lo cual por esta vez he podido, e incurrir en esta reinteradas inasistencias y faltas al trabajo*); that is, the overall effect is one of deference and respect.

When responding to a request for a service, however, Peruvian speakers, like their Venezuelan counterparts, preferred SPS and mitigators over aggravators. This might have been due to the idea that accepting a request does not threaten the interlocutor's need not to be imposed upon, but rather satisfies his or her need to be liked and/or met with approval. When reprimanding, Peruvian participants, like their Venezuelan counterparts, chose SPS (solidarity) strategies, thus emphasizing the power differential between Boss (+P) and Employee (-P). They also preferred to threaten the interlocutor's negative face—that is, his or her desire to be respected and not imposed on. In this study, then, the Peruvians' rules of rapport can be summed up as: 1) Don't impose; 2) Give Options; 3) Be friendly, in that order—a marked difference from the politeness system used by their Venezuelan counterparts, but similar to the U.S. American politeness system.

In analyses of both Venezuelan and Peruvian discourses, qualitative but not statistically significant differences were found between male and female participation. Females were more verbose, mitigated their participation more and expressed their willingness to cooperate more than males. Males, on the other hand, did not mitigate their participation as much and preferred to impose their will rather than negotiate or convince. Since age and social class were not controlled variables, these differences were not analyzed.

Developing Students' Understanding of the Perspectives that Motivate Discourse

Results from sociolinguistic research can help us develop students' awareness of different cultural perspectives and consequently of different linguistic practices. Olshtain and Cohen suggest five steps for presenting and practicing speech acts (1991, 161-162): 1) diagnostic assessment; 2) model dialog; 3) evaluation of the situation; 4) role-play activities; and 5) feedback and discussion. For purposes of illustration here, we focus on classroom analysis of one speech act: reprimanding.

Step I. Diagnostic assessment allows the teacher to see where students are, "to establish the students' level of awareness of speech acts in general and of the particular speech act to be taught" (161). For this purpose, students might be given the description of a situation followed by three possible statements from which they would choose the one that would be most culturally appropriate to perform a given function—in this case, reprimanding an employee in the workplace.

Example: You are the boss. One of your employees has not been coming to work on time, has been leaving early and has not been completing his/her work. You call him/her to your office to address these issues. Which of these approaches will you take?

> a. *El horario de trabajo en esta oficina no se está cumpliendo y esto me tiene muy preocupado. Esta compañía tiene grandes responsabilidades y los horarios hay que cumplirlos. Si los empleados llegan tarde, se van temprano, y no cumplen con sus obligaciones, la compañía se puede ir a la quiebra.*

> b. *Mira como ... el trabajo tienes que conservarlo porque lo necesitas, y además tienes que dar*

ejemplo a las demás compañeras, no puedes llegar tarde al trabajo, porque si te imitan todas las demás harían lo mismo, ¿no? Tienes que esforzarte. Quizás tengas algunos problemas en la mobilidad o eres floja.

c. Le he mandado llamar porque he notado de que está incumpliendo reiteradamente el horario de trabajo, está llegando demasiado tarde por la mañana y está saliendo usted demasiado temprano. Y por otro lado, el cumplimiento de sus obligaciones: En cuanto a labor que debe desempeñar, veo que está dejando mucho que desear. Yo quisiera saber qué explicaciones da usted sobre el particular.

If students choose option (a) it is worth pointing out that this strategy exhibits preference for an indirect reprimand as observed in the use of impersonal reference (*El horario de trabajo en esta oficina no se está cumpliendo* and *los horarios hay que cumplirlos*) and a non-confrontational tone. In fact, upon hearing it, the interlocutor can very easily simply agree with the boss and walk away. If used in a real-life situation then, option (a) might be interpreted either as vague and/or lacking assertiveness and authority, and consequently not culturally appropriate within the Venezuelan culture, though probably so within the Peruvian culture. If students choose option (b), the teacher or students might point out that this boss offers advice, states the employee's obligation, moralizes, assumes the employee's possible reasons—all SPS, implying +P -D between the boss and employee. Students might comment that the boss' use of the term 'floja' might be insulting and/or patronizing and not appropriate here. Along these lines, it might be pointed out that this reprimand would seem more appropriate between a homemaker and a maid than between a boss and an employee in the workplace, and consequently is jarring in this context. If, on the other hand, students choose option (c), they will be expressing preference for a more assertive, authoritative and hierarchical perspective displayed in the use of SPS (presentation of facts, expression of concern, request for justification), strategies that are reflective of the tendencies of both Venezuelan and Peruvian participants as described in the aforementioned research.

After a series of such exercises, teachers might respond to their students' choices in each task. According to students' responses, Olshtain and Cohen (161) tell us that the "teacher should plan teaching goals and procedures" which would normally involve the teacher's explanations and further activities to help students identify and understand the different perspectives that motivate use of different stylistic strategies and politeness systems when reprimanding. One of these activities might involve introducing students to the appropriate routine formulae for reprimanding (see **Appendix B**).

Step II. Model dialogues illustrate actual participation of other-culture representatives in a reprimanding situation. The dialogue could be a sample of authentic discourse or simulated authentic discourse—that is, a dialogue produced for pedagogical purposes which has a high probability of occurrence in real communicative situations between native speakers (Rogers and Medley). Presented here is a sample of authentic discourse between a Peruvian boss and her employee (this dialogue took place as a response to the participant task previously described). Before and after listening to the dialogue, students are to perform in pairs the following tasks designed to help them develop their sociocultural awareness.

A. Pre-listening. You will listen to a conversation between a Peruvian female boss and her female employee. The boss calls the employee to her office to deal with the issue of the employee's poor performance. Before you listen, discuss with your partner the following questions:

    1. Who has more/less power in a boss-employee relationship? Justify your response.

    2. How is this more/less power reflected in the way a boss and his/her employee relate to each other? Give examples.

Before listening to the conversation, list in the "*Antes de escuchar*" column the types of information you expect to hear in each category.

	Antes de Escuchar	*Después de Escuchar*
1. List things the boss might complain about.		
2. List expressions that the boss will use in his/her presentation of the complaint		
3. List expressions that the employee will use in his/her response.		
4. Give types of evidence the boss will present.		
5. Give reasons/justifications/arguments the employee will provide.		
4. List some demands the boss will make.		
5. Will the problem be resolved? How?		

B. Post listening. Now listen to the conversation and, in the right column, record as much as you can from what you hear.

Jefe	*Señorita,¿cómo es posible, toda esta semana ha estado llegando tarde, ¿tiene algún motivo? porque usted no dice nada. Ud. llega tarde no más y el trabajo se atrasa. No estoy contenta con usted.*
Empleada	*Le ruego que no me llame la atención en esa forma. Tenga la ... llámeme en otra forma la atención no ... no así con esa cólera, esa indignación.*

Jefe	*Pero señorita fíjese la ... el trabajo se atrasa. Yo no puedo seguir con usted. Fíjese, la compañía es inmensa, muy grande, y si us ... a ... como usted faltaran otros empleados, bueno no sé adónde iríamos a parar.*
Empleada	*No. Pregúnteme primero por qué es que he llegado tarde, cuáles son los motivos, pero no no no se moleste en esta forma. Primero pregúnteme para eso trabajo bastantes años en la empresa.*
Jefe	*Señorita pero todo tiene un límite. Yo quisiera saber bueno los motivos. A ver, me hubiera dicho desde el principio, pero no así toda esta semana.*
Empleada	*No, es que tengo a una de mis hijitas enferma y entonces he tenido que estar yendo y llevándola adonde el doctor pero ya todo se va a solucionar. No me llame la ... en esa en esa forma la atención*
Jefe	*Gracias. Está a prueba conmigo.*

Step III. Evaluating the situation. After students listen to the dialogue and complete the chart above, it would be helpful to guide class discussion around the following questions:

1. From your point of view, who has more power in this conversation and how is it expressed? Did this reflect your expectations? Explain.

2. What kind of relationship exists between the boss and the employee? How do you know this? Present evidence from the dialogue to justify your answer.

3. How does the boss present her complaint? Is she rude or polite? Present evidence from the dialogue to justify your answer. Did her reprimand reflect your expectations? Explain.

4 How does the employee respond to the reprimand? How does she feel about the reprimand? Why do you think she reacted that way? Explain.

5. Do you think a male employee would respond in the same way? Justify your response.

6. What do you think a male employee would say in a similar situation? And what values, beliefs do you think his response would reflect? Justify and illustrate.

7. How does the boss react to the employee's response? Illustrate. What values, beliefs does she reflect?

8. Is the relationship between the boss and the employee hurt in any way as a result of this interaction? Justify, illustrate.

9. What similarities and/or differences do you find between the interaction of the boss and

the employee in this dialogue and what you would expect it to be between an American boss and his/her employee? Explain.

10. Have you ever reprimanded anyone who worked for you? How was your reprimand similar to or different from the one in this dialogue?

11. Have you ever been reprimanded by your boss? How was your reaction similar to or different from that of the employee in this dialogue?

In the discussion of these questions it is important to bring up the personalization/familiarization of the interaction, where the employee attempts to break down the distance inherent in a boss-employee relationship and establish a woman-woman, solidarity-based relationship in which she even reprimands the boss for the way her reprimand was phrased! Along these lines, the boss' threat of the employee's positive face (*No estoy contenta con usted*) needs to be highlighted, since this act may have triggered the employee's reaction. In turn, discussion of the boss' threat to the employee's negative face (*Yo no puedo seguir con usted,* and *Está a prueba conmigo*) which, interestingly enough, had no major effect on the employee, should be discussed in terms of how this might reflect this culture's perspectives. These are topics that merit discussion for the purpose of comparison and contrast with the U.S. American culture, within which respect for one's negative face is a priority. The teacher might also find it useful to point out the role of 'advisor/counselor/moralizer' assumed by the boss (*y si us ... a ... como usted faltaran otros empleados, bueno no sé adónde iríamos a parar*) which contributed to lower the power differential, and how this again reflects the culture's perspectives—that is, the need to create solidarity rather than distance between the interlocutors.

In the discussion of this discourse segment, it is important to emphasize that this is only a sample of a female boss-female employee interaction within the Peruvian culture and cannot be generalized to all female boss-female employee interactions in Peru, nor to all boss-employee interactions in Peru, much less to all boss-employee interactions within the Spanish-speaking world. To compare and contrast perspectives between Venezuelans and Peruvians, the reader is referred to an additional dialogue sample in **Appendix C**.

Step IV. Role-play activities allow learners to experiment with appropriate, effective and acceptable ways to approach different situations in different speech communities. It should be borne in mind, however, that even after illustration and discussion of the different frames of participation, stylistic strategies and preferred politeness systems of Spanish-speakers of different cultures, students will still tend to revert to their own sociolinguistic patterns and will participate in these situations using their own sociocultural perspectives. The purpose of these activities is not to change students' perspectives, but rather to increase their level of awareness and sensitivity to different ways of behaving in different types of situations. For this purpose then, students prepare and rehearse the role-play situations in pairs or small groups and later dramatize them in front of the class for feedback and discussion.

1. El/la secretario(a) irresponsable. Trabajo en parejas. Ud. *es el/la jefe de una empresa y está bastante molesto(a) porque su secretario(a) no está cumpliendo con su trabajo: no ha escrito las cartas que Ud. le pidió ayer, no ha enviado unos paquetes que tenían que salir esta mañana y todos los días llega tarde. Llámelo(a) a su oficina y hable con él/ella.*

2. Su hermano(a) menor. Trabajo en parejas. Su hermano(a) menor no sabe usar computadoras pero usó la suya ayer sin su permiso. Hoy Ud. la quiere usar pero se da cuenta que no funciona. Llame a su hermano(a) y pregúntele qué pasó. El/ella no le da importancia al asunto.

Step V. Feedback and discussion is the last step recommended by Olshtain and Cohen as necessary because "students need to talk about their perceptions, expectations, and awareness of similarities and differences between speech-act behavior in the target language and in their first culture. Such feedback."…helps all participants become more aware of speech act behavior and helps them recognize areas of interference..." (161-162). Along these lines, it is advisable to guide students' thought along the following lines:

1. How did you perceive your participation and that of your interlocutor(s) in these situations: Passive? Aggressive? Rude? Polite? Assertive? Not assertive? Explain.

2. How easy/difficult was it for you to participate in this fashion? What values that are not your own did you emphasize? How did you do so?

3. How was your participation in this situation different from what it would have been if you had role-played it in English? What values would you have emphasized and how would you have done so? Explain.

4. If you faced a similar situation in real life, what features in your interlocutor's language would you be attentive to and why? And, how would you tailor your language to be culturally appropriate in your response?

5. Do you think your culture is superior/inferior or better/worse than the target culture because you do things differently? Explain.

When discussing the answers to these questions, it is important to emphasize that having similar or different values or perspectives is neither intrinsically good nor bad, but that different cultures perceive life and personal relations in a fashion that is completely satisfactory to them. Consequently, what is good for a Venezuelan Spanish speaker is not necessarily so for a Peruvian Spanish speaker or for an English speaker, for that matter. But it is because of these differences that cross-cultural interactions enrich our lives.

The importance of this last stage cannot be underestimated, as it is vital to developing an understanding of different speech communities' perspectives and practices and avoiding the creation of stereotypes. Along these lines, it should be noted that while the rules of rapport mentioned by Lakoff (1. Don't impose; 2. Give Options; 3. Be friendly) hold within the cultural framework, values, and beliefs of U.S. American society, this same order should not necessarily be expected from other cultures with different values and belief systems.

Conclusion

We began this discussion by seeing how two people speaking the same language but coming from different sociocultural backgrounds completely misunderstood each other. Each had a different perspective of the situation and a different approach to behavior in it. Each participated within a different frame, used different stylistic devices and preferred (different) rules of politeness. The result was, in essence, failed communication. The boss was participating within a 'this is business' frame whereas the employee preferred a 'this is friendly' frame. The boss used solidarity politeness strategies emphasizing his power and authority (talking down), whereas the employee used deference politeness strategies emphasizing indecision. As a consequence, the power differential was emphasized and the employee's positive and negative faces were threatened. We then examined results from sociolinguistic research on the linguistic behaviors of two groups of native Spanish-speakers in service-requesting and -reprimanding contexts and presented suggestions on how one might apply these results in actual teaching situations to help develop students' awareness of the different cultural groups' perspectives as reflected in their linguistic practices.

As Olshtain and Cohen say: "What we are after is the development of an awareness of sociocultural and sociolinguistic differences that might exist between one's first language and the target language. Such awareness will often help explain to both teachers and learners why sometimes there is unintended pragmatic failure and breakdown in communication. If we are aware of it, it might be easier to find the appropriate remedy" (164). Developing just such an awareness has been the goal of this chapter.

Works Cited

Blum-Kulka, Shoshana, Juliane House, and Gabriele Kasper. "Investigating Cross-cultural Pragmatics: An Introductory." *Cross-Cultural Pragmatics: Requests and Apologies.* Shoshana Blum-Kulka, Juliane House, and Gabriele Kasper, eds. Norwood: Ablex Publishing Corporation, 1989. 1-34.

Brown, Penelope and Stephen Levinson. *Politeness. Some Universals in Language Use.* Cambridge: Cambridge University Press, 1987.

García, Carmen. "*La expresión de camaradería y solidaridad: cómo los venezolanos solicitan un servicio y reponden a la solicitud de un servicio.*" *Estudios sobre el discurso español.* Madrid: Editorial Gedisa, 2001 (forthcoming).

_____. "Who's the Boss: How Venezuelans Reprimand and Respond to a Reprimand." *Hispanic Linguistics.* 2001 (forthcoming).

_____. "Making a Request and Responding to It: A Case Study of Peruvian Spanish Speakers." *Journal of Pragmatics* 19 (1993): 127-152.

Gumperz, John, J. *Language in Social Groups.* Stanford: Stanford University Press, 1971.

Hymes, Dell. "Models of the Interaction of Language and Social Life." *Directions in Sociolinguistics: Ethnography of Communication.* J.J. Gumperz and D. Hymes, eds. New York: Holt, Rinehartand Winston, 1972. 37-71.

Lakoff, Robin Tolmach. "The Logic of Politeness; Or, Minding Your P's and Q's." Papers from the Ninth Regional Meeting of the Chicago Linguistic Society, 1973.

_____. *Talking Power.* New York: Basic Books, 1990.

National Standards in Foreign Language Education Project. *Standards for Foreign Language Learning: Preparing for the 21st Century.* Yonkers, NY: American Council on the Teaching of Foreign Languages, 1996.

Olshtain, Elite and Andrew Cohen. "Teaching Speech Act Behavior to Nonnative Speakers." *Teaching English as a Second or Foreign Language.* Marianne Celce-Murcia, ed. New York: Newbury House, 1991. 154-165.

_____. "Face in Interethnic Communication." *Language and Communication.* Jack C. Richards and Richard W. Schmidt, eds. New York: Longman, 1983. 156-188.

Rogers, Carmen V. and Frank W. Medley, Jr. "Language With a Purpose: Using Authentic Materials in the Foreign Language Classroom." *Foreign Language Annals* 21, v (1988) 467-88.

Scollon, Ron and Suzanne Wong Scollon. *Narrative, Literacy, and Face in Interethnic Communication.* New Jersey: Ablex Publishing Company, 1983.

Appendix A
Transcript Notation

A. Simultaneous utterances:

[[are used to link together utterances that start simultaneously.

B. Overlapping utterances:

[is used to indicate beginning of overlap; and] to indicate end of overlapped utterances.

C. Contiguous utterances:

= is placed between utterances with no time gap uttered by different speakers or to link different parts of a speaker's utterance that has been carried over to another line because of an interruption.is placed when more than one speaker participates immediately after a just-completed utterance.

D. Intervals:

(0.0) is placed to measure pause lengths (measured in tenths of a second).is placed at point of interruption. An utterance was considered to be interrupted when the speaker started making an utterance and changed its content and/or form.

E. Characteristics of speech delivery:

. marks fall in tone

, marks continuing intonation

? marks rising intonation;

?, marks weaker rising intonation

! marks an animated tone

↑↓ marks rising and falling shifts in intonation.

> < marks that the enclosed utterance is delivered at a faster pace

Capital letters mark increased volume in the production of a given word or words of the utterance

::: marks lengthened syllable; each : marking one "beat".

<u>Underlining</u> marks emphasis.

(LF) marks laughter

(( )) encloses description of gestures or other non-verbal information.

F. Transcriber doubt:

( ) is used to mark unintelligible utterances.

Appendix B
Routine Formula For Reprimanding

Siento tener que decirle(-s)/decirte/ comunicarle(-s)/comunicarte que...	I'm sorry to tell/announce that.
La verdad es que ...	The truth is that...
Pero, ¡qué falta de responsabilidad!	But, how irresponsible!
¡Esto es el colmo!	This is too much (the last straw)!
Pero, ¿cómo pueden hacer esto?	But, how can they do this?
¡Ésta es la última gota!	This is the last straw!
¡Esto no puede ser!	This can't be!
¡Uds. hacen lo que quieren y yo soy el pagano!	You do what you want and I have to pay!
¡Esto no tiene ni pies ni cabeza!	This is absurd!
No sirve para nada.	It's good for nothing!
Voy a poner el grito en el cielo.	I'm going to hit the ceiling.
Pero, ¡qué barbaridad!	But, this is terrible!
Pero, ¿Ud./tú está(-s) loco(a)?	What, are you crazy?
Pero, ¿Ud./tú cree(-s) que yo soy tonto(a)?	What, do you think I'm a fool?
¡Qué se/te ha(-s) creído Ud./tú!	What do you think you are!
¡De ninguna manera voy a aceptar esto!	There's no way that I'm going to accept this!

Appendix C
Sample Workplace Dialogue #2: Venezuelan interlocutors

In discussion, the teacher may wish to note the type of interaction between the boss and the employee, and compare/contrast it to that of the first dialogue in terms of the informal tone of the interaction, the frames of participation, the stylistic strategies and the rules of politeness and how these factors reflect this particular speech community's perspectives.

Jefe	*Hola ¿cómo estás Enrique?*
Empleado	*Muy bien Celeste, y tú ¿cómo estás?*
Jefe	*Muy bien.*
Empleado	*¿Me llamabas para algo?*
Jefe	*Bueno sí chico. Estoy: algo preocupada porque:: bueno, he observado que estás llegando tarde (0.2) demasiado seguido, y veo que también sales del trabajo antes de la hora normal y quisiera preguntarte si tienes alguna razón. te podríamos ayudar, no sé, tienes algún problema o, por qué no me lo has dicho si lo tienes. debiera preguntarte si ( ).*
Empleado	*Cónchale Celeste me, me sorprende, pero en verdad mira, a: tengo dos días nada más llegando tarde. tú sabes que mi problema es las huelgas que ha habido últimamente, los paros, las marchas, el tra el tráfico está terrible. he tenido que salir más temprano - tú sabes que con estos rumores de golpe de estado a cada rato mira yo prefiero ir a buscar a los muchachos temprano y llevarlos a la casa temprano ¿no?, y bueno y lo que ha pasado son dos días nada más. yo me imagino que bueno tú conoces la situación no?*
Jefe	*=Ajá. entonces yo no sé qué llamarás tú a estar retrasado. porque para mí mediahora ya es bastante tarde, aun quince minutos. además de que uno viviendo en Caracas uno sabe que para llegar a tiempo uno tiene que tomar en cuenta todas esas contingencias que se pudieran presentar no?, del tráfico, de todo eso y entonces realmente no lo veo justificado. esto no no me parece completamente justo.*
Empleado	*Bueno ni justo me parece a mí porque fíjate yo no puedo estar (0.2) yo no yo no sé cuándo, cuándo hay una marcha cuándo hay - cuándo - tú sabes que yo tengo que pasar por la universidad todas las mañanas, y de vez en cuando cierran toda la avenida y es cuando a ellos se les antoja. yo no sé si has escuchado que cierran no? sobre todo tú sabes que ya - yo creo que la materia, que las contingencias > ( ) < que yo puedo salir temprano, pero los avatares y los accidentes no los puedo: [[no los puedo*
Jefe	*=[[Bueno mira, yo por mi parte?, quizás eso te ayudaría, yo evito pasar cerca de la*

plaza Venezuela, precisamente porque si hay algún disturbio en la universidad y no verme involucrada en ese en ese desorden.

Empleado   *Yo solamente paso ahí y yo no tengo, no tengo salida.*

Jefe   *Y quizás lo de ir a recoger a tus hijos, no podrías hacer otro arreglo de que fueraotra persona o algo así? porque realmente ( )*

Empleado   *=Mira, sabes que mi esposa está muy mal ¿no?, entonces ella no, ella está de reposo y la cosa se me complica un poco. Claro, bueno también te digo sabes que ha pasado durante dos días nada más ¿no?, tampoco - sabes que ahorita la situación del país no está como para - y me da miedo pues dejarlos solos, uno no sabe lo que puede pasar no? pero: yo estoy preocupado por el problema no creas. ahora si mira, mi trabajo, yo creo que yo he realizado mi trabajo como es debido o sea a pesar de que he perdido tiempo, imagínate, no salgo almorzar para recuperar el tiempo perdido.*

Jefe   *Ah bueno. quizá::s me: me complace un poquito más ¿no? pero de todos modos yo creo que vas a tener que buscar otra solución porque a pesar de la situación del país, una empresa es una empresa y y el primer objetivo es es ser eficiente [no?,*

Empleado   *[Bueno pero yo soy eficiente a pesar de llegar tarde ¿no?*

Jefe   *Bueno.*

Chapter 4

Analyzing Cultural Products in Practice

Nancy A. Humbach, Miami University, OH

All cultures produce objects that provide a window to perspectives, practices, and often the personalities of their creators. By guiding language learners to observe and analyze a culture's products in their geographical, historical and traditional contexts, we help them master a lifetime skill that will serve them in developing insights into cultures they will experience in the future. Edward T. Hall, in his book *The Hidden Dimension*, considers that objects reflect "those uncommon, unstated experiences which members of a given culture share [and] communicate without knowing" (x). Objects produced by a people may reflect the culture broadly and locally—in terms of geography, history, lifestyle, belief systems and values—as well as convey the status, experience, creativity and even the sense of humor of their individual producers.

Age, lack of world experience and often the lack of training in observation skills can limit students' ability to analyze objects from another culture. Unless they receive preparation, they are often unaware of the process of creating stereotypes in their own culture (even though they are usually able to list of number of those held for other culture groups). Therefore, the teacher must provide guidance through practice in observation and analysis within the context of that specific cultural world to help learners develop a perspective that enables them to view the physical in terms of the reality of the culture's members (Eder 3). Lesson models provided here illustrate ways in which teachers can assist students in their development of a contextualized perspective.

What Is a Product?

What do we mean by "products" of a culture? Products include any materials or objects produced by a people. We can include literature, architecture, art, music, and crafts, as well as artifacts important in everyday life—tools, signs, menus, schedules, advertisements, folk remedies and recipes – in short, anything—produced by a culture. Literary works need not be limited to what we traditionally study as undergraduates, but can and should include children's literature, formal forms of folktales, myths and legends, short works, poetry, non-fiction, essays and drama to name a few (see Bacon & Humbach; Vidal, this volume). Short stories, often no more than a paragraph or two, may offer humor as well as the portrayal of universal concepts. Poetry such as Marti's "*Versos sencillos*" is accessible to beginners, as are short works by Enrique Anderson Imbert, for example. Guadalupe Loaeza's hilarious accounts of shopping, marketing and other aspects of women's lives in Mexico are also a good choice. Latino writers in this country (Anzaldúa, Delacre) offer various views of the lives of Spanish-speaking people living in the United States. Francisco Jiménez' autobiographical writings (*Cajas de cartón, La mariposa, El regalo de Navidad/ The*

Christmas Gift) leave the reader changed through the glimpse he offers of the life of a child of migrant farm workers.

Angeles Mastretta (*Mujeres de ojos grandes*) offers views of women's lives through several genera-tions in a story format of ideal length for most classrooms. One chapter of this work, for example (25-28), tells the story of a young woman without marriage prospects who finds a way to establish her status within the community: While window-shopping at "La Princesa," a well known jewelry store in Puebla, she inquires about an item in the window. Later that day, a gentleman arrives at her home with a proposal of marriage from a now-absent suitor who has just been called to Spain. She accepts the proposal, a grand wedding takes place with a stand-in groom, and she then leaves imme-diately to join her new husband in Spain. Following a year of letters about her new life, she returns to Puebla, a very respectable widow. As a widow, she is easily accepted into a society that had reject-ed her as a spinster. But the story leaves the reader with the gnawing suspicion that she was never really married and that the wedding was a ruse to ensure her acceptance by a rigid society.

Francisco Jiménez' *El regalo de Navidad*/ The Christmas Gift and *Cajas de cartón*, his anthology of autobiographical stories, depict the richness and close relationship of the family. He writes of the struggles to survive, of the roles of various family members, and especially of the "pecking" order and responsibility held by older children who, in turn, care for their younger siblings. From these read-ings, students can gain a sense of the meanings of privacy, solitude and *familia*. In *Las niñas bien* Loaeza depicts the wealthy Mexican woman's shopping trips to Florida, her reliance on her cell phone and charge cards, and the ways she deceives her husband when the bills arrive. In *Compro, luego existo*, she writes about a shopaholic who visits the markets in Valle de Bravo. One might use Loaeza's writings, Jiménez' portrayal of his mother, and Mastretta's vignettes of women to structure a unit in which students compare the lives of women in different cultures and consider the influences of tradition on the socioeconomic structure of society.

Language is, of course, the principle cultural product and as such must be taught not simply as grammar and vocabulary, but as communication within a cultural context. Many non-native speakers of Spanish have experienced, for example, what is sometimes a frustrating dialog in a restau-rant: The server asks "*¿Más café?*" and the diner responds with "*Gracias*" but is promptly confused when the waiter walks away without serving more coffee. What the customer does not realize is that in this context, implicit in the word *gracias* is the message of "*No, gracias*." Indeed, the meaning of a word resides in its cultural connotation.

For the purposes of this article, we will focus on items such as household objects, crafts, photo-graphs and print materials. Most teachers return home from travels with a wealth of such authentic realia; however, often these collections go unexploited in terms of classroom use: Teachers may not know what to do with these items, or they may feel they have no time to prepare activities with which to use them, or they may believe discussion of them in Spanish is too difficult for their classroom learners. However, as we will demonstrate, with a little planning it is possible to practice language and enhance language experiences while exploring the cultural meanings implicit in words and objects.

During trips with students, and later with teacher-participants in the AATSP's *Encuentro con Puebla* (See Bacon & Humbach, this volume), the use of the "*Búsqueda de tesoros culturales*" was useful in bringing focus to cultural products. In the case of teachers, all were given a list of *tesoros* (*molcajete, calaca, esquela*, etc.) that served as a starting point for conversations with native informants during a two-hour "living laboratory." The Living Laboratory concept, originally conceived by Eugene and Geraldine Savaiano, directors of Wichita State University's National Defense Education Act Institutes in the early 60s, was applied in this project to allow pairs of participants to spend time with a native informant visiting sites of interest and gathering information specified in the "*Búsqueda*" (see **Appendix**). The initial reaction of participants on seeing the objects and materials on the tesoros list is typically a barrage of questions about the meanings of certain words, such as *Xoxtla, talachería, jarcería*, for which native informants and others are to be consulted. This cultural scavenger hunt invites participants to use the language in context, gather information, and understand that research is not necessarily based on reading. In class, during the *Encuentro* stage, participants receive guidance in the creation of classroom materials using these artifacts. It is important to note that many items on the tesoros list are not for purchase and must be secured through oral negotiation or via photographs, video or other means.

Rebecca Eppley, a middle-school teacher in Galion, OH, and a participant in the 1995 National Endowment for the Humanities workshop co-sponsored by the University of Cincinnati, used cultural products such as these to create a series of learning centers for her students.[1] Based on the model of the science laboratory exam, she arranged objects (or photographs of objects) and artifacts such as menus, bills, and programs, in approximately twenty stations. Working in pairs, students viewed her display as a "window on Puebla" and, using their language and observational skills, they became detectives, responding to questions prepared by their instructor: A bill from a restaurant would perhaps be followed by questions about what Eppley ate, how much it cost, where the restaurant was located, the name of the server. Eppley piqued their interest in learning more by demonstrating similarities with the students' own culture. For a study of arts and crafts, students responded to questions such as why there were so many crafts, why so many of the crafts were miniatures, why Mexicans made skeletons in humorous poses, how *papel picado* was made, and were then asked to consider crafts in their own culture—who made them, what they were like, and how technology was related to handicrafts. Also included were objects or photographs of some of the elements of the city that demonstrated clear differences, such as foods, buildings, hours and days when events took place. By creating boxes of cultural materials related to specific places, Eppley provided students opportunities to observe, analyze, categorize, and relate cultural artifacts as amateur anthropologists while becoming observers of their own culture as well (see **Figure 1** for an example of the contents of an artifact box). Likewise, Mari Haas, in *The Language of Folk Art*, uses a selection of craft items accompanied by materials that invite students to analyze their meaning, origin and other aspects. Her work suggests a model that teachers can follow as they assemble and prepare their collections for use in the classroom.

Figure 1. Cultural Artifact Box

crafts	advertisements	music/tapes, cds
phone books	forms/applications	programs/plays, etc
driver's training manuals	printed instructions	tickets/passes
maps	transportation	ads for films
cookbooks	decorative items	entertainment guides
food boxes/wrappers	magazines	flyers
bills	banking forms	stamps
menus	invitations	TV guides
Ids	comics	schedules
spices	celebrational materials	art
cooking utensils	phone cards	literature
prepared foods	phone books	textbooks
currency	matches/napkins	
home remedies		

Photographs, copies and/or video of all the above plus:

instructions (phones, ATMs, self serve machines)	table settings
store signs (-ería)	foods (market)
decorations, store windows	foods (as served)
processes (food, craft production)	types of clothing
items posing danger to students (facón, blow gun, machete)	houses, schools
items used and produced locally (molinillo)	celebrations

Suggested Products and Themes

Edward Hall's books, *The Hidden Dimension* and *The Dance of Life*, are important resources for understanding the ways in which cultures view space and proxemics and time. Using insights from these works, the teacher can plan classroom lessons around products of the culture to examine cross-cultural perspectives. The structure of cities and neighborhoods as seen in maps and photographs, for example, reflects attitudes toward personal space as well as housing preferences and transportation patterns. Further, accompanied by photographs or video images of people walking or talking together or simply sitting on park benches, such depictions provide a sense of how people use public space and interact within it. In photographs of housing, inside and out, showing yards and exterior structures (or lack thereof), we can explore both notions of "togetherness" and privacy through class discussion or student research. Several years ago, for example, I led a group of non-Spanish-speaking adults to Tlaquepaque, Guadalajara, where we visited the parents of a young doctor in our city. When we arrived at the home, my fellow travelers tried to convince me that the exterior door, for all appearances the entrance to a warehouse, could not possibly be that of a private home. Or, if it were a home, how could a doctor's family live there? But when the *señora* opened the door, a collective gasp arose. We were ushered into a lush patio where vines, hanging thick as curtains from a second-floor balcony, provided verdant shade for a restful area filled with the refreshing sounds of a bubbling fountain.

I later used photos of this door and of the home's interior in class, first inviting students to guess what was behind the door. Students were thus confronted with their own culture's tendency to prefer demonstration of wealth both inside and outside a home. Once they had exhausted their guesses, they were shown the photograph of the interior and asked to make comparisons with homes in their community. They discussed the virtues of the interior patio for privacy as opposed to the lawns, porches or patios of homes they knew. Their ideas led to research into housing styles in different areas of the Hispanic world and into the relationship between housing and climate. As one student remarked, "Hey, that's the perfect house for a hot climate! It's stone, you can be outside most of the time, the fountain sounds cool, and you can't hear much from the street. And besides, you don't have to worry about how you dress because you're in your own house."

How different cultures use time is also a reflection of values. Students usually learn that "now" is *ahora*, until they arrive in a country where *ahora* or *ahorita* likely means "in a (very non-specific) while." According to one's perspective, which is more important, meeting an appointment or spending time with a family member or acquaintance? When is being "on time" most critical? Why do some wedding invitations indicate "*en punto*" after the hour? How is the use of time related to the use of space? Newspapers are excellent sources of information regarding perceptions of time, as they contain television schedules, store and business hours, times for recreational activities and social events. Schedules can provide us with a realistic idea of what happens in the general daily schedule, and television-programming schedules reveal much about the patterns and lifestyles of their target-audience families. By inviting students to think about why we have the "six o'clock news," the "soaps" in the early afternoon and so on, we provide an advance organizer that sensitizes them to possible differences as they peruse a television guide from another country. The schedule of daily routines is reflected in an abundance of cultural products: Theater ads tell us when people partake of public entertainment; restaurant menus often give the times for *comida* and *cena*; traffic signs tell us when one might park in a given area and when parking is restricted, giving hints about rush hour traffic. Students may be asked to keep a log of times they encounter and begin to form hypotheses about the organization of a day—weekday or weekend—and once again, pose questions to native informants to test out their accuracy. In some cities, businesses still close for several hours in the afternoon (one sign in a Mexico City store indicates the hours, followed by "*más o menos*."); in other cities, the midday closing is being replaced by a schedule similar to that of the United States (see Galloway, this volume). Students might thus give thought to how such changes impact family time, traffic patterns, recreation, television schedules, school schedules and other aspects of life.

The teacher who travels has an excellent opportunity to photograph signs and collect tape- or video-recordings around the theme of schedules. For example, during a visit to a target culture, we might ask a number of students when they begin school and when they end their day. In some countries, there will be three shifts for students, leading to further questions and investigations about overcrowded schools, the importance of education to students, and perhaps government regulations and the need for students to work to support their families. These "man-on-the-street" interviews are excellent material for listening practice because the students are essentially answering the same questions in a variety of ways. They also constitute authentic contacts with peers from the culture. The teacher might even use the students in the video as a springboard for developing e-pal relationships for classroom learners.

Indeed, photography, both still and video, provides teachers with an infinite range of possibilities. Overhead transparencies, computer images, illustrations for printed materials, or video images from websites, all bring alive much of what we experience as sojourners in another culture. Through the photographer's perspective, we view details of life of the inhabitants and practitioners of a culture. Further, videotaping or photographing the context and process in which products are used not only reveals their function but also hints at and clarifies their role and value and their "logic" within a system. A grocery ad, combined with seeing, smelling and tasting the actual ingredients, followed by a cooking demonstration, can activate sensory experience, as well as show the time and cost of preparation of a typical family dish. A store receipt combined with photos of the signs for "cashier" and of people paying and receiving their goods, illustrates the procedure of paying before retrieving purchases in many Hispanic cities, for example. A collection of recipes that make up a Sunday dinner can be combined with photographs of markets, foods and prices. Students can prepare shopping lists using the recipes and then decide who will go to the *lechería, frutería, carnicería*, etc. They can incorporate mathematics through the metric system of weights and measures and the use of currency; they can incorporate the procedures of shopping, getting the purchases back home, storing or preparing foods with certain tools; finally, they can decide in which order the dishes must be served, and by whom, as they prepare the meal or parts of it.

The Process of Analysis

The analysis of objects challenges learners to use critical-thinking skills to build on information or images they have experienced. They may be asked to imagine a scene, based on prior knowledge, make suppositions about facts or allusions and brainstorm with peers in a setting where the teacher encourages them to consider everything a possibility. Students continue to build communication skills as they record, report, and discuss their observations. The process of analysis, however, must be carefully planned to include advance organizers, observation, development of a hypothesis, search for evidence, adjustment of hypothesis, presentation of data, and suggestions for further study.

Building observation skills takes practice. Students need to begin their process of analysis by observing the product and describing it in detail. Fleming suggests a three-step observational model: 1) classify, 2) authenticate, 3) describe. This process can require students to perform such tasks as listing characteristics and possible uses, drawing the object, or writing a descriptive paragraph— either individually or as part of cooperative groups. The teacher must be prepared to authenticate the object or, ideally, to provide resources to allow learners to conduct the authentication themselves.

Following a period of study and description of the object, students are ready to proceed through the following process: 1) develop a hypothesis; 2) gather information; 3) test the hypothesis and, in the event the hypothesis cannot be proven, 4) determine what they would need to know or do in order to approach a decision. As they begin to speculate and search for evidence, learners should be encouraged to share their ideas with a group or with the class as a whole. A variety of resources can be gathered, including video, printed matter, Internet resources, personal testimony from native informants or e-pals and, of course, the teacher. The teacher must take into account the need to provide the three types of communication: *interpersonal* (built into group activities), *interpretational* (interpretation of the object and discussion in groups or with the class) and *presentational* (students report on their findings regarding a portion of their hypothesis).

Teachers should note their own critical role in providing guidance while students prepare their hypotheses as, left to brainstorm without direction, it will be easy for students to stray and the task can lose effectiveness. Students must be led to consider why such a statement was made; what are the potential consequences of such a conclusion; and is there a more logical choice? While not all hypotheses can be proven absolutely, it is important for students to acquire enough information and receive sufficient guidance so as to develop skills in analysis. The management of this type of activity progression is critical, as each step must be planned carefully and elicit good information for students to transition to the next step. Students might be required to read, complete vocabulary searches, scan, gist, summarize in written or oral form, and so on. Each task should be clear and its role in the process should be understood; moreover, a communicative format or set of language-use parameters should be built into the tasks so that students are aware of how they are to practice expressing themselves at each juncture. Along the way, learners must have the opportunity to ask questions, to test a hypothesis, all within the scope of their level of language development.

The following is a sample progression of tasks on the theme of "Sunday dinner." The recipe cards for the dinner menu are purposely out of order. The teacher might decide to begin with a view of the entire menu and then break up the menu, giving a recipe to each group, along with the following instructions:

> *Hoy vamos a ver un menu más o menos típico para una comida. A veces vamos a trabajar en grupos y a veces van a trabajar solos. Quiero que piensen en las preguntas o ideas que tengo escritas en la pizarra. En comparación con una comida/ cena en su casa, ¿qué les parece el número de platos? ¿la dificultad de la preparación? ¿El número de ingredientes? ¿De qué país son las recetas?*

CAFÉ DE OLLA ESTILO MEXICANO
1 litro de agua
60 gramos de café
140 gramos de piloncillo
Se pone al fuego el agua y el piloncillo. Cuando éste se deshace, se añade el café tostado y molido no muy fino. Cuando se hierve un mintuo se retira del fuego, se mezcla muy bien, se tapa la olla y se deja en un lugar cerca del fuego hasta que se asienta, o sea, hasta que el café ha quedado en el fondo de la olla. Se cuela y se sirve.

LECHE QUEMADA

2 litros de leche
675 gramos de azúcar
1/4 cucharadita de bicarbonato
Se pone al fuego en una olla honda 1/4 de litro de la leche y el azúcar. Cuando se cambia a un color dorado, se agrega poco a poco la leche restante, que ya habrá hervido con el bicarbonato. Se deja hervir sin dejar de removerse, hasta que al levantarla con una cuchara haga hebras. Se vacía al platón.

ENSALADA TRICOLOR

5 elotes tiernos
5 aguacates
5 granadas
1/8 de litro de aceite
2 yemas]
vinagre, sal y pimienta al gusto
Con las yemas y el aceite se hace mayonesa, se sazona de vinagre, sal y pimienta. Se le agregan los elotes cocidos y desgranados y se ponen en una ensaladera. Se le forma una franja de la granada y se adorna de tiritas de aguacates, formando una bandera mexicana.

ARROZ BLANCO

225 gramos de arroz
115 ramos de manteca
85 gramos de mantequilla
225 gramos de queso crema
1/2 cucharadita jugo de cebolla
2 tazas de agua frí
2 tazas de leche
6 chiles verdes poblanos
115 gramos chícharos cocidos
sal al gusto
El arroz se remoja 15 minutos en agua caliente. En seguida se lava en agua fría hasta que salga el agua limpia. Entonces se escurre bien en un colador y se fríe en la manteca al mismo tiempo que la cebolla. Antes de que dore se quita la manteca y se agregan dos tazas de agua fría. Cuando se consume se pone la leche y sal al gusto. Cuando empieza a resecarse, se agregan los chícharos cocidos y los chiles asados sin la piel, las venas y las semillas y rellenos de queso. Se tapa la cacerola, dejándose hervir a fuego lento hasta que esté suave, seco y separado un grano de otro. Entonces se le agrega la mantequilla en pequeños trocitos. En cuanto se incorpora bien, se vacía al platón y se sirve inmediatamente.

SOPA MEXICANA

1 pechga de pollo
1 cebolla
1 cucharada de manteca
6 cucharadas de puré de jitomate
1/2 cucharada de jugo de cebolla
2 litros de caldo de pollo
1/2 aza de crema
2 guacates
115 gramos de queso crema
tiritas de tortillas fritas

Se cuece la pechuga en 3 litros de agua con la cebolla, sal y pimienta. Cuando está cocida, se parte en cuadritos. En la manteca se fríe el puré de jitomate y el jugo de cebolla. Se agrega el caldo colado, sal y pimienta. Se deja hervir 15 minutos y se retira del fuego. Cuando ya se va a servir, se agregan las tiritas de tortillas fritas a la sopera con el caldo. Luego se agrega la crema, los cuadritos de la pechuga, los aguacates y el queso cortado en tiritas.

ADOBO

900 gramos de lomo de cerdo
56 gramos de maneca
6 chiles anchos
2 cebollas
2 dientes de ajo
1/2 cucharadita de oregano
1 hoja de laurel
4 cucharadas de vinagre
2 azas de caldo de la carne
2 cebollas para adornar
3 aguacates
1 manojo de rábanos
sal y pimienta al gusto

Se pone a cocer el lomo con una cebolla, sal y pimienta. Los chiles se tuestan ligeramente y se remojan. Se muelen con la cebolla, los ajos y el oregano. Se fríen en la manteca. Se agrega el lomo ya cocido, el caldo, el vinagre y el laurel. Se deja hervir hasta que se espesa el adobo y cubre bien el lomo. Se vacía al platón y se adorna con ruedas de cebolla separadas, tiritas de aguacate y flores de rábano.

BUDIN DE ELOTE
6 elotes
6 huevos
1 taza de leche
1/2 taza de crema
140 gramos de mantequilla
1 cucharada de azúcar
1 cucharada de sal
3 cucharadas de pan molido
Se bate la mantequilla hasta que acreme y se agregan los granos de elote molidos en crudo, los huevos uno a uno, la sal, el azúcar y la leche. Se vacía a un molde engrasado y espolvoreado con el pan molido. Se cuece a horno de calor suave. Ya cocido se vacía al platón. En el centro se pone la crema batida sazonada con sal y pimienta.

To begin, the teacher might ask students to complete a vocabulary search for a number of cognates. These activities can all be done together, particularly in a block schedule, or the teacher might decide to do one or two each day until the unit is completed. It is important for students to understand that it will not be necessary to comprehend every word; rather, the teacher must caution them to look for broader concepts by skimming, scanning and gisting. By assigning groups, the task is viewed as less overwhelming and opportunities abound for interpersonal and interpretational language use.

*1. Los cognados. Muchas veces podemos leer más de lo que creemos, simplemente pensando en los cognados. Recuerda que un cognado tiene una palabra equivalente casi parecido en otro idioma. Por ejemplo: teléfono=*telephone. *Busca los cognados para cada palabra de la lista.*

vinegar	coffee	pulverized, ground
salt	adorn, decorate	tomato
cream	bicarbonate, baking soda	chile peppers

2. ¿Dónde los encuentro? En Estados Unidos tenemos la costumbre de comprar comida en un supermercado. En otros países uno puede visitar el 'super' o también puede hacer las compras en tiendas especializadas. Busca la tienda en donde se puede comprar cada cosa en la lista de compras.

Ingredientes

cebollas
lomo de cerdo
pechuga de pollo
crema
aguacate
café
huevos
elote
jitomate
ajo
mantequilla
leche

Tiendas

a. carnicería
b. frutería
c. mercado de verduras
d. lechería
e. sección de bebidas
f. sección de ingredients para hornear

The following activity can be completed in groups in jigsaw fashion, with each group completing a list. Students might also practice shopping for amounts listed in the recipes.

3. Lista de compras. *Prepara una lista de cosas de cada categoría que vas a necesitar para preparar la comida.*

carnes	frutas/verduras	productos lácteos	ingredientes secos

4. La influencia prehispánica. *Además del español, el idioma de seguna popularidad en México es el nahuatl, la lengua de los aztecas y de varios grupos del Valle de México. Muchas palabras de uso diario encuentran su origen en nahuatl, y algunas de estas también se usan en inglés. A ver si puedes adivinar las palabras en inglés para las palabras de origen nahuatl.*

nahuatl	inglés
cacahuate	corn
aguacate	tomato
elote	avocado
jitomate	peanut

Respuestas: *cacahuate-maní, cacahuete=*peanut*; aguacate, palta [Cono Sur]=*avocado*; elote, xilote=*corn*; jitomate=*tomato

[Pronunciation note: *En nahuatl, se usa el sistema fonética española, con la excepción de la 'x' inicial que se pronuncia como 'sh' en inglés.]*

5. *Otra comida muy popular por todo el mundo también viene de la Mesoamérica prehispánica. En nahuatl, la palabra es 'xocolatl.' ¿Cuál será la palabra en español?*

At this point the teacher will want to verify that students understand what is intended from the recipes. The decision about what they are to understand should be based on language background. Students are now prepared to analyze the menu in context.

Actividades de poslectura. *Acabas de leer las recetas que van a usar para una cena especial el sábado que viene. Contesta las siguientes preguntas sobre el menú. Recuerda que tienes que adivinar en algunos casos, preparar otras preguntas y comprobar tu hipótesis. Usa las siguientes preguntas para guiar la formación de tu hipótesis.*

1. ¿Piensas que es mucha o poca comida? ¿Por qué?

2. ¿En qué orden crees que se sirven los platos? ¿Por qué?

3. ¿Cuál es el postre? ¿Por qué lo escogiste?

4. *¿Cuáles platos se preparan en el horno? ¿Mencionan una temperatura? ¿Por qué crees así? ¿Qué puede indicar esta información?*

5. *Investiga anuncios de comida y trata de decidir cuál plato cuesta más/ menos. Compara los precios de la misma comida en tu ciudad con los que en cuentrasen el periódico. ¿Son parecidos? Si el sueldo mínimo en México (de por medio) es a[30] pesos el día, ¿qué puedes adivinar sobre la posibilidad de incluir carne en la dieta diaria?*

6. *¿Quiénes serán los invitados a esta comida? ¿La familia? ¿Los amigos? Investiga las costumbres familiares durante los fines de semana, en especial los domingos. Luego haz los cambios necesarios a tu hipótesis. [Students may question native informants, e-pals, students in their school.]*

7. *En tu opinion, ¿Cuánto tiempo se necesita para servir y comer esta comida? ¿Por qué? ¿Por qué se sirve una comida tan grande? Prepara unas preguntas que podrían hacerles a tus 'informantes' sobre la costumbre de la comida. Un concepto que debes investigar es el de "la sobremesa."*

8. *¿Existe algo parecido a esta comida en tu familia? ¿Cuáles son unas diferencias en las costumbres? ¿Por qué? ¿Cena la familia junta? ¿Por qué sí o no?*

9. *¿Cuánto tiempo se necesita para preparar esta comida, más o menos? ¿Te parece mucho o poco trabajo? ¿Por qué?*

10. *En dos recetas se mencionan los colores de la bandera mexicana. ¿Por qué?*

La hipótesis. At this point, the teacher must provide guidance in the formation of a hypothesis about the meal, suggesting perhaps the following aspects of the project to the class at large or dividing the class into small groups and assigning a topic to each one. Groups or individuals may prepare a presentation of the hypothesis, the evidence they have gathered, and also comments on what they might need to arrive at a more concrete analysis.

•Content of the meal and its preparation

•Traditional influences (use of corn, *chiles*, colors of the flag)

•The meal as a possible gathering of family members

The concepts the teacher is trying to impart here are that in many Mexican homes a large meal served on weekends is a way for the family to spend time together; the meals often last several hours, with the family talking around the table during and after each course (*la sobremesa*); food preparation is very often a laborious task, with most dishes being made "from scratch" using few pre-prepared ingredients. Students might investigate how these customs are changing and why: Growth of female employment (the former serving class is now entering manufacturing or business), lack of time, changes in tastes, economic trends—all are factors. Obviously not every factor can be investigated;

the teacher may choose to focus on one or two of them or, alternatively, spiral the activities through several levels of language instruction. If students keep portfolios of their work from year to year, the material can be used to stimulate the next level of investigation as well as motivate each learner through observation of individual language growth.

Teacher-prepared materials, such as videos or photographs that show meals in private homes can provide some of the validation of learners' hypotheses. Native informants can also be asked to submit answers to e-mail questions, visit the class to talk about family customs, respond to inquiries about the menu. Further, as teachers help prepare students for the formation of their hypotheses, it is important to keep in mind that there will likely be no universal agreement on outcomes, as we all perceive the world around us according to our own experiences and tend to judge accordingly. However, it is important that learners understand that "judgment" is neither our goal nor our right; rather, the rationale for a behavior comes from the distinct history, tradition, geography, socio-economic factors and values system of the culture under study. We are helping students develop an authentic perspective of another culture, one that allows us to see "difference" as neither good nor bad. Debunking Whorf's theory that two brains will have similar reactions to an experience, Edward Hall states that each person utilizes a selective screening process related to personal sensory patterns and that "experience...cannot be counted on as a stable point of reference"(x). Because the individual possesses a personal set of cultural and sensory filters, no two people will experience an event in precisely the same way. It is important, therefore, to recognize differences in opinions or perceptions, provide additional information if students wander too far from a likely hypothesis or direct them to sources of data on the topic.

The teacher must play the role of "cultural referee" as well—to caution students against judging another culture's product or practice by the standards of their own culture. The late H. Ned Seelye often suggested that students fold their hands in normal fashion, then open their fingers and refold them, this time placing the opposite thumb on top. The question that follows relates to how it felt—were they doing a "different" thing? Or were they simply doing the same thing in a different way? Simple reminders to students that we do not always perceive events in the same manner can take the shape of questions such as the following:

- How does climate/geography affect [choice of foods, building materials, design of buildings, choice and/or color of clothing, time schedules]?

- How do we see indications of a difference in values [for example, historical influence in relationships within families, choice of housing, meal structure]?

- What role does technology [or the lack thereof] play in this event [or artifact, such as the *alebrije*]? Is there an indication about the importance of time?

- Would this [house, activity, meal, city design] fit in our town? Why or why not?

Throughout their research, students must be guided to return to their original hypothesis for validation and modification as necessary, according to new information gathered. How they present their information can be controlled by the teacher, who will take into account not only the level of language development, but the particular aspects of language targeted for practice. Thought must be given to opportunities for practicing communicative skills (interpersonal, interpretational and presentational). By using cooperative groups, each type of skill can be included, each chosen to match the developmental level of the learner.

To illustrate the task progression, we use here a flyer handed out on a street corner in Mexico (**Figure 2**). The activities that follow designate the instructional level at which each might be used most successfully: N=novice, I=intermediate, A=advanced.

Antes de leer. Familiarize students with Puebla, the kinds of buildings in the colonial style of architecture, the incorporation of azulejos and talavera. Information can be found on many websites related to the city of Puebla.ii Try to include photographs of typical restaurants (la Fonda de Sta. Clara, for exampleiii). Explain to students that they will be asked to prepare hypotheses about a restaurant and the food served there. Divide students into groups of three and give the following:

Figure 2. La Fonda de Teresita

1. Preparen una lista de los colores que se ven en la foto [de una pieza de talavera, un azulejo, un edificio]. (N)

2. Describan el edificio (número de pisos, la puerta, los adornos). (N) *¿Parece viejo ocontemporáneo?* (I) *¿Por qué?* (I)

3. ¿Cuáles son las ventajas/desventajas de una estructura colonial? (I-A) *en comparación con un edificio de uso similar en su ciudad (e.g. el correo)?*

4. *¿Cuáles son unas diferencias entre esta estructura y otra similar en su ciudad?* (I)

5. *¿Cuál sería la relación de esta estructura a la historia y la tradición?* (I-A)

6. *¿Qué opinión tienen Uds. de este edificio? ¿Por qué?* (N-A)

7. *¿En qué parte de la ciudad se encuentra? Es de un barrio típico, de un centro turístico, del centro de la ciudad?*

Explain to students that they will be working with an advertisement for a new restaurant. Their task will be to form hypotheses regarding the appearance of the restaurant, the food served, typical clientele, meal costs and methods of payment. They are to look at the ad, make some predictions about what the restaurant is like, about the food served and other information necessary for someone who might want to eat there. Teachers may wish to provide information about some of the foods listed and alert students to the fact that they will likely find dishes that are closely related to prehispanic cooking. If a word list is provided, teachers may want to provide photographs of dishes or ingredients from cookbooks, personal photo collections or Internet websites. Once again, students work in groups to prepare responses they will share with the class as a whole. Note that some of the activities listed may be deleted if students have not yet learned the skills (number 6, for example).

Novice:

1. *¿Cuál es el nombre del restaurante?*

2. *¿Cuál es la dirección?*

3. *¿Cuál es el teléfono?*

4. *¿Cuándo se abre? ¿Qué comidas se sirven?*

5. *¿Cómo se puede pagar? ¿Tarjeta de crédito? ¿Efectivo?*

6. *Con unos compañeros, haz un pequeño drama en el que piden una comida en el restaurante.*

Intermediate: all of the above plus

7. *Usa la imaginación y prepara una lista de adjetivos que describen el lugar según su impresión. ¿Por qué crees así?*

8. *¿Quiénes comen en este restaurante? ¿Serán turistas? ¿De dónde serán los turistas? ¿Gente del pueblo? Preparen una defensa de tus ideas.*

9. *¿Por qué crees que estos platos son populares?*

10. *En el drama, [No. 6], pidan información sobre la preparación de un plato.*

Advanced: All of the above plus

> *11. Prepárate para convencer a otra persona que coman en este restaurante. Describe el ambiente, los platos, y por qué quieres comer aquí.*

> *12. Pide una definición de un plato y de su preparación antes de escogerlo.*

> *13. Termina la frase: Si comiera en este restaurante, yo escogería [escamoles] porque…*

> *14. En un grupo de tres o cuatro,bHablen entre sí para decidir si éste es un restaurante de alta categoría o no. ¿Por qué?*

Formación y comprobación de la hipótesis. The following activities are directed toward guiding hypothesis formation and validation.

> *1. Forma una hipotesis sobre uno o más de los siguientes temas:*

> > *a. El ambiente del restaurante, incluyendo los sonidos, olores, colores* (N)

> > *b. La clientela* (N)

> > *c. El menú [¿Qué tipos de comida se encuentran? Si es un menú turístico, ¿quiénes son los turistas?]* (N)

> *Busca varias personas que tengan información sobre Puebla y este restaurante. Prepara una lista de preguntas que procuren averiguar su hipótesis. Házles las preguntas y compara la información. Se puede llevar a cabo por medio del Internet, un guía turístico, un informante, fotos del maestro.*

> *2. ¿De dónde vienen nuestras comidas tradicionales? ¿Vienen de la historia? ¿Llevan la influencia del clima o de la geografía? Prepara una plática sobre el tema, invitando a los colegas a participar.* (I-A)

> *3. Prepara un dibujo de su concepto del restaurante. Puedes escoger el exterior o el interior.* (N)

> *4. Prepara un menú usando las comidas del anuncio. Si quieres averiguar los precios, busca otros precios en los menús del Internet.* (N-A)

> *5. Si tu maestro es el "informante," preséntale tu trabajo y pídele sus opiniones.* (N-A)

As follow-up, the teacher may have further information about the restaurant, recipes for some of the dishes served, or even photographs from books or websites. Students may also want to prepare one or more of the dishes and take a "virtual trip" to the restaurant. On the flyer, there is also a map indicating the restaurant's location, which can be used by students to practice giving and getting directions.

What cultural information is transmitted here? First and foremost, there is the concept that old is not worthless. Pride in colonial architecture (as opposed to the "new is better" attitude in the U.S.) is an important aspect of this culture. Foods served are reminiscent of prehispanic diets, indicating the importance of heritage, tradition, ethnic identity, climate and geography. Corn, for example, is a staple in the Mexican diet of today, just as it was in prehispanic times (García Rivas 165-87). In fact, the enormous variety of dishes requiring corn attests to its plentiful growth, perhaps the inventiveness of the cooks, and its role in the diet. From displays in the National Museum of Anthropology in Mexico City, we see that corn prepared with lime (*tortillas*) in prehispanic days had a beneficial effect on the preservation of teeth and bones, a benefit now nullified by the addition of sugar to the diet. Today, we see Mexican corn everywhere, even as snacks on street corners. Indeed, there are many legends and sayings surrounding corn, such as: *Tiene las manos en la masa* ("He has his hands in the tortilla dough" = he's involved in the event, affair). Students should be encouraged to relate their findings to their own cultural background, always keeping in mind the heritage of family.

Getting Students Involved

Cooperative learning activities take varied forms (Shrum and Glisan, 182-204). Learning stations, information-gap and jigsaw activities are all ways in which students can maximize their language production while employing authentic cultural artifacts as a topic of discussion. Using the ad for *La Fonda de Teresita,* for example, the teacher can prepare two versions, each of which will lack pertinent information. Pairs of students then provide the missing information for each other. For the jigsaw, a reproduction of a photograph such as that in **Figure 3**, can be cut into several pieces; students then divide into groups of three or four, according to letters (a, b, c, d); those with the same letters gather as a group to memorize the contents of their picture before returning to their "home group" to share the information and complete a worksheet with questions regarding the contents of each of their portions.

All students are capable of undertaking a more thorough analysis of any object in question as long as the teacher structures activities to meet the language level of the students and to guide them through clear objectives. The use of an artifact collection does just that, by providing students artifacts along with activities that guide them to make statements with their analyses or match items to list of functions or people who produce them or to geographical sources. Depending on the level of language skills, the process can be adjusted to make the activity challenging yet totally doable.

If students see the products in use or observe photographs of a location, such as *La Fonda de Teresita*, the are better able to imagine the product in its own setting. This kind of information can provide validation of a hypothesis or indicate a need to modify and look further. Small groups or the whole class can begin to form a plan that will move them from the item at hand to the next stage. For example, are all restaurants in a certain area like *La Fonda de Teresita*? Are the foods served there typical of most restaurants? How might we find the answers to these questions? Teachers should encourage students not to base the proof of a hypothesis on one artifact or piece of evidence alone, however. Rather, learners must be encouraged to make their search a protracted one that will eventually yield clues that lead to a better understanding of a concept or perspective. For example, the humor demonstrated in a craft item such as an *alebrije* (colorful wooden figure from Oaxaca) or *calacas* from Mexico, in reflecting the experience and perspective of its creator also reveals something about that creator's culture in a broad sense.

Consider the photograph in **Figure 3**, for example. This wood carving, an *alebrije* from the town of Tilcajete in Oaxaca, Mexico, is an example of a craft that allows the observer to consider many aspects of life in that town. The town itself is the subject of an article in *Smithsonian Magazine*[4] and its wooden figures have become famous throughout the world. What can we speculate about the life of the creator of this piece? Is he imaginative? Possessed of a sense of humor? Does he have time to produce figures in laborious detail? Since these are all obviously true, what can we suppose about his life, the way he earns a living? What other figures like this one might we find? A quick search for "*alebrije*" on the Internet yielded 129 sites with photographs and historical information not only about the figurines themselves but also about the towns where they are crafted in cottage industry by farmers living fairly isolated from the capital city of Oaxaca. Similarly, a molinillo, the wooden utensil used to whip hot chocolate, can give students a place to begin study of the importance of chocolate in prehispanic cultures.

Figure 3. Alebrije by Porfirio Sosa Gutiérrez, Tilcajete, Oaxaca, México.

Photograph by N. Humbach

The unit, as students might design it, could include the role of chocolate in today's diet, myths relating to the arrival of chocolate on Earth, recipes for other foods that require its use, and finally the preparation of hot chocolate in class.

Understanding the Notion of Change

Because cultures are dynamic, equally important to any cultural study is the analysis of change. Projects that require students to interview those of other generations regarding changes in living patterns, attitudes and habits are often done in social studies classes and the language teacher might piggyback this kind of project with one that mirrors changes in the target culture. As has been previously noted, lifestyles within the U.S. have shown a great deal of change over the last fifty years. Through interviews of several generations of relatives, students have access to such changes as the number of cars per family, the number of televisions (or other material goods), alterations in meal schedules and in food and eating habits in general, the evolving role of women in society and so on. In discussions with grandparents or community members of that age, with parents and with peers, students are better able to see the progression of these changes. Change in other cultures can be captured to some extent not only through the use of Hispanic film and literature of different decades, but through other authentic sources—from reflective feature articles and Op-Ed pieces in Hispanic newspapers and magazines, to photo galleries, political slogan-and-poster archives, and most especially through advertising-through-the-ages collections—all available via the Internet on websites of Hispanic news media, political and religious organizations, and a great number of businesses. In using such strategies, the critical element is that of guiding students to understand that cultures are dynamic and that lifestyle patterns are continuously changing as peoples create and respond to their world and to the peoples around them.

Obviously, differences also exist between socio-economic classes and ethnic groups within a country. In the end, our goal is to prepare students to reject stereotypical statements about behaviors, attitudes, or products of other cultures. One way to have the effect of stereotypes hit home is to examine with students what it means to be typecast in their own school or cultural setting, through terms such as "dumb jock," "Asian genius," "blonde cheerleader," "band nerd" and so on[5] and to then share with students the comments of "Latino" students regarding how they feel stereotyped, both positively and negatively, for their heritage. If given the opportunity to consider their own experiences before being introduced to similar, yet different, concepts in other cultures, learners may find the notion of "difference" far less startling.

Conclusion

Access to authentic materials is critical to the development of skills in cultural analysis. Through their use, students learn both similarities and differences between their own and target cultures while developing communication skills in Spanish to make comparisons, establish connections with other disciplines and work with communities. Access to native informants, ideally in person, but also via the Internet, can provide students access to the culture through the language of its people to help learners reach the understanding reflected in Rudyard Kipling's poem, "We and They."

We and They[6]
Father and Mother, and Me,
Sister and Auntie say
All the people like us are We,
And everyone else is They.
And They live over the sea,
While We live over the way,
But—-would you believe it? —They look upon We
As only a sort of They!

We eat pork and beef
With cow-horn-handled knives.
They who gobble Their rice off a leaf,
Are horrified out of Their lives;
While they who live up a tree,
And feast on grubs and clay,
(Isn't it scandalous?) look upon We
As a simply disgusting They!

We shoot birds with a gun.
They stick lions with spears.
Their full-dress is un-.
We dress up to Our ears.
They like Their friends for tea.
We like Our friends to stay;
And, after all that, They look upon We
As an utterly ignorant They!

We eat kitcheny food.
We have doors that latch.
They drink milk or blood,
Under an open thatch.
We have Doctors to fee.
They have Wizards to pay.
And (impudent heathen!) They look upon We
As a quite impossible They!

All good people agree,
And all good people say,
All nice people, like Us, are We
And everyone else is They:
But if you cross over the sea,
Instead of over the way,
You may end by (think of it!) looking on We
As only a sort of They!

Notes

[1] Rebecca Eppley presented her concept of learning centers in Puebla, 1996, at a gathering of the participants of the NEH workshop co-sponsored by the University of Cincinnati and directed by Susan Bacon and Nancy Humbach.

[2] See for example: www.pud.upaep.mx/puebla/index_eng.html and www.talavera.com.

[3] La Fonda de Sta. Clara: http://www.fondasantaclara.com.mx.

[4] Barbash, Shepard (text) and Vicki Ragan (photos). "These magicians carve dreams with their machetes." *Smithsonian Magazine*, May 1991, 118-129. Last updated 16 April 1996.

[5] See, for example, activities in Chapters 9-10 of Humbach and Ozete, *Ven conmigo* 3. Holt Rinehart Winston, 1995.

[6] Rudyard Kipling, "We and They." *The Complete Verse*. London: Kyle Cathie, Ltd., 1990. 631-32.

Works Cited

Eder, Elizabeth K. "Seeing the Invisible: Exploring Culture through Objects." *Hidden Messages: Instructional Materials for Investigating Culture*. Barbara Finkelstein and Elizabeth K. Eder, eds. Yarmouth, ME: Intercultural Press, 1998. 3-27.

Finkelstein, Barbara and Elizabeth K. Eder, eds. *Hidden Messages:Instructional Materials for Investigating Culture*. Yarmouth, Maine: Intercultural Press, 1998.

Fleming, E. McClung. "Artifact Study: A Proposed Model." *Material Culture Studies in America*. Thomas J. Schlereth, ed. Nashville, TN: American Association for State and Local History, 1982. 162-73.

Garcia Rivas, Heriberto. *Cocina prehispánica mexicana*. México: Panorama Editorial, S. A. de C. V., 1996.

Jiménez, Francisco. *Cajas de cartón*. Boston: Houghton Mifflin Company, 1999.

_____. *El regalo de Navidad/*The Christmas Gift. Boston: Houghton Mifflin Company, 2001.

Haas, Mari. *The Language of Folk Art*. Englewood Cliffs: Prentice Hall, 1996.

Hall, Edward T. *The Hidden Dimension*, NY: Anchor/Doubleday, 1982.

_____.*The Dance of Life: The Other Dimension of Time*. NY: Anchor Books, 1983.

Humbach, Nancy A. and Oscar Ozete. *Ven conmigo*3. Austin: Holt Rinehart Winston, 1995.

Loaeza, Guadalupe. *Las niñas bien*. México, D.F.: Aguilar, León y Cal Editores, S.A.deC.V., 1994.

_____.*Compro, luego existo*. México, D.F.: Alianza Editorial, "Editorial Patria,"1992.

Mastretta, Angeles. *Mujeres de ojos grandes*. México: Aguilar, León y Cal Editores, S.A.deC.V. 1990.

Menser, David G. "Ideas and Objects: The Artifact Kit." *Social Education* 30 (May 1966): 343 45.

Storti, Craig. *Figuring Foreigners Out: A Practical Guide*. Yarmouth, ME: Intercultural Press, 1999.

Appendix
Búsqueda de tesoros poblanos (Puebla, México)

cuatro tarjetas postales
tres timbres
una lista de precios
un santoral
un metate
un molcajete
un camote (dulce)
unas tortas de Santa Clara
tres esquelas (periódico)
una calaca
un molinillo
un anuncio (de la calle)
tres tarjetas de negocios
anuncios para tres negocios que no hay en su ciudad (copias del guía telefónica)
tres boletos de museos o de funciones
un programa de una función teatral/musical
tres remedios caseros
una receta casera (favor de no usar recetario)
un milagro de plata
guía del cine
gestos para indicar distancia a
    1) Amozoc
    2) Atlixco
    3) Izúcar de Matamoros
tres gestos más
dos dichos poblanos
tres paquetes de comida que se puede llevar
chocolate en tablilla
un azulejo
la leyenda de La Llorona (contada por un poblano)
otra leyenda de Puebla
nombres de tres frutas que no se encuentran en los Estados Unidos
nombres de 7 chiles
recomendaciones para los 6 platos más típicos de Puebla
un periódico de Puebla
tres recibos/notas de compras (restaurantes, tiendas, etc.)
tarjeta LADATEL
reglas para la pronunciácion de la X en México (Ejemplos: Cacaxtla, Xoxtla, Atlixco, Huexotitla

10 palabras indígenas de uso común
fotos de tres platos comunes (tarjetas postales)
una calavera de azúcar
una bandera mexicana
¿Qué se compra en...?

una talabartería	*una lencería*
una jarcería	*una bonetería*
una abarrotería	*una talachería*

Chapter 5

Understanding Culture Through Music: Products and Perspectives

Paula R. Heusinkveld, Clemson University

In one sense, music is a universal language that transcends linguistic and cultural boundaries to touch every person who hears it. We do not need to understand the words of a song written in Italian, Spanish, or Japanese to enjoy the melodic line, the rhythm, the musical style, and the rich blend of sounds made by various instruments, including that of the human voice. Music can evoke strong emotional responses such as joy, melancholia, light-hearted cheer, or nostalgic reflection. Because these emotions are universal, the appeal of the music that elicits them is also universal. For this reason, music can serve to break down cultural barriers and create bonds of understanding.

At the same time, any given piece of music is a product of a specific culture or sub-culture. The use of characteristic musical instruments, harmonies, rhythms, and styles can help us identify a particular piece of music as being Caribbean, Andean, Brazilian, or Chinese. Even within a culture, varying musical styles can reflect the uniqueness of a particular sub-culture, region, or ethnic group. Music of the United States, for example, includes Appalachian clogging tunes, Negro spirituals, cowboy ballads, and New Orleans-style jazz. In Hispanic countries we find an astonishing variety of musical styles, ranging from Spanish flamenco to lively Mexican mariachi music, from pulsating salsa rhythms to the haunting melodies of Andean panpipes.

The lyrics of a song are a culturally authentic text, constituting a potential goldmine of cultural information. The words selected by the composer may reflect the unique dialect or expressions of a particular region, ethnic group, age group or social class; the theme of a song the group's perspective, prevalent attitudes, values and shared beliefs. Lyrics may refer to geographic landscapes, foods, heroes, religious figures, holidays, historical events, legends, superstitions, or other elements of a specific culture or sub-culture. Most songs, therefore, despite their potential for universal appeal, have special meaning for people from the culture in which they originated. Each piece of music is a product of the culture where it was produced, and this product reflects a cultural perspective.

For these reasons, music is an ideal vehicle for integrating important cultural lessons into the foreign language class. Over the past several decades, foreign language practitioners have increasingly come to appreciate the effectiveness of music as a valuable resource to enhance lessons in both language and culture. Further, the undeniable appeal of music makes it a powerful motivational tool in the classroom, a stimulating vehicle for listening or pronunciation practice, vocabulary reinforcement, grammar study and directed conversation activity.[1]

Although any song or jingle – even one created expressly for the language class – can accomplish many of these linguistic objectives, a culturally authentic song has rich dimensions that are lacking in artificial classroom-designed compositions.[2] A song created by a member of a particular culture conveys a wealth of information and reveals insights about that culture, even as it reinforces language and entertains and inspires our students. As our National Standards call for the fuller integration of culture into our foreign language classes, it makes sense to consider more frequent, extensive and varied uses of culturally authentic musical composition.[3]

Not surprisingly, authentic musical texts are apt to be more difficult than simple songs or jingles created for the foreign language class (or even more difficult than conversational samples or many types of written documents). The vocabulary is richer and more complex, and cultural references, directed to an in-group listener, will often be unfamiliar to the language learner who does not share the in-group's frame of reference. Further, a singer performing for a native audience may be less attentive to careful articulation of words, and the accompanying background music may make comprehension more difficult.[4] Despite these challenges, though, the pedagogical benefits of working with a culturally authentic song easily justify the effort, as this chapter will demonstrate.

In the pages that follow, we will consider a variety of strategies that incorporate culturally authentic music into the foreign language class. Going beyond the study of individual songs, we consider the broader issue of the role that music plays in our lives, either in our own culture or another. The chapter is organized into several major sections: First, we propose a series of classroom activities designed to heighten students' awareness of music in their own lives and in the cultures of the Hispanic world. Second, we briefly discuss some of the factors that teachers should consider when selecting culturally authentic music. Third, using the Dominican song "*Ojalá que llueva café*," we present a sample lesson plan that completely integrates linguistic and cultural learning objectives. Finally, we will see how a lesson based on a culturally authentic song integrates all of the "Five Cs" of the *National Standards*.

Music Self-Awareness Survey

The more fully we understand the many roles of music in our own lives, the better we are able to comprehend the close relationship between music and culture in Hispanic countries. Indeed, many cross-cultural educators maintain that the first and most important step to cross-cultural understanding is "cultural self-awareness," that is, awareness of what distinguishes our own culture from others. It has been this writer's experience that the two-part Musical Self-awareness Survey that follows is time well spent. Although by no means a prerequisite to listening to and enjoying Hispanic music, these questions do increase students' understanding of the role of music in their own culture, making all further study of Hispanic songs more meaningful. Experience suggests that this survey works best in a think/ pair/ share format. After receiving the list of printed questions, students briefly formulate individual answers, compare notes with a partner, and then share with the entire class.

Parte I – Tus preferencias y tus perspectivas musicales

1 ¿Dónde escuchas la música? Indica todos los lugares donde escuchas la música:
❑ tu cuarto ❑ la discoteca ❑ fiestas ❑ reuniones familiars ❑ la playa ❑la iglesia
❑ la escuela ❑ restaurantes/ cafés ❑ eventos deportivos ❑ la clase de español
❑un campamento de verano ❑ consultorio del medico ❑ otro _____

2. ¿Qué otras cosas haces mientras escuchas la música?
❑ estudiar ❑ comer ❑ bailar ❑ cantar ❑ descansar ❑ conversar con amigos ❑ meditar
❑ pensar ❑ rezar ❑ correr/ caminar ❑ limpiar la casa ❑ otro _____

3. ¿Con quién(es) escuchas la música?
❑ familia ❑ amigos ❑ tu novio/-a ❑ parientes ❑ solo/-a ❑ los maestros
❑ compañeros de la escuela ❑ compañeros de trabajo ❑ compañeros de la iglesia otro

4. ¿Qué estilos de música te gustan más/ menos?
❑ jazz ❑ rock ❑ country ❑ rap ❑ popular ❑ reggae ❑ blues ❑ salsa ❑ tecno
❑ mariachi ❑ clásica ❑ópera ❑ samba ❑ tango ❑ polka ❑ sitar ❑ flamenco
❑ folclorica ❑ otro _____

5. ¿Cuáles son tus artistas musicales preferidos? (cantantes o grupos)

6. ¿Qué aspectos de la música te importan más?
❑ el ritmo ❑ los instrumentos ❑ la melodía ❑ la letra (las palabras) ❑ la calidad de la voz
❑ el/la cantante ❑ el estilo ❑ la harmonía ❑ el sentimiento otro_____

7. ¿Tocas un instrumento musical? ¿ Cuál instrumento? _____

8. ¿Te gusta cantar las palabras mientras escuchas una canción?

9. Cuando hay una reunión de tu familia, ¿se escucha la música? ¿Qué tipo de música se escucha? ¿Cantan juntos a veces?

10. ¿Cuáles son los temas más comunes de las canciones que escuchas?
❑ el amor ❑ el desamor ❑ la amistad ❑ el amor por la patria ❑ la naturaleza
❑ la fe o la religión ❑ temas sociales, la protesta ❑ la política ❑ temas cómicos
❑ otros _____

11. ¿Cuáles son las emociones que puedes sentir al escuchar la música?

☐ alegría ☐ tranquilidad ☐ nostalgia ☐ ganas de bailar

☐ melancolía ☐ inspiración ☐ reflección meditativa ☐ unidad con otras personas

☐ relajación   felicidad ☐ indignación ☐ patriotismo ☐ otro _____

12. Si no eres de los Estados Unidos, ¿hay un estilo de música que te guste a ti, pero que la gente de tu comunidad en los Estados Unidos no sabe apreciar? ¿Cuál es?

Parte II – Canciones que conoces. Trata de nombrar una canción en cada categoría.

1. Esta canción es magnífica música para bailar.
2. Es buena música para una noche romántica con un amigo/ una amiga muy especial.
3. Es una canción que aprendiste cuando eras un/a niño/a, y todavía la recuerdas.
4. Te gusta cantarla con tu abuelo(a) o con otro pariente mayor.
5. A tus padres les encanta la canción, pero a ti te parece fuera de moda.
6. A ti te encanta la canción, pero a tus padres no les gusta; dicen que es moderna / extraña.
7. La escuchas (o cantas) con tus amigos en fiestas o reuniones de amigos.
8. La aprendiste en algún campamento, tal como "Girl Scouts."
9. La aprendiste en la escuela primaria.
10. La asocias con el patriotismo o el amor a la patria.
11. La asocias con el orgullo/la lealtad a tu escuela.
12. La asocias con la fe o con tu religión.
13. La asocias con la Navidad.
14. La asocias con otro día festivo.

These questions are accessible to first- and second-year Spanish students since they are framed mostly in the present tense, require limited vocabulary, and deal with concrete topics that are familiar to them. Most of the musical vocabulary in the survey consists of cognates (*el ritmo, la melodía, el estilo, los instrumentos musicales*) easily recognized by first-year students. Thus, the survey offers practice with basic vocabulary while raising students' awareness of the various roles of music in their own lives. It should also generate curiosity about the musical tastes of others of either their own or other cultures.

Ethnographic Interviews on Music

Using the same questions as in the two-part survey described, we may now conduct ethnographic interviews regarding musical tastes in the Hispanic world. To help students gain confidence in asking questions, we begin by inviting one or more native speakers to class. Students can take turns asking the guest(s) questions from the above survey and then, working in small groups, compile the results. What conclusions can they draw about similarities and differences in their own musical tastes and those of the native speaker? In a modified version of a Venn diagram, individual students can record information on musical tastes in three columns as follows:

Me gusta a mí	*Nos gusta a los dos*	*Le gusta al invitado (cubano)*
tecno, fusion	rock, jazz, pop	salsa, merengue
Eric Clapton	Ricky Martin	Celia Cruz, Pablo Milanés

The middle column shows what students have in common with our Hispanic guest in terms of musical taste. The column on the right, indicating the musical tastes of our guest, may include musical styles and artists unfamiliar to Anglo-American students. As follow-up, students could do an Internet search to learn more about popular Hispanic styles and performers mentioned by the native informant.

After one or more in-class interviews, students should feel confident enough to interview Hispanics in the community. If there is a significant Hispanic population in the area, they can work individually or in pairs to find their own informants—ethnic restaurants are an excellent place to look, for example. If the Hispanic population is sparse, the teacher can build up a list of native-speaker volunteers with phone numbers. The international student office of a nearby college is an invaluable source of names of native informants, offering the additional advantage of having the students listed by countries. Every possible effort should be made to find native informants from a variety of Hispanic cultures and subcultures.

This writer's experience has shown that the results of such an assignment easily justify the effort. These interviews generally yield an abundance of cultural information while providing a marvelous opportunity for students to interact with native speakers. The two-part survey above has proven to be quite manageable as an interview format. At the beginning of each interview, students should ascertain the name, age, and country of origin of the informant; then, with a printed copy of the questions, students can ask the questions orally and fill in the answers. Having students write down the answers (rather than use a tape-recorder) assures on-the-spot comprehension and allows for clarification if necessary.

Part I of the survey tends to bring out the universal appeal of music whereas Part II is more apt to elicit names of songs particular to the culture of our informant. Since our students will probably not be familiar with the songs named in Part II, they should solicit further information. For example, if the native informant names a patriotic song, students should investigate something about its theme, origin or lyrics. A tape recorder could be an option at this point to allow the informant the chance to sing a song of his or her choice. As a variation on the original interview, students could take the lyrics of a particular song previously studied in class (or possibly from the internet), and ask the native speaker to help them understand its significance in his or her culture.

The assignments and class activities that follow these interviews will depend on the linguistic level of the students and the amount of time available. The following are several possibilities:

1) Brief compositions in the present tense, using the verbs *gustar* and *encantar* with the appropriate indirect object pronouns and articles: "*Luis Robles, un hombre puertorriqueño de 34 años, siempre escucha la música en fiestas con su familia. Le encanta la música romántica, especialmente las canciones de Jenifer López. También le gusta bailar la salsa, con la música de Willie Colón. No le gusta nada la música mexicana de los mariachis...*"

2) In a more advanced class, students could draft the composition in the past: "*Luis Robles dijo que cuando era un niño le gustaba escuchar...*"

3) Students form small groups to share information orally. Working together, they draw conclusions about musical tastes in various Hispanic regions, and then share their conclusions with the entire class.

4) Students give brief oral reports on what they learned, possibly including an audio clip of a song sung by their native informant.

5) As a follow-up assignment, students could turn to the Internet to learn about artists and musical styles that are unfamiliar to them.

Through these interviews and related activities, students should come to realize that Hispanic cultures, like U.S. culture, have produced a tremendous array of musical styles that reflect different subcultures, appeal to different groups, and serve different purposes. An interesting observation that emerges from these interviews is that in Hispanic cultures there exists a much larger body of songs spanning several generations; that is, songs that are familiar to young and old alike. This is probably because of the prevalence of multi-generational family gatherings, and because music is almost always an important element of these events. Parents and teens in Hispanic cultures may be somewhat less likely to clash over musical taste than typical Anglo-American families. The repeated exposure to older songs at family gatherings and the pleasant memories associated with these occasions may help to explain this. Even so, Hispanic young people are sure to have their own favorite current artists.

Also interesting are the songs that our native informants associate with patriotism. Patriotic songs vary widely from one Hispanic region to another, but they are certain to reveal interesting facts about national or local history. For example, in a recent class interview, a young man from the oil-rich state of Veracruz, Mexico recalled learning a song in primary school about Lázaro Cárdenas, the Mexican president who nationalized the Mexican oil industry in 1938. Other native informants have cited their national anthems when asked about songs that inspire patriotism. Class discussion of patriotic songs in various Hispanic countries helps students realize that national/ regional pride is an important element of every culture.

Song-Title Association Activities

Another activity that heightens students' awareness of music as a product of a culture involves word associations derived from song titles. In this vocabulary activity, students work in small groups to make word maps based on titles of two familiar American songs, "Happy Birthday to You" and "The Star-Spangled Banner." After writing the title of the song in the center of a piece of paper and drawing a circle around it, students brainstorm all the words they associate with that song. "The Star-Spangled Banner" could prompt students to think the Fourth of July, baseball, hot dogs, United States, patriotism, parades, red, white, blue, etc. "Happy Birthday" prompts words like candles, balloons, cake, ice cream, party, friends, gifts, and children. During the activity, the teacher circulates through the room to help students find Spanish equivalents to difficult vocabulary items. In a multicultural classroom, students from other nations would be asked to create a semantic map based on their own national anthem or another song associated with a traditional holiday in their culture.

The objective of this activity, aside from building and reinforcing vocabulary, is to help students realize the extent to which familiar songs may be associated with specific events or holidays characteristic of a particular culture. For example, three Mexican students, when asked to make a semantic map of the Mexican birthday song, "*Las Mañanitas*," included words such as *serenata, madrugada, guitarra, cantar, felicitaciones, La Virgen de Guadalupe, santo, and chocolate con pan*. "*Las Mañanitas*" is traditionally sung as an early-morning serenade beneath the window of the person whose birthday or saint's day is being celebrated, and is followed by an invitation to come in for hot chocolate. It is also sung every year on December 12, in honor of the Day of the Virgin of Guadalupe. As another example, a Colombian who was asked to make a semantic map based on his national anthem mentioned soccer, *arepas* (a traditional Colombian food), and red, yellow, and blue (the national colors of Colombia). Clearly, these word associations do much more than build vocabulary: They teach us valuable lessons about cultural practices, even as we study a song as a cultural product.

In another similar activity, students choose a song that is meaningful to them and that reflects some aspect of their culture, present or past (distant or recent). They choose from the song four or five key words or phrases that are the most significant and try to give them their best translation into Spanish. Students then write these "palabras clave" vertically on a sheet of paper and for each, write under columns such as the following the images, sounds, aromas, feelings that this song evokes in them.

<u>Escucho</u>   *<u>Veo</u>*   *<u>Me siento...</u>*

Or they may simply use this song as the centerpiece of a semantic map, in which the categories above serve as associational spokes. Students may use their finished lists to explain to someone from a Hispanic country what this song means to them and the people of their culture and what scenes it evokes.

The musical surveys, the ethnographic interviews, and the song-association exercises just described are all activities that heighten students' awareness of their own musical tastes, of the variety of musical tastes of others, and of the close connections between music and culture in preparation for learning about the variety of musical styles in the Spanish-speaking world.

This variety of musical styles of the Hispanic world reflects profound cultural differences between countries, regions and ethnic groups. To illustrate this concept, we might consider the following intriguing exercise. The teacher plays a short segment of flamenco music, followed by Mexican mariachi music, or Andean pipe music followed by Caribbean merengue. Students are asked to describe the music and react to it, possibly using a teacher-distributed word bank of adjectives to facilitate the task. Spanish flamenco music, for example, is *melodramático, intenso, exacto, melancólico*; Mexican mariachi music, on the other hand, is *sentimental, transparente, alegre, bullicioso*. Andean panpipe music is *melancólico, penetrante, solitario, misterioso*, in contrast with ebullient salsa or merengue rhythms from the Caribbean. Clearly, these contrasting musical styles reflect profound cultural differences among their various Hispanic countries of origin.

Selecting Music for Adolescent Language Learners

Given the tremendous range of musical genres that exist in the Hispanic world, how do we decide which songs to use? Our choice of songs will depend largely on our pedagogical objectives. We might select a song for its characteristic Latin rhythms, its poetic or easily comprehensible lyrics, its association with a particular country or region, its treatment of a particular theme, or its appeal to adolescent or young adult students.[5] Although this writer has a special fondness for traditional folkloric music and has used it successfully in Spanish classes at all levels, we cannot ignore the affective appeal of recent popular recordings for our adolescent students. A newly-released Latino hit song can achieve several cross-cultural objectives: It can heighten curiosity about the target culture, build empathy, break down stereotypes, and increase students' motivation to seek further information.

Research suggests that at the early stages of language learning, adolescents respond more positively to cultural similarities than cultural differences. This seems to be especially true of 14- and 15-year-olds who feel a strong need to establish identity as part of their own peer group. As one writer has stated, "Emphasizing the ways in which the lifestyles of speakers of the target language coincide with our own seems to enable students to identify in a positive way with members of the foreign culture. In other words, perceived similarity contributed toward the establishment of positive first impressions – impressions which, once formed, are not easily changed."[6]

Willis and Mason argue convincingly that popular music can motivate our students for both linguistic and cultural learning. The affective aspect of the music, they maintain, is what students notice first. Purcell contends that if the music itself is not appealing or if the audio quality of the recording is poor, the language or culture lesson that the teacher wants to illustrate will not come across. This was recently confirmed in my own class when I played a song that illustrated perfectly the use of the Spanish future tense, but was accompanied by a cliché rock-and-roll ballad rhythm straight out of the 1950s. The lesson flopped, only increasing students' stereotypes about the boring music that must appeal to aging Spanish professors, not to mention stereotypes formed about Hispanic cultures! My marvelous examples of the future tense got lost between the scratchy grooves of the record.

In recent years, thanks to the World Wide Web, music from throughout the world is more accessible than ever before. The words "Latin music" under any major search engine yield hundreds of web sites that include information on recent Latin hit tunes, biographical sketches of contemporary Latin artists, reviews of recent albums, sound clips, links to the websites of individual artists, information about musical styles, MP3 downloads, and more. Because of the large market of Hispanic Internet users, many sites now offer the choice to select English or Spanish text, making these especially useful in the language class.[7] A search with the words of any song title will often yield its complete lyrics, such as those to the song "*Ojalá que llueva café*," featured in the next section of this chapter.[8]

Latin Rhythms: Designing a Lesson Around a Song

A song that has significant cultural content as well as popular appeal for adolescents may be ideal for our purposes. Such is the case with the 1989 international hit song, "*Ojalá que llueva café*," by Dominican composer Juan Luis Guerra.[9] The words are delivered fast, so this is admittedly not the best song for auditory-comprehension exercises. The driving merengue rhythm, however, is a delight, and with the printed text, students can learn a great deal about life in rural areas of the Dominican Republic as they enjoy the infectious, happy music.

The most appealing aspect of this song is the music itself, so students will hear the whole song before they start to identify the words. The pedagogical approach suggested here is modeled on the "whole language approach" to teaching a song, as described by Barry and Pellisier. In their words, the strategies used "approach the song holistically, that is, they are more concerned with an overall appreciation of the song as a conveyer of cultural themes than they are with teaching vocabulary or grammatical structures."[10] We begin by considering the overall effect of the song and gradually focus on more specific details. It should be understood that all classroom activities related to this song are conducted in Spanish.

Pre-listening activities: Activating background knowledge. Just as it is important for students to engage in pre-reading activities when studying a printed text, they benefit from activities that prepare them for the song they are about to hear. The activities suggested here represent only some of the many possible approaches to a culturally authentic song.

After informing students that they will be listening to a song that mentions foods and food crops, we invite students to recall some of their own favorite foods. In a think/ pair/ share activity, students make a list of ten to twelve favorite foods and beverages. Then, as a class, students brainstorm to create a list of crops that are grown in their region.

Brainstorming. According to an old popular American song, sometimes it rains "pennies from heaven." Expanding on this idea, students are invited to fantasize. Using the structure "*Ojalá que llueva...*" students work in pairs to write down marvelous things they would like to see fall from the heavens. Students may choose to mention favorite foods or other items. It is likely that their wish list will include CDs, video games, and so on, thus contrasting sharply with the simple wishes for basic foods expressed in the song they are about to hear. While this song is excellent reinforcement of the subjunctive, if the class has not yet studied the use of this structure, simply teach the phrase "*Ojalá que llueva*" as a lexical item. This works perfectly well, just as students learn to say "*me gustaría*" long before they study the conditional tense. As a follow-up, students can report on the wishes of various group members, using the verbs *desear/ querer/ esperar* as follows: "*Kevin espera que llueva CDs de Cristina Aguilera; Brittany quiere que llueva ropa elegante de Calvin Klein.*" These sample sentences offer excellent contextualized practice with the subjunctive. At the same time, they will provide a basis for comparisons with the simple wishes of Dominicans as expressed in the song.

Expanding on background knowledge, predicting. With a large map of the Caribbean, the teacher helps students locate the Dominican Republic. Students are given one minute to write any words, facts, or names of people they associate with the Dominican Republic. They are then encouraged to share whatever knowledge they may have about this country. Based on their knowledge of the region, what might the climate be like? Can they guess what food crops might grow in this climate? Is the singer more likely to mention French fries or rice? What do students know about music from the Caribbean? Can they guess what music from the Dominican Republic might sound like? What musical instruments might we expect to hear? Throughout this discussion, the teacher can supply pertinent vocabulary as needed, especially cognates such as "*isla tropical*" or "*música rítmica.*" To provide further orientation to the setting, the teacher can tell students they will hear three places named in the song: Villa Vásquez, Los Montones, and La Romana. La Romana, well marked on maps, is where Bill Clinton vacationed in April 2001 to play golf at an exclusive resort—quite a contrast to the lyrics of this song! Villa Vásquez is a small population of about four or five thousand people, of which about twenty-five percent are unemployed (*desocupados*).

First audition: Emotional responses and general observations. The first audition of the song focuses on its overall emotional effect. Students can listen with their eyes closed without paying particular attention to the words. They should then be invited to react: How does the song make you feel? Do you like it? Why or why not? Does it make you want to dance? What mood do you think the composer was in when he wrote this song? Based on the mood of the music, what do you think the song might be about? Would you like to listen to this song in your home? These questions address the affective aspects of the song, or those that will catch the students' attention first. There are no right or wrong answers here – just emotional responses. Students will almost certainly react positively to the song's *merengue* beat and lively tempo. These first questions, then, establish that we like this song and create motivation for further study.

Other questions, designed to sharpen students' observational skills, focus on various elements of the music itself: Do you hear any musical instruments? If so, what are they? What types of singers do you hear? Why do children sing the chorus of the last stanzas? What do they represent? How would you describe the rhythm? Is the tempo lively, slow, or in-between? Is the rhythm similar to what you would expect for a song from the Caribbean? Students may be interested to learn that the characteristic rhythm of this song, the *merengue*, originated in poor rural areas of the Dominican Republic in the mid-nineteenth century, and helped to rally peasants in their fight for independence.[11]

Another line of questioning helps students place the song in context. In a think/ pair/ share activity, students fill in a brief worksheet with questions about where they might hear the song, and what sorts of people might listen to it: *¿Piensas que esta canción es mejor para bailar, cantar, o escuchar? ¿Dónde se podría escuchar esta canción – en una discoteca, en una iglesia, en un concierto,en un festival folclórico, o en un restaurante elegante? ¿Crees que esta canción será popular en cinco, diez o veinte años? ¿Con qué grupos de gente podría ser popular esta canción?* After sharing their impressions with a partner, they summarize for the whole class. These questions are useful in the study of any culturally authentic song, not just "*Ojalá que llueva café.*" Even when a song contains no specific cultural references, questions such as these help to sharpen students' cross-cultural observational skills. As the late Ned Seelye explained in his classic volume, *Teaching Culture*, we need to cultivate in our students the ability to determine whether a behavior pattern (or in this case, a song) is associated with a specific age group, gender, socio-economic class, etc. within a given culture.[12] If we choose to teach a contemporary popular song, then students need to understand that this is a style that may have special appeal to a particular age group within a particular Hispanic culture at a certain moment in time, namely, the present.

Second audition: Focus on aural comprehension. With the second audition of the song, students concentrate on the words. Working in pairs or small groups, they try to decipher as many words as possible. With the rapid merengue beat of "*Ojalá que llueva café,*" this will be difficult, so students should be forewarned not to expect to understand everything. The numerous words specific to the Dominican Republic present additional challenges. It is wise, therefore, to help students focus on what they do understand, rather than on the words they miss. Moreover, it is advisable to have students listen to one stanza at a time with the teacher recapping each one after students have given their input. After each stanza, various groups can share what they heard and the teacher can write a composite list of words on the board. Almost certainly, students will understand the title, "*Ojalá que llueva café,*" as well as scattered words throughout the song. Comprehension can be enhanced considerably with either/or questions; for example, *¿Dónde se espera que llueva – en la ciudad o en el campo? ¿Cuál comida se menciona en la canción - las papas o la yuca?* For written reinforcement, students could complete a brief worksheet with true/ false statements, in which false statements are corrected; e.g., "*Se espera que llueva en la ciudad.*" As a follow-up exercise based on the key words they have understood, students form hypotheses about the content of the song: What seems to be the main theme? Do you know a song in your own language that expresses a similar theme or idea? Have you ever felt an emotion similar to the ones expressed in the song?

Third audition: Further consideration of the lyrics and theme. For the third audition of the song, students are given the printed lyrics with lines numbered to facilitate discussion. For this particular song, students also receive a glossary in Spanish of regional vocabulary and place names (see **Appendix B**)[13] With lyrics in hand, students work to understand the content of the song: How many place names can they find? How many foods are mentioned? Working in groups, students can make three separate columns for words that refer to foods, place names, or nature. Pooling the information from various groups, the teacher lists the words on the board and places an asterisk beside the names of unfamiliar foods. Would students like to try any of these new foods? Which foods would students select if they were in a restaurant in the Dominican Republic? Which crops are mentioned that are not common in the United States?

In another activity, students work in pairs to seek contrasts in the song, such as *llanura* vs. *montaña/ cerro*, *aguacero* vs. *seco, sufrir* vs. *cantar*; they can also seek words that personalize the land, such as grooming terms: *vista, peinar.* What do these convey about the perspectives/attitudes of the peasant farmers toward their land? Worksheets can reinforce both vocabulary and grammatical structures found in the song as well. For example, a worksheet in matching format with definitions in Spanish (and/or pictures downloaded from the Internet) can help to reinforce the regional vocabulary. Students could also write definitions of words found in the song, or they could answer simple either/or questions: *¿Qué es una batata – una legumbre o una fruta? ¿Qué es pitisalé – una fruta o una carne?* Other worksheets can target a variety of grammatical structures, such as in the following examples.

Present subjunctive. For present subjunctive, students complete open-ended sentences: "*El cantante espera que...para que...; Los campesinos quieren que...para que...; Es lástima que los dominicanos...; Es dudoso que los dominicanos...*"

Conditional tense. Another possibility would be to complete sentences in the conditional tense: "*Si yo viviera en la República Dominicana,..., or Si realmente lloviera café..., Si estos campesinos tuvieran más dinero....*"

Ser/estar. For a quick review of ser/estar, students could use ser to write sentences describing the Dominican Republic, and estar to tell the location of various towns or to describe the mood of the singer. At a more basic level, students could simply fill in the blanks, with sentences such as "*Los campesinos dominicanos _____ muy pobres*" or "*La República Dominicana _____ una isla que _____ en el mar Caribe.*"

Comparisons. With the following elements, students form sentences using comparisons. *La isla de Cuba/ grande/ Hispañola. Los campesinos dominicanos/ tener / dinero/ yo. Cultivar/ café/ República Dominicana/ Estados Unidos.*

Direct object pronouns. Students answer questions about what the Dominicans do with various food products, using the direct object pronoun. *¿Qué hacen los campesinos con el café? (Lo beben/ lo cultivan/ lo recogen/ lo muelen/ lo venden, etc.) ¿Qué hacen con las batatas? (Las siembran/ las cultivan/ las cocinan/ las comen, etc.)*

Indirect object pronouns. Given an either/or question, students answer using the indirect object pronoun: *¿Qué les sirven las mamás dominicanas a sus hijos – papas fritas/ arroz; mermelada/ miel; hamburguesas/ pitisalé?* For further practice, we could compare what Dominican mothers serve their children with typical United States teenage fare: *¿Qué te sirve tu mamá de almuerzo los sábados?*

These exercises are just a small sampling of the enormous possibilities as, clearly, a teacher would not necessarily choose to use all of these. The point is that we can use song lyrics to illustrate or reinforce virtually any grammar point. Furthermore, the activities associated with this or any other song can be scaled up or down in difficulty, depending on the level of the students. In other words, music and other cultural products need never compete for time with grammar lessons; rather, both reinforce each other to enhance communication skills.

After ascertaining that students understand the lyrics, we explore the theme of the song. Working in small groups, students prepare a list of all the things the singer is wishing for. Students are then asked to compare the "wish list" of the Dominicans with their own: "*El cantante espera que llueva café*" versus "*Kevin quiere que llueva CDs de Cristina Aguilera*." Students should be struck by the contrast between their own materialistic wishes as privileged U.S. residents and the simple wishes for basic foods as expressed by the subsistence farmer. Are the Dominicans who sing this song probably rich or poor? How can we tell? Why do these people wish for coffee? Do they really want it to rain coffee, or do they want it to rain so their crops can thrive?

A quick think/pair/share exercise can guide learners to consider the relative importance of the weather in industrialized urban societies or agrarian rural cultures. Students complete statements about their own reactions to the weather and share their responses with a partner and then with the class: "When it rains, I feel...because...;" "When the sun shines, I feel...because...;" "If it doesn't rain at all this month, I will feel..." Follow-up questions guide students to go deeper: How important is weather to you? If it didn't rain for a month, how would that affect your life personally? What would you be able to do or not be able to do if it didn't rain? Do you think weather might have a different meaning to the people in this song? If it rained every day for three weeks, how would that affect your life? How might it affect the livelihoods of the people of this song?

To stimulate higher-order thinking, students can work in small groups to discuss in Spanish provocative statements about the song: Each group takes one statement, discusses it thoroughly, and then reports back to the class, arguing for or against the statement. These statements (written in Spanish) might include the following: "The peasants really want it to rain coffee;" "The peasants are so ignorant and naïve that they really believe it can rain coffee;" "The people are lazy, and just want things handed to them;" "If they are hungry, they can just go to the store and buy something to eat;" "These people are probably unhealthy from drinking too much coffee;" "These people are obsessed about food / the weather." Other types of statements in Spanish could lead students to an understanding of the theme of the song. Again working in groups, students could decide on a scale of one to five the extent to which they believe the statement expresses the theme: "This happy song can lift the spirits of people who have a difficult life;" "This song shows the rich imagination of some people who live in extreme poverty;" "This song could give people a sense of connectedness with others who are experiencing hardships similar to their own." Distracter statements could also be included here: "This song shows the greed of the Dominican people;" "This song just gives farmers an excuse to start dancing instead of doing their work."

As students discuss the song, they should notice the sharp contrast between the underlying motif

of hunger and the infectious, happy music. Do students think these people are sad, happy, or both?
Students could work in pairs to complete statements in Spanish, such as: "I think these people are
sad because…;" "I think these people are happy because…;" "The music makes them feel better
because…;" "Sometimes when I'm sad, music makes me feel…;" "When I listen to happy music, I
feel like…;" "When I listen to music with other people, I feel…;" "I sometimes feel like dancing
when I'm sad because…"

Through these exercises and class discussion, students should conclude that the music in "*Ojalá
que llueva café*" serves as an emotional release that could mitigate somewhat the pain of hunger in the
Dominican countryside, joining people together even in hardship. But the theme of the song goes
beyond food, hunger, or poverty: The lyrics convey a sense of magical realism as well as poetry,
affirming that poverty does not preclude developing a rich imagination to dream. What fun to
imagine food falling magically from the sky! Even as this song reflects the perspective of Afro-
Hispanic peasants in the Dominican Republic, it taps into universal truths about the power of imagination and of music to uplift the human spirit. Indeed, all students should be able to recall a time in
their own lives when music lifted their spirits. We can help students explore further the emotive
powers of music as they practice the preterit and imperfect tenses in the following assignment:

> Think of a time when you were feeling "down" and music made you feel better and/or more
> connected with other people. 1) Describe the initial scene; 2) give the series of events that hap-
> pened; 3) tell how you reacted and how you felt; 4) tell the type of music or the song you lis-
> tened to; and 5) tell how you suddenly felt as a result.

At some point in all of these activities, we definitely want the students to sing and, once students are thoroughly familiar with the lyrics, they should be eager to participate. Experience has
shown that the actual singing will be more successful if students try to imagine that they are
Dominican peasants fervently wishing for food. With this leap of the imagination, students seem to
sing with greater conviction.

Expansion activities. The *merengue* is just one of several Latin rhythms that emerged in a culture of rural poverty among an oppressed minority. Throughout Latin American, a number of musical styles have arisen spontaneously to give oppressed people a sense of connectedness, to help them
survive alienation and harsh conditions. Students might enjoy researching the roots of Latin
rhythms such as the Cuban *son*, Brazilian *samba*, or Colombian *cumbia*, or music of similar origins
in their own country. In the United States, for example, jazz, Negro spirituals, blues, rock, rap,
punk, and 60s folk songs all have their roots in similar stories of sadness, abandon, misunderstanding,
protest or revolution.

Jigsaw. To help students discover additional information related to this song in a cooperative
learning format, a "jigsaw" group dynamic is recommended. The class is divided into four
groups: A, B, C, and D. Each group is assigned a different topic to research on the Internet as
follows: A) la República Dominicana, B) el merengue; C) Juan Luis Guerra and D) foods of the

Caribbean, including those dishes mentioned in the song. After individual students in each group collect information from the Internet, group members work together to prepare a paragraph that summarizes the most interesting facts they found. The members of each lettered group become "experts" on their topic. In the second phase of the jigsaw, students within each group count off from one to four. The class re-groups, with all the number 1's together, the 2's, and so forth. In each new group, there will be at least one member from each of the previous lettered group (e.g. A –1, B-1, C-1, and D-1). Now students teach each other information they learned in their previous groups. Students could complete brief worksheets on all four topics.[14] As an alternative to the second phase of the jigsaw, each group could report orally to the whole class on the most interesting information they found on their assigned topic.

Original song. Using the same rhythm and melodic line, students write an original song in Spanish, beginning with the words "*Ojalá que llueva...para que...*" Students could work individually, in pairs, or in small groups to create and perform the song for the class.

Original story. Students write a story about the life of a poor farmer in the Dominican Republic. For a touch of magical realism, they might want to imagine what would happen if the wish expressed in the song came true, that is, if coffee actually rained from the sky.

With all these activities related to just one song, we have achieved a variety of linguistic and cultural objectives. Students have practiced their Spanish extensively; they have learned a great deal about the Dominican Republic; they have become motivated to hear more Hispanic music. Furthermore, this instructional unit accomplishes a number of important cross-cultural objectives: 1) It heightens students' curiosity about another culture and helps to cultivate positive attitudes toward that culture. 2) It helps students develop understanding for people of another culture. 3) It increases students' motivation to seek more information about the target culture. 4) It helps students become more discriminating, observant listeners. 5) It heightens students' awareness of contrasts between their own culture and another. 6) It promotes students' understanding of music as a product of a specific culture, and of the close relationship between music and culture. 7) It helps students appreciate the universality of music. Finally, imagine how proud the teacher will feel when students blurt out spontaneously in perfect subjunctive form, "*¡Ojalá que llueva pronto!*"

With slight variations, the kinds of activities suggested here for "*Ojalá que llueva café*" can be adapted for use with any culturally authentic song, be it a contemporary popular hit, a traditional children's song, or a folkloric tune from a specific region. Over a period of time, teachers would be wise to select songs of varying styles and regions. Since "*Ojalá que llueva café*" has a rapid tempo with words that may be difficult to understand, a slow romantic ballad with clear lyrics could be an excellent choice for the next song.

Another approach would be to develop an instructional unit based on several songs with similar themes, rhythms, or regional settings.[15] The famous Colombian song, "*Moliendo café*" ("Grinding Coffee") works especially well as a companion lesson to "*Ojalá que llueva café.*" The lyrics describe an old man on a coffee plantation who continues to grind coffee long into the twilight to forget his sorrows. Although the theme is rather melancholy, the samba rhythm is ebullient. Just as in "*Ojalá que llueva café*," joyous music with a lively beat provides an emotional release from difficult conditions and a sense of connection with others experiencing the same hardship.[16]

Music and the National Standards

Whether we teach just one song, a variety of songs, or an instructional unit based on several similar songs, the activities described in this chapter demonstrate the total integration of linguistic and cultural instruction. Furthermore, the unit on "*Ojalá que llueva café*" not only incorporates all of the "Five Cs" described in the 1996 *National Standards for Foreign Language Learning* (Communication, Cultures, Connections, Comparisons, and Communities),[17] but it can effectively help us broaden our conceptual understanding of the *Standards*. The unit clearly gives students practice in all modes of communication, as they listen to the song, interpret information from the Internet, exchange ideas with each other, and present their ideas in both oral and written form. Yet, aside from these classroom notions of "communication," students were made part of real communication through the voices of a people.

The cultural components of this lesson go far beyond the specific elements that identify "*Ojalá que llueva café*" as being from a particular country. Surely, part of the lesson is to help students identify the characteristic merengue rhythm, the regional vocabulary, and the references to specific foods, places, and landscapes that make this song a cultural product of the Dominican Republic. Further, the lesson helps students learn of the perspectives of rural Dominicans who find emotional release in music and in dreaming, despite their hunger and their poverty. But beyond these specific lessons about Dominican culture, the unit helps to cultivate a cross-cultural openness, through heightened awareness of their own culture and through deepened understanding of universal human needs not only for food, but for camaraderie, joy and expression of the creative mind.

The entire unit presented here is filled with a rich web of Connections. In connecting with music through the activities described, learners connect language and culture learning by connecting with the geography, history, agrarian economy and creative expression of the song's origins. Moreover, the universal appeal of "*Ojalá que llueva café*" helps to break down cultural barriers, so that students can feel connected to Dominicans and indeed to music enthusiasts throughout the world who are touched by this delightful music. Most significantly, students come to realize that the song itself is a means of helping people feel connectedness with others who share similar difficult circumstances. Through song, learners thus connect to a Community—one that although far from them in physical distance, can touch them through its words and rhythms and melodies to share its message. Throughout these lessons, as learners share their points of view and their own experiences, they build a sense of community in the classroom. Through an appealing song, students become part of a community of listeners that transcends cultural boundaries. And as they conduct their ethnographic interviews outside the classroom, they reach out into their own communities to interact with those of other cultures.

Both in the ethnographic interviews and the unit on "*Ojalá que llueva café*," students make all manner of comparisons between their own culture and another. To begin with, students compare musical tastes, attitudes, and listening habits of native informants from various Hispanic countries. Later, students compare a variety of musical styles from within the Spanish-speaking world. In our discussion of "*Ojalá que llueva café*," we compare much more than foods, crops, landscapes, or musical styles. More significantly, we compare the aspirations, dreams, and flights of imagination of Dominican peasants with our own.

Throughout this unit, we have seen that even as music reinforces language learning, it can give us new insights into the lifestyles, attitudes, and perspectives of a particular culture. Indeed, music reflects the soul of a people. At the same time, music has universal appeal, with the power to delight and inspire our students. It may make us want to dance, march, clap our hands with joy, reflect in quiet meditation, or wipe away a tear. Music transcends linguistic and cultural barriers to reach all socio-economic classes, all age groups, and all ethnic groups. Ultimately, culturally authentic music in the foreign language class does much more than integrate lessons in language and culture. It can enrich the lives of both teachers and students, helping them to become more sensitive human beings.

Notes

[1] For example, Purcell (1992) demonstrates the use of Spanish songs to reinforce pronunciation, intonation, vocabulary and grammar. Willis and Mason (1994) recommend the use of contemporary Latin popular music to teach language and motivate students. Leith (1979) uses popular songs as a starting point for advanced conversation activities. Abrate (1983) and Failoni (1993) propose a wide variety of strategies for using music to teach both language and culture. For ideas on using music for FLES, see Sporborg, J. D. (1998). These are only a few of the helpful articles available on this subject.

[2] Just as many printed texts are created expressly for use in the foreign language class, imaginative Spanish teachers with musical talent have composed songs designed specifically to teach language and motivate students. These songs definitely have their place in the curriculum. For further information on some of these resources, see the **Appendix A**

[3] See National Standards in Foreign Language Education Project, 1996.

[4] In her excellent 1992 article, Galloway discusses at length the challenges of working with an authentic print text.

[5] Various articles in the professional literature offer suggestions for language and culture lessons based on music ranging from traditional folk songs to the latest popular mega-hits. Using the example of Costa Rica, Griffin (1988) recommends studying Latin American culture through a country's folk music. Barry and Pellisier (1995) use music to explore ethnic and immigrant issues. Hamblin (1988) and Conrad (1991) recommend using popular songs with both contemporary and historical themes to teach about the culture of France and Germany respectively. Delière and Lafayette (1985) describe a unit they developed on French culture based on several contemporary songs with a similar theme. Gatti-Taylor (1980) proposes using contemporary songs whose lyrics convey attitudes characteristic of Italian culture. In the same article she presents an excellent discussion of the various objectives that can be achieved through music.

[6] See Cooper (1985), p. 68; also Hahn (1980).

[7] Some sites for Latin music that have proven popular with Spanish students include the following: www.sonymusiclatin.com - User selects English or Spanish text to read detailed biographies of artists. www.picadillo.com - Text in English and Spanish, with links to WebPages of Latin artists.www.universal.com.mx - Catalogue of contemporary popular music from throughout Latin America. Text is all in Spanish, as website is based in Mexico City. Links are available to other Hispanic sites.

[8] See the following website to listen to and read the lyrics of "*Ojalá que llueva café*": http://www.colby.edu/personal/b/bknelson/ojala/index.html

[9] Juan Luis Guerra (b. 1957) uses an adaptation of the merengue beat to sing of the poverty in the Dominican countryside. His 1989 mega-hit, "*Ojalá que llueva café*" propelled him to international fame. He now uses this international stature to promote awareness of Dominican issues, especially rural poverty and the need for education.

[10] See Barry and Pellisier, pp. 17-18.

[11] The *merengue* gradually moved from the countryside to the poorest neighborhoods of Santo

Domingo. This sensuous dance music was accepted by polite society only after it became a commercial success abroad, especially in the United States. The merengue is now considered the national dance of the Dominican Republic. For more information on this and other Latin American rhythms, see Leymarie (1997).

[12] See Ned Seelye (1992), Chapter 3.

[13] This glossary can be found on an excellent website designed by Professor Ricardo Ureña of the University of Massachusetts. The copyrighted website is http://www-unix.oit.umass.edu/~urena/jlg.

[14] Grateful acknowledgement is made to my students Maribel Doucette and Margaret Ana Luna, who proposed this idea as part of a class project in a master's level course, "*Integración de la música en la clase de español*," for the University of Southern Mississippi in Morelia, Michoacán, Mexico in July 2000.

[15] The professional literature offers excellent suggestions for instructional units based on several thematically related songs. Heusinkveld (2001) proposes a unit based on songs of nostalgia, including the songs "*Guantanamera*," "*México Lindo*," and "*Mi Viejo San Juan*." Delière and Lafayette (1985) describe a unit based on three French songs dealing with the theme of vacations.

[16] In fact, several characteristic Latin rhythms have their origins in the Afro-Caribbean slave culture. Brought to Brazil by West African slaves, the *samba* was originally a fertility dance. (The word *samba* derives from *semba*, or "womb" in the Bantu language.) The dance gradually lost its sacred character and moved to the poor neighborhoods of Rio de Janeiro. Despite high society's initial disapproval of this sensuous dance, the samba rapidly gained popularity, eventually becoming the national dance of Brazil. The *cumbia*, a rhythmic dance with a strong beat and simple harmonic patterns, was created by slaves chained together by one ankle. Unable to move one foot, they devised a dance that involved a shifting of weight from one foot to the other, accompanied by a gentle swaying of the hips. For fascinating information on the origins of these and other Latin rhythms, see Leymarie (1997).

[17] See National Standards in Foreign Language Education Project (1996).

Works Cited

Abrate, Jayne Halsne. "Pedagogical Applications of the French Popular Song in the ForeignLanguage Classroom." *Modern Language Journal* 67 (1983): 8-12.

Anton, Ronald J. "Combining Singing and Psychology." *Hispania* 73 (1990): 1166-70.

Barry, Sue, and Sidney Pellissier. "Popular Music in a Whole Language Approach to Foreign Language Teaching."

Robert M. Terry, ed. *Dimension '95: The Future is Now.* Valdosta, GA: SCOLT Publications, 1995. 13-26.

Conrad, Bernd. "Contemporary and Historical Contexts in Popular Music: Theory and Implementation of an Intermediate Level Course." *Die Unterrichtspraxis* 24 (1991): 18-30.

Cooper, Thomas C., ed. *Research Within Reach: Research-guided Responses to the Concerns of Foreign Language Teachers.* Athens, GA: ACTFL/ SCOLT Task Force on Research in Foreign Language Education, 1985.

Delière, Jacques, and Robert C. Lafayette. "*La clef des chants: Thèmes culturels et techniques pédagogiques pour l'enseignement de la civilisation par la chanson.*" *The French Review* 58 (1985): 411-25.

Failoni, Judith Weaver. "Music as a Means to Enhance Cultural Awareness and Literacy in the Foreign Language Classroom." *Mid-Atlantic Journal of Foreign Language Pedagogy* 1(1983): 97-108.

Galloway, Vicki B. "Toward a Cultural Reading of Authentic Texts."

Heidi Byrnes, ed. Languages for a Multicultural World in Transition. Lincolnwood, IL: National TextbookCompany, 1992. 87-121.

García-Saez, Santiago. "The Use of Song in Class as an Important Stimulus in the Learning of a Language." ERIC Document Reproduction Service No. ED 240 872, 1984.

Gatti-Taylor, Marisa. "Songs as a Linguistic and Cultural Resource in the Intermediate Italian Class." *Foreign Language Annals* 13 (1980): 465-69.

Griffin, Robert J. "The Folk Music of Costa Rica: A Teaching Perspective." Hispania 71 (1988): 438-41.

Griffin, Robert J. "Teaching Hispanic Culture through Folk Music." *Hispania* 60 (1977): 942-45.

Hahn, Sidney L. "Let's Try a Positive Approach." *Foreign Language Annals* 13 (1980): 415-17.

Hamblin, V. L. "Integrating Popular Songs into the Curriculum." *The French Review* 60(1987): 479-84.

Heusinkveld, Paula. "Teaching Hispanic Culture through Music: The Theme of Nostalgia." C.

Maurice Cherry, ed. *The Odyssey Continues: Dimension* 2001. Valdosta, GA: SouthernConference on Language Teaching, 2001. 65-78.

Leymarie, Isabel. *La música latinoamericana, ritmos y danzas de un continente.* Barcelona: Claves, 1997.

Leith, William D. "Advanced French Conversation through Popular Music." *The French Review* 52 (1979): 537-51.

National Standards in Foreign Language Education Project. *Standards for Foreign LanguageLearning: Preparing for the 21st Century.* Lawrence, KS: Allen Press, 1996.

Nuessel, Frank, and Caterina Cicogna. "The Integration of Songs and Music into the ItalianCurriculum." *Italica* 68 (1991): 473-86.

Purcell, John M. "Using Songs to Enrich the Secondary Class." *Hispania* 75 (1992): 192-96.

Seelye, H. Ned. *Teaching Culture: Strategies for Intercultural Communication.* Lincolnwood, IL: National Textbook Company, 1992.

Sporborg, James Douglas. *Music in Every Classroom: A Resource Guide for Integrating Music Across the Curriculum*, Grades K-8. ERIC Document Reproduction Service No. ED 430861, 1998

Trapp, Elizabeth A.B. "Break Down Inhibitions and Build Up Understanding with Music, Music, Music." *Hispania* 74 (1991): 437-38.

Willis, Bruce Dean, and Keith Mason. "*Canciones en la clase*: The Why and How of Integrating Songs in Spanish by English-speaking and Bilingual Artists." *Hispania* 77 (1994): 102-09.

Appendix A. Resources for Music in the Foreign Language Class

Anton, Ron. *Via Music Communications.* P.O. Box 42091, Cleveland, OH 44142. TEL: 1-800-222-0189 or 216/529-8049, http://www.viamc.com.

Cantos y Ritmos: Spanish Chants, Rhythms and Rhymes. www.teachersdiscovery.com Teacher's Discovery, 2741 Paldan Dr., Auburn Hills, MI 48326, 1-800-832-2437.

Díaz-Perera, Hilda Luisa. "*Cuando Te Miro: A Collection of Folk and Pop Songs from Latin America.*"TEL: 1-800-CANTARE; FAX: 305/261-0103; www.hispanicmusic.com.

Gessler Publishing Co., 15 East Salem Ave., 2nd Floor, Roanoke, VA 24011TEL: 1-800-456-5825 or 540-345-1429.

Grupo Cañaveral, P.O. Box 521866, Miami, FL 33152. www.hispanicmusic.comTEL: 1-800-CANTARE Email: info@hispanicmusic.com

Lozano, Patti. *Music that Teaches Spanish! Original Songs, Rhymes, Creative Activities.*

_____. *More Music that Teaches Spanish: Original Songs, Rhymes, Creative Activities.*

_____. *Spanish Grammar Swings! An Interactive Songbook.* Dolo Publications, Inc., 2001. 12800 Briar Forest Dr. #23, Houston, TX 77077. TEL: 281/491-4552; FAX: 281/679-9092; email: dolo@wt.net.

MacArthur, Barbara. *Sing, Dance, Laugh, and Eat Tacos.* TEL: 1-800-832-2437.Teacher's Discovery, www.teachersdiscovery.com.

Medina, Jorge. *Nostalgia: México Lindo y otras canciones.* Cassette tape w/ lyrics.3037 Creekside Dr., Seneca, SC 29672 TEL: 864/882-8238 FAX: 864/656-0258.

México de mis recuerdos, Comunicorp,6203 Liberty Hill, Dallas, TX 75248.Video with 10 songs about Mexican cities. TEL 672/ 716-0290 diegolastra@prodigy.net.

Orozco, José Luis. De Colores and Other Latin-American Folk Songs for Children. New York: Dutton Children's Books, 1994.

Songs and Rhymes. Education in Motion, P.O. Box 224, Chico Rivera, CA 90660.

Sporborg, James Douglas. *Music in Every Classroom: A Resource Guide for Integrating Music Across the Curriculum,* Grades K-8. Teacher Ideas Press, 1998. P.O. Box 6633,Englewood, CO 80155-6633. TEL 1-800-237-6124. ED Document 430-861

Teach to the Beat, 1268 Pear Wood Way, Uniontown, OH 44685. TEL: 216/896-2756.

Tipton, Stacey. "Musical Spanish." www.musicalspanish.com; smtipton@bellsouth.net

Vibrante Press, 2430 Juan Tabo, Suite #110, Albuquerque, NM 87112.

Appendix B

Ojalá que llueva café

Juan Luis Guerra

1 *Ojalá que llueva café en el campo*	I hope that it rains coffee in the countryside,
2 *que caiga un aguacero de yuca y té*	that a shower of manioc and tea will fall
3 *del cielo una jarina de queso blanco*	from the sky, a sprinkling of white cheese
4 *y al sur una montaña de berro y miel*	and to the south, a mountain of cress and honey,
5 *oh, oh, oh-oh-oh,*	Oh, oh, oh, oh,
6 *ojalá que llueva café.*	I hope it rains coffee.
7 *Ojalá que llueva café en el campo*	I hope it rains coffee in the countryside
8 *peinar un alto cerro (d)e trigo y mapuey*	Combing a high hill with wheat and mapuey,
9 *bajar por la colina de arroz graneado*	Going down the hill full of grains of rice
10 *y continuar el arado con tu querer.*	And continuing the plowing with your loved one.
11 *oh, oh, oh-oh-oh.*	Oh, oh, oh, oh.

12 *Ojalá el otoño en vez de hojas secas*	I hope that the autumn, instead of with dry leaves
13 *vista mi cosecha de pitisalé*	Will dress my harvest with pitisalé
14 *sembrar una llanura de batata y fresas*	To sow a plain with yams and strawberries,
15 *ojalá que llueva café.*	I hope it rains coffee.
16 *Pa' que en el conuco*	So that in the little plot of land
17 *no se sufra tanto, ay ombe*	People won't suffer so much, hey, man,
18 *ojalá que llueva café en el campo*	I hope it rains coffee in the country
19 *pa' que en Villa Vásquez oigan este canto*	So that in Villa Vásquez they hear this song
20 *ojalá que llueva café en el campo*	I hope that it rains coffee in the country/
21 *ojalá que llueva,*	I hope it rains,
22 *ojalá que llueva, ay ombe*	I hope it rains, oh man!
23 *ojalá que llueva café en el campo*	I hope it rains coffee in the country
24 *Ojalá que llueva café.*	I hope it rains coffee.
oh, oh, oh-oh-oh.	Oh, oh, oh, oh.
25 *Pa' que to(dos) los niños*	So that all the children
26 *canten en el campo*	Can sing in the country,
27 *ojalá que llueva café en el campo*	I hope it rains coffee in the country
28 *pa' que en La Romana oigan este canto*	So that in La Romana they hear this song
29 *ojalá que llueva café en el campo*	I hope it rains coffee in the country
30 *ay, ojalá que llueva,*	Oh, I hope it rains,
31 *ojalá que llueva, ay ombe*	I hope it rains, oh man,
32 *ojalá que llueva café en el campo*	I hope it rains coffee in the country
33 *ojalá que llueva café.*	I hope it rains coffee.

Ojalá que llueva café is from the album *Ojalá que llueva café* – 440 by Juan Luis Guerra Copyright 1995 by Karen Publishing Co. 7060-62 N.W. 50th St., Miami, FL 33166 Distributed by POLYGRAM LATINO U.S., a division of *Polygram Records,* Inc.

Glossary of terms:[1]

The name of Juan Luis Guerra's group, "440," comes from the number of vibrations per second of the note "concert A," or the "A" above "middle C." This is the note to which musicians tune their instruments.

Batata – a sweet tuber, not to be confused with the Spanish *patata* (called papa throughout Latin America). In Cuba this vegetable is called boniato and in the United States, "sweet potato."

Cibao (adj. *cibaeño*) – Name of the principal valley of the Dominican Republic, located in the north, between the Central and Western ranges or mountains. It is a fertile valley traditionally dedicated to agriculture.

Conuco – Word of taino origin that refers to a small parcel of land, frequently dedicated to subsistence agriculture.

Jarina – When flour is sifted, the result is, metaphorically speaking, a sprinkling of flour. Thus the term "jarinita" has come to mean a light rain shower in the Cibao valley.

Mapuey – The *mapuey* is a tuber used in the preparation of *sancocho*, a typical Dominican dish.

Pitisalé (*petit-salé*) – This is a kind of bacon (could be pork or goat meat) which is salted and dried in the sun and used to season various dishes.

La Romana – Third-largest city in the Dominican Republic. Its name comes from one of the traditional industries in the city (the romana is the balance used to weigh the freshly-cut sugar cane).

Taino – Indigenous peoples who inhabited the islands now known as Puerto Rico and Hispañola.

Villa Vásquez – A municipality located in the northwest of the Dominican Republic.

Yuca – The yucca is the name of an edible root from the plant of the same name. Rich in starch, it was used by the taino people to make a kind of bread called "*casabe*."

[1] Grateful acknowledgement is made to Professor Ricardo Ureña of the University of Massachusetts, who has provided all this information and more in Spanish on an excellent website: http://www-unix.oit.umass.edu/~urena/jlg

Chapter 6

The Five C's of Legends and Folktales

Susan M. Bacon, University of Cincinnati

Nancy A. Humbach, Miami University, OH

Long before the coinage of the five Cs associated with the *National Standards for Foreign Language Education*, teachers have enjoyed presenting culture in contexts that can be exploited to include many facets of language learning. What teacher has not, for example, used a song to teach vocabulary, to introduce or reinforce a grammar point, or to present certain rhythms or musical styles? [See Heusinkveld this volume.] The elementary-school teacher has a "bag of tricks" or "magic can" with artifacts that children can touch and observe to imagine their origin and use; the high-school teacher has a bulletin board with photographs, calendars, refrains and proverbs, all of which illustrate not only linguistic phenomena that enter into Communication and Comparisons, but also Communities (the language that goes beyond the classroom), Cultures (the products, practices and perspectives of groups of people), and Connections (the reinforcement of other learning through interdisciplinary activity). For example, when students recognize the *calabaza* (gourd) as a logical receptacle for drinking *mate* tea, they approach understanding of the importance of local agricultural products in everyday customs. When students compare the functions of language, such as requesting permission or apologizing, they may become more attuned to performing the function in their first language. By listening to music from other lands, students may connect rhythms, styles and instruments with those of music familiar to them.

Teachers have always included in their lessons the products of the target culture, such as music, foods, crafts, everyday documents and artifacts and have instructed students in conventional practices of certain contexts through role-plays, assimilators, TPR and audio-motor units. Learning about the products and practices of a culture gives students insight into the perspectives of a people that would not be accessible through simple study of grammar and vocabulary. For example, when students learn about the *sobremesa*, they begin to appreciate the social significance of mealtime. When they practice *saludos*, they compare the Hispanic custom of shaking hands or kissing the cheek with their own habits of greeting. Despite the many efforts to include culture in language classrooms, however, the challenge has always been that of maintaining balance and cohesion between cultural and linguistic presentation. The pressure to ensure that students are prepared for the next "grammar exam" may cause us to lose sight of the very essence of language learning: language is culture.

The present chapter demonstrates the use of a particular cultural product, the legend or folktale, to embody all facets of the Cs and the Ps in such a way that students and teachers enrich their understanding of culture and both model and apply linguistic phenomena. First, we present a rationale for using legends as a medium to teach language and culture, demonstrating its practice with several examples. Then, we report on a four-year program involving K-12 teachers in the teaching of legends and folktales. Finally, we present a sample unit that guides the reader through the steps of preparing to use a legend in teaching. We believe teachers and students alike benefit from this approach.

Rationale for the Use of Legends in the Foreign Language Classroom

Everyone loves a good story. Canadian researcher Kieran Egan (1979, 1986), for example, stresses that middle-schoolers are easily attracted to legends and myths because of the characteristics of their stage of development. Characterizing this age group as "romantic" learners, Egan encourages teachers to find ways to include story-telling materials that speak of adventure and heroes in all areas of teaching. When learners use imagination to feel what it would be like to be another person, they begin to treat others with as much respect as they would wish to be treated themselves. As further corroboration of the attraction of tales and legends, we need only witness the popularity of the Harry Potter stories by J. K. Rowling (1998, 1999, 2000) not only among adolescents but also among many adult readers, young and old. The need to imagine and escape seems to be inherent to the human psyche.

The five standards proposed by the National Standards in Foreign Language Education Project are easily integrated into the teaching of legends and folktales. In second-language instruction, legends provide a superb context for making information meaningful to learners (connections). For example, animal legends incorporate real and imaginary creatures, descriptions, and emotions; architectural legends expand descriptive vocabulary—colors, dimensions and measurements; topographical legends help students make comparisons between their own environment and that of others. Legends are traditionally oral literature, the use of which encourages students to become good listeners (communication). The story, therefore, provides the context for instruction of vocabulary, syntax and functions of language (comparisons). Students are encouraged to explore extra-classroom resources for use of Spanish in personal enjoyment and enrichment (communities). Most importantly, legends transmit cultural perspectives—the values, beliefs and worldviews of groups as reflected in their laws, art, language, daily routines and lifestyles.

Legends and Folktales in the Hispanic world[1]

Legends and folktales were originally oral literature whose purpose was to communicate history and values from one generation to the next. The story tended to evolve and adapt itself to the historical context in which it was told, which is why we can find so many versions of the same legend. A good example of this change through time is that of *La Llorona*: The colonial Mexican version is markedly different from the versions told today along the Río Grande or in the Chicago *barrios*. However, if we examine the historical, political and geographical contexts of the legend, we gain insights into the social practices of the time, the perspectives on law and justice, and the products that exemplified the culture.

An eighteenth-century Mexican version of *La Llorona* relates an event during the Spanish conquest in which an indigenous woman falls in love with a Spaniard of wealth and nobility. After several years of living with the woman and fathering three of her children, the Spaniard abandons her to take a wife of his own station. The first woman is devastated and, in her despair, stabs her children to death. Because of this dastardly act, the woman is barred from heaven and condemned to the eternal search for the souls of her babies. Even today, it is said, she often appears at night by the edge of a river or lake, sobbing inconsolably. But children especially should beware, because in her search for her own children, *La Llorona* has been known to take the souls of others. Many versions and testimonials related to the legend are available on the Internet (**see Appendix A, Web Resources**).

The tragic story of *La Llorona* has been used through the centuries as a didactic tool by parents, the Catholic Church, and those who would warn against falling in love with someone above one's station. Historians believe the Mexican version derives from the story of the Aztec Cihuacóatl, the "first goddess" who threw her many children into a canal or river. In Aztec culture, death by drowning (or sacrifice by drowning) was considered a sacred means of dying, as it was believed that the souls of the drowned ascended to the highest level of "heaven." Some believe that the early legend of Cihuacóatl was meant as a prophecy of the Spanish conquest in that it symbolized the loss of Aztec children to the conquerors. The colonial version in which *La Llorona* stabs her three children appears to be an example of the syncretism[2] of Aztec and Spanish cultures: For the Spaniards, the dagger or sword was a symbol of power and nobility; for the Aztecs, water was a symbol of purity. Even in the United States, *La Llorona* is known to most children of Mexican heritage as a fearful specter, although they are probably unfamiliar with the story's evolution from ancient to modern times. The legend of *La Llorona*, which is most appropriate for middle-school and older adolescents, includes the human fascination for the macabre, the universal themes of love, deceit, and sorrow, Anglophone parallels in the form of the "bogeyman," the didactic purpose of the time in which it was popular, and syncretic elements of colonial Mexico. Moreover, the story presents many opportunities for connection to other disciplines: Students can locate and investigate sites where *La Llorona* has appeared (geography); they can relate elements of a particular version to its setting and era (history); from the names of characters, places, and so on, they can derive the profound influence of indigenous cultures on modern-day Mexico; they can examine the psychological connections of dreams and human emotions; they can investigate female depression and its relationship to infanticide or search for parallels in literature from other countries. The rich cultural connections of the legend are almost limitless.

From eighteenth-century colonial Mexico sprouts a quite different and more mundane legend: *La Casa de los Muñecos* relates the story behind the construction of a grand house whose façade is adorned with gigantic Romanesque figures (see **Appendix A, Web Resources**). As the legend goes, the city council first denied don Agustín permission to build his house on the grounds that his plan called for an edifice that would be taller than the municipal building. Don Agustín circumvented the city council by requesting permission directly from the King. As a final act of petulance, he not only built his house, but decorated it with caricatures of the members of the city council. The themes of the legend are universal: money, power, honor and revenge. However, through the legend, we also gain a glimpse of the practices and products that give insight into the culture of the era: the ways of obtaining permission and dealing with authority reflect the underlying belief system that wealth is mightier than the law; the beautiful ceramic *talavera* that decorates the *Casa de los Muñecos* reflects the evolution of the artisanry from the Moors in Spain to its distinctive Mexican use in architectural façades. The architecture, though influenced by Spain, is more ornate, reflecting the Mexican baroque style. By examining the plan of the colonial house, students can imagine both the grandeur and the inconvenience of living in the 18th Century.

Some folktales reflect the need to explain natural phenomena important in daily life, such as those that depict the origin of corn or chocolate. An Argentine/Paraguayan tale relates the origin of yerba mate as a symbol of friendship and good will: Yací, the Moon goddess longs to visit the earth and explore the spaces she cannot see from the sky. One night she transforms herself into a woman and descends to acquaint herself with the marvels of the jungle. When suddenly she is attacked by a ferocious jaguar, she realizes that she cannot transform herself back into her former self. Just as the jaguar lunges toward her, an old man kills the beast with an arrow. Yací re-ascends into heaven, but that night she appears in the old man's dream. She rewards him with the *yerba mate* plant, and instructs him to share it with whomever should cross his path. Today, the *yerba mate* is the drink of choice among many people who live in the Southern Cone (see **Appendix A, Web Resources**). By examining the climate, topography and agricultural practices reflected in this legend, students gain insights into why certain foods are so important to their producers. Further, they can investigate how changes have occurred in eating and drinking habits through improved communication, transportation and agricultural techniques.

Other tales explain the formation of topographical features, such as volcanoes. In the legend of *Los novios*, we learn the story behind the creation of the volcanoes Popocatéptl and Ixtaccíhuatl in central Mexico (see **Appendix A, Web Resources**). In *Los novios*, the volcanoes are anthropomorphized as star-crossed lovers, one a heroic Aztec warrior, the other a beautiful princess. In the story, we see the traits of fidelity and courage that were important values in pre-Columbian culture and that persist as such in modern Mexico. Even today, some risk their lives climbing Popocatéptl to deliver an offering to placate the gods in hopes that the volcano will remain dormant. Whether superstition or faith, the act reflects the belief that one can intercede to influence the future. Students can investigate other practices that reflect the syncretism of organized religion and indigenous practice in modern Mexico, such as *el día de los muertos*.

Other examples of syncretism of two or more worlds abound in Latin American legends that reflect both Spanish and indigenous values. The story of *El ñandutí*, relates the creation of the Paraguayan lace bearing its name, and highlights the merit of indigenous artisanry. The legend underscores the power of friendship between a Spanish woman and her Paraguayan soul mate. Although the legend has its origin in the colonial era, the practice of making *ñandutí* lace persists today. Students can trace the use of the *mantilla* in Spain to its unique Paraguayan designs and uses (see **Appendix A, Web Resources**). Other times, a legend will spoof the Spanish heritage to extol the virtues of indigenous peoples. In *Los cadejos* from El Salvador, good (the *campesinos*) conquers over evil (the Creole landowners) through the invervention of a single familiar animal, the dog. Students can relate the legend to present-day conflicts over land ownership in Latin America. As another example, the Colombian legend, *El dorado*, demonstrates the futility of the search for imagined treasure. Again, the indigenous peoples seem to be the victors who succeed in hiding their treasure from the conquerors. Today many indigenous groups in Latin America preserve their language and traditions despite the predominance of the Spanish heritage. Students can discuss how the preservation of cultural heritage in the U.S. has been considered both a virtue for the founding families and an obstacle to acculturation for indigenous and immigrant groups.

The legends summarized here are just a few examples of how this type of literature can be used to spark interest and curiosity, provide the cultural context for language learning and help students develop a deeper knowledge and appreciation of the values and beliefs of cultures through the ages. The products and practices depicted in them allow insights into perspectives and historical relationships of communities of peoples. Moreover, the comparisons and connections they afford to other fields of study help students see relationships to their own culture.

The Legends of Mexico NEH Project

In 1994, the University of Cincinnati was awarded a major grant from the National Endowment for the Humanities to fund the "Legends of Mexico K-8" project. In addition to University support, other funding was subsequently awarded by the American Association of Teachers of Spanish and Portuguese (AATSP) and the Central States Conference (CSC). The purposes of the institute were to help participants 1) improve and maintain Spanish-language skills; 2) improve understanding of Mexican culture and how it can be communicated to children; and 3) gain expertise in adapting authentic materials for teaching in grades K-8.[3]

The first summer consisted of a five-week program that began in Cincinnati and ended in Puebla, Mexico. During the week in Cincinnati, twenty-five teachers participated in an intensive workshop to learn the art of storytelling and to use the story as a point of departure for creating a unit of instruction. MaryAnn Brewer of Dallas served as the bilingual storyteller and Mari Haas of Columbia University Teachers College was our pedagogical expert. Participants learned how to create a storyboard, locate and assemble artifacts related to the story, and create synesthetic activities to reinforce and exploit the story. We were particularly interested in using the story as a starting point for content-based teaching (reading, math, science, social studies). Once participants were fully steeped in theory and technique, the teachers and project directors traveled en masse to Puebla, Mexico, were we were met by two additional professors, Francisco Jiménez[4] of Santa Clara University, an expert in Mexican Civilization and successful writer of short stories for children and adolescents, and Aitor Bikandi-Mejias,[5] an expert in Spanish civilization and syntax. The project directors were responsible for the FL Methods course.

The course of study for the institute provided for the written and oral-interview collection of legends from prehispanic Mexico, peninsular Spain, and post-conquest Mexico. Participants were encouraged to search for indications of the blending of cultures, the creation of new legends, and the retention of old traditions. It was expected that through their studies participants would come to an understanding of the meaning of the conquest in contemporary Mexican culture. We were housed in the beautiful Hotel Colonial, a building that dates from the 18th century and is steeped in its own legends and myths. For two of the four weeks, participants stayed with families in Puebla.

The focal point of the institute was each participant's investigation of at least three Mexican legends for the creation of classroom ethnographic units consisting of songs, dance, interviews, artifacts, photographs, stories and so forth. To help them in this endeavor, each pair of participants was assigned a native-speaker *acompañante* (local teachers and other professionals) who served as conversation partner and informant and accompanied them as they investigated their projects and learned more about the Puebla and its environs. Several of the informants also joined us for lunch where they served as conversation leaders at their tables.

Mornings were devoted to formal classes in Spanish language, Mexican civilization, and materials preparation. Language classes were proficiency-oriented, with special emphasis on the communicative and educational needs of children. In addition to formal class presentations, the civilization course included weekends to Mexico City/Teotihuacán, and Vera Cruz. The Materials Preparation class combined the theory of FL acquisition in children with authentic texts and artifacts that participants gathered on site. The writing component consisted of the continued use of dialogue journals to encourage participants to reflect on and express their ideas about their classes, experiences, and investigations throughout the institute and to explore their impressions of and reactions to their own adaptation to Mexican culture. This self-monitoring and examination of the process of cultural adaptation served as another unifying thread throughout the institute.

Following the summer in Mexico, participants prepared and presented at least one workshop to other teachers in their school or district on the preparation of authentic materials for content-based instruction. Several participated in local, regional or national conferences and several now regularly hold Spanish or bilingual storytelling hours at local libraries and schools. The outcome of the first year of the institute was the compilation of twenty-five units or modules for the teaching of Mexican legends.[6]

The second year of the grant consisted of a one-week reunion of participants and professors in Puebla using a workshop schedule that allowed for a variety of formal presentations and participant input. Sessions included presentations on how Mexican civilization is reflected through its legends, such as *La Llorona*. This summer workshop also provided several "*Cuéntame*" sessions for informal storytelling in which participants shared legends *en familia*. By holding these sessions, we encouraged participants to prepare a legend different from the one they had prepared the previous summer to see how they had matured in their storytelling techniques. Without exception, individuals had developed their own unique styles that included ample gestures, intonation, facial expressions, and visual effects. One participant told the story of the Mexican version of Cinderella using the rhythm of a rap song. She explained that her students could relate to that style of narration better than any other. Another participant brought her students' illustrations of a legend she had told to her classes the previous year. In all, it was evident that participants had continued exploring and developing their narrative techniques.

Teacher-participants also used this time to discuss what they had done during the school year and to share their successes and frustrations in incorporating what they had learned from the institute. Some mentioned that they had had to lower their expectations to better ease their students into learning language through content. One expressed disappointment that her school administrators did not want her to speak Spanish in the classroom. Both of these teachers, however, said they had finished the year feeling a degree of success in overcoming initial difficulties. One of the most moving accounts came from a middle-school teacher who had dreaded beginning the year with a particularly unruly group of eighth- graders. Despite her initial misgivings, she began the year by telling them a story, thus engaging their interest and seducing them into the realm of legends. By the end of the year, the students hugged her and said they wanted her 'to be their teacher forever.' A seventh-grade teacher who worked with a team of teachers on an integrated curriculum related that her students had awarded her a prize for being "the teacher who always spent her summers learning something new to be able to teach it to her students the next year." These moving accounts sparked a lively discussion among the teachers about how much they appreciate the small but significant demonstrations that prove they have made a difference in students' lives.

Participants wrote in Spanish about how they had used legends in their classes during the last year, how they had benefited from the institute, and what suggestions they would make for improvement of the institute. This writing activity not only served as an evaluation of the program but as a means to contrast participants' current writing ability with that they had demonstrated the previous year. The essays ranged from thoughtful to elated, as some of the passages excerpted here illustrate. The following participant had expressed serious reservations about her Spanish-language skills at the beginning of the institute; at the end, however, we see that even though she focuses on professional benefits, she also comments on how she gained confidence in her communicative abilities.

> *Como otra participante ya había dicho, estoy de acuerdo que la experiencia del año pasado me ha cambiado en maneras que son difíciles de describir, pero son profundas. En esta página comentaré más de los cambios profesionales.*

> *Durante el año escolar pasado, leí de nuevo el libro escrito por Curtain y Pesola, y traté de integrar sus ideas en la enseñanza de las leyendas. Algunas ideas suyas copié, haciéndolas de la misma manera sin cambios, mientras otras modifiqué un poco.*

> *Además, a través de mi experiencia aquí, por primera vez tuve la experiencia de trabajar con otros para hacer una presentación acerca de asuntos literarios. Primero, otro profesor y yo presentamos la unidad que había preparado como proyecto. En el invierno, María Elena y yo dimos una presentación a los profesores de leyendas extranjeras en Cleveland.*

> *Mientras estaba en México el verano pasado, compré mucha realia para usar en mis clases. La*

usé bastante, especialmente en mi presentación de la unidad "El niño espíritu." Noté que mientras me servía de la realia, a los niños les interesaron mucho, se animaron, tuvieron preguntas. Los dibujos y las fotos me han ayudado bastante en la instrucción, hasta cierto punto. Pero la realia siendo real, captura la imaginación y el interés de todos los alumnos, aún los que generalmente no parecen beneficiarse de todo lo que está pasando en el aula de clase.

Si tuviera que participar de nuevo en el programa, buscaría las leyendas más fáciles que pudiera encontrar, o bien las que podría modificar para que las contara en una manera fácil. Esto haría porque tengo solamente alumnos del séptimo y octavo grado, principiantes que estudian el español por primera vez y están en un curso titulado "el español de exploración." El curso dura sólo medio año, y lo que me gustaría más es que tengan una buena experiencia con la lengua, que vean las similaridades entre las dos lenguas y que compartan en las culturas como puedan.

He beneficiado mucho del curso. Lo que he notado, al llegar aquí este año es que no tengo miedo de hablar a los latinoamericanos ni a los profesores latinos.

Another participant voiced personal benefits she derived from the program when she wrote, in part:

...Les quisiera dar las gracias a las personas que escribieron el programa, y si lo pudiera hacer otra vez, mil veces yo sí me inscribiría.

Yo por lo menos aprendí mucho sobre México, la cultura y la gente de este programa. En parte, esta reunión es como una reunión de familia. Ésta siempre será mi familia de Puebla y en los pocos días en los cuales estuvimos juntos otra vez, aprendí cómo poder usar las leyendas en otras formas.

Ésta ha sido la mejor clase y la mejor experiencia de mi vida...

In the late summer of Year Three of the project we opened the forum to teachers of all levels for a one-day workshop on the campus of the University of Cincinnati. Invited scholars discussed current issues in Mexican civilization and culture and new ideas for teaching content in Spanish K-12. Mary Ann Brewer guided participants through techniques for telling stories to children and young adults.[7] Previous participants led breakout sessions to help newcomers create units of instruction and prepare legends to present to the entire group. Thus, the tradition of legends and the art of storytelling were further disseminated. In the project's fourth and final year, both organizers and participants gave numerous workshops around the state and country. As the project gained notoriety, requests came in from all over the world to receive the Units of Instruction that participants had created in their first year of the program. By all measures, the project was a success.

Developing Lessons around a Legend

As we have seen, the Spanish-speaking world provides a wealth of legends, folktales and myths that are still passed from generation to generation. Interestingly, they also form an important part of the curricula of Spanish-speaking students from kindergarten through graduation. Mexican students not only learn their rich heritage of tales, but are encouraged to develop both oral and written story-telling skills. Students at secondary through postsecondary levels continue to study legends and folktales and their manifestation in literature.

Aside from the heritage connection, legends connect people across cultural and generational boundaries through universal messages that are as important and true today as when the stories were first told. It is this aspect that brings the tales alive, that helps students relate the past to the present and to understand the universality of human dilemmas, trials and tribulations. Ideas of love, honor, greed, trust and friendship are but a few of the universal themes that are evident in legends—versions of Romeo and Juliet, for example, abound. The aforementioned legends of the Mexican volcanoes and the story of *Los amantes* de Teruel are common examples of legend types (see **Appendix B** for general considerations in choosing, developing and telling legends).

The story of *La Casa de los Muñecos* is an excellent example of a tale that offers myriad opportunities for developing language within a cultural context. The house, situated in the historic downtown of Puebla, Mexico, faces the *ayuntamiento*. Because of its proximity to the town hall, the Zócalo and the Cathedral, it is obvious that the owner was a man of great wealth and importance. And so it is told that this gentleman, don Agustín de Villavicencio, had promised his wife, the lovely doña Ana, a beautiful home two stories high. She, of course, was thrilled and immediately announced the impending construction to all her friends and family.

But then as now, building a house requires a permit of sorts, and Puebla was no exception in demanding the approval of plans. Naturally, the *regentes* (fifteen plus the mayor) were adamant that no structure could be built higher than the *ayuntamiento*, which at that time was only one story. At the refusal of his plans, both don Agustín and doña Ana were devastated. Doña Ana was so upset that she took to her bed but her husband, angered by the council, decided to go directly to the top authority. Following a refusal of the plans by the viceroy, don Agustín went to, as Mexicans would say, *el mero mero*. He arrived in Spain, went directly to Toledo, and was admitted to the King's presence. After he presented his case, the King, aware of his visitor's great wealth and importance, granted permission to build the home according to plans. Don Agustín returned to Puebla where doña Ana received the news with great rejoicing.

And so the house was built – two stories (not counting the ground floor, of course) – one story higher than the *ayuntamiento*. But don Agustín added some decorative touches. Puebla, still known for its production of *talavera* and *azulejos*, was about to be known for yet another work of art: Don Agustín commissioned *azulejos* for the façade of the house, but also ordered sixteen murals of semi-nude Greco-Roman figures, all with the faces of the sixteen *regentes*. And so, from that day to this, the members of city council can look out on the *Casa de los Muñecos* and see the results of a self-styled act of civil disobedience. Using the story of *La Casa de los Muñecos*, we may divide the unit of instruction into pre- and post-reading or listening activities, using both advance organizers and culminating tasks (see the process illustrated in **Appendix C**).

Pre-listening/reading. The Internet provides many resources on Puebla, its geography, photographs of the city and its buildings and also the *talavera* industry (see **Appendix A, Web Resources**). Before looking at a site, students could write a list of the uses of tiles and talavera in their homes and school and compare their appearance and use to those of the Puebla sites.

We can also prepare our students for the idea of protesting a governmental decision by asking them to consider similar situations in their hometown. Perhaps they have participated in a protest or know someone who did. As we make this connection to civics and social studies, we are also providing a skill that may prove useful to them in the future.

Because we cannot forget the language structures, this is a perfect time to review the verb tenses in which the story is told. We should remember that folktales are often told in the present indicative as well as the past, making this story accessible to more than just the advanced student. Usually key vocabulary, such as *ayuntamiento* or *talavera* can be illustrated or explained through analogy, thus serving as advance organizers for the story. Also, by supplying some key concepts, such as *honor*, *dinero, venganza,* and *vergüenza* students can speculate on the theme of the story. By the time the preparation is completed, they should be able to say that the story explains the origin of a house with an unusual façade and involves certain familiar themes.

Listening and reading. Since legends are inherently oral, they lend themselves to listening even before reading. The teacher, knowing the level of the students, can accompany storytelling with appropriate visuals and gestures to help students understand. By preparing and practicing the legend with a storyboard, the teacher will develop skills that can be applied to any legend. The oral version should include sufficient redundancy to help reinforce key points in the narration, so that students may begin to fill in details, such as *la casa tenía no sólo un piso sino dos pisos.*

As students read or listen to the tale, they can be encouraged to do a number of things to help them organize their thoughts, review what they have learned and make predictions about the outcome. Story maps and charts are useful tools in these activities. For example, students may keep a character chart on which they note adjectives related to the attributes of each of the main characters. Before they begin to read, they might list in columns some of the following information:

Lo que ya sé	Lo que quiero saber	Lo que voy a saber	Lo que supe

The first column is based on the advance organizers and presentation of key words. The last column is to be completed at the end of the unit and will serve not only to confirm predictions, but to help students see how much they have learned as a result of the unit. This type of activity provides critical-thinking skills and also opportunities for students to interact in pairs or small groups. The chart itself can serve as a model for a presentation to a small group or to the class as a whole.

As students hear or read the story, they may also be asked to link events and decisions to character attributes. For example, we know that don Agustín is proud, wealthy, influential, and that he is stubborn and unwilling to take "no" for an answer. By listing these characteristics, we also find elements in the story that confirm each of these traits. To prove he is wealthy, for example, we can indicate the size of the house and its location. For his stubbornness, we might note his trip to Spain to seek the approval of the King.

Personaje	Características	Acciones
don Agustín	rico	quiere construir una casa grande
doña Ana		
el Sr. López		
el Rey		

Post-listening/reading activities. A variety of post-reading/listening activities are available to test comprehension of main events and details. Here are some examples:

- **Who might have said...?**
  ___ *Soy una persona de bien y merezco una casa grande y elegante.*
  ___ *Con todo permiso, tenemos que negarle el permiso.*
  ___ *¡Qué vergüenza!*

Although the first two statements easily identify don Agustín and Sr. López, the last statement asks for inference. It could have been doña Ana when she found out she had to cancel her party; it could be don Agustín when he was denied permission. Or it could be Sr. López and other members of the ayuntamiento when they saw their caricatures on the façade of the building.

- Reorder the words to make logical statements (and indicate whether the statement is *cierto o falso.*)

    Construir/ Don Agustín/ le/ al/ casa/ pidió/ Sr. López/ para/ una/ permiso.

    →*Don Agustín le pidió permiso al Sr. López para construir una casa. (Cierto)*

- Reorder the events according to the chronology of the story.

> *Éste le dio su permiso.*
> *Se lo contó a Ana, su esposa.*
> *Don Agustín quería construir una casa.*
> *Cuando el ayuntamiento le negó su permiso, decidió pedirle permiso al rey.*
> *Le pidió permiso al jefe del ayuntamiento.*

> →*Don Agustín quería construir una casa. Se lo contó a Ana, su esposa. Le pidió permiso al jefe del ayuntamiento. Cuando el ayuntamiento le negó su permiso, decidió pedirle permiso al rey. Éste le dio su permiso.*

- Complete statements as a prewriting activity.

> *Don Agustín de Ovando y Villavicencio vivía ...*
> *Era una hombre muy...*
> *También era muy feliz porque...*
> *Pero un día decidió...*
> *Por eso,...*
> *etc.*

- Tell how the following words (from Word Box or word strings) fit into the story.

> *honor – orgullo – venganza – vergüenza*
> →*Don Agustín quería proteger su honor.*

Extension Activities. Of all the post-reading/listening activities, extension activities bring home the moral of the story and help students understand the commonalities between all people. With *La Casa de los Muñecos*, there is a plethora of possibilities for students at all levels. Teachers in the NEH program developed some; however, others who have used the story have added. Here is a list of some of the activities with the grade level in which each was used.

- Prepare a drawing of *La casa de los Muñecos*, relating it to your own hometown. Caption the drawings with statements about the political figures. Here the "*muñecos*" depicted local politicians who were currently in the news as a result of some hotly contested issues (Grade 7).

- Build a model of a colonial house, complete with patio, tile roof and *azulejos*. Discuss why this style of architecture fit the times and the climate. Describe the modifications you would make if you were to live in this house in your own hometown (Grades 6-10).

- Write letters to the editor of *El Sol de Puebla*, supporting or protesting the newly erected house. Write another letter to the editor of your local newspaper to support or protest a controversial building or project (Grade 10).

- Role-play the meetings between don Agustín and his wife, the city council, the king. Use appropriate register and forms of address for language functions such as complaining, asking permission, granting or denying permission (Grades 10-postsecondary).

- Draw the sequence of events of the story and find suitable sentences to describe the scenes in an envelope of story strips (Grades 7-9).

- Role-play doña Ana's conversations with her friends and with her maid in her efforts to retrieve her deposit for her housewarming celebration (postsecondary).

- Role-play the reactions of the city-council members and the townsfolk to the semi-nude figures gracing the house (Grades 10-post secondary).

- Design a mural for your school. Include figures of teachers and students and write captions to describe their qualities and contributions to the school (Grades 7, 8).

- Design your own *azulejos* after viewing a number of designs on the Internet (or ideally by seeing real *azulejos*). Indicate where you would use these azulejos in your home or other buildings you know (Grades 1-6).

- Create a poem using some of the terms from the story. For example:

  > *Éramos ricos y poderosos,*
  > *pero ahora estamos tristes y solos.*
  > *Queríamos una casa grande,*
  > *pero no tenemos más que un estante.*
  > *¡Qué vergüenza!*

- Trace the evolution of *azulejos* from the Moorish occupation of Spain to their use in colonial Mexico. Compare the designs, colors and uses. Use a timeline to indicate dates of historical events (Grades 10-postsecondary).

- Investigate art as social protest in Mexico through the murals of Rivera, Orozco and Siqueiros (Grades 10-postsecondary).

- Investigate the oldest building in your town or neighborhood. How does it compare in age, structure and maintenance with the *Casa de los Muñecos?* What does this tell you about North American and Mexican perspectives on time and age (Grades 6-9)?

- Examine how Mexican culture views time, how the old and new can exist together and be venerated. Compare how the notion of time includes social relationships as well as historical relics (Grades 9 and above).

- Mount plans for a peaceful protest of a public (or perhaps private) project in your home-town, school or university. This may be presented in writing, as a debate, or simply as a plan of action. How does your plan differ from don Agustín's and why (Grades 10-post-secondary)?

- Describe what you as a regente would do if you saw yourself caricatured on a building. Discuss what politicians and other public figures do when attacked in this manner and why. How does your reaction differ from theirs (Grades 11-postsecondary)?

- Rewrite the story from a different point of view: that of a regente, a neighbor, doña Ana, the maid or the butler, the viceroy or the king (Grades 10-postsecondary).

- Take a Spanish proverb, such as *Más vale pájaro en mano que cien volando* or *No hay mal que por bien no venga* and develop a legend that could use the proverb as its final sentence and moral (Grades 11-post secondary).

Each time this story is presented in another classroom, new ideas for activities are formed. In the end, students have grown in their language skills (communication); they have explored culture throughout the activity; they have learned that we have many things in common with other people (comparisons), and they have learned something about civil disobedience and ways to approach the government to change laws or minds (connections, communities).

Conclusion

In the authors' experience, teachers are sometimes skeptical about using legends and folktales with older students. We have found, however, that learners of all ages enjoy a good story. One of the best personal testimonies came from a teacher in Southwestern Ohio who had taught for nearly thirty years and thought that her seemingly suave and sophisticated high school students would hate legends. Nevertheless, she prepared and presented a unit. The reaction? Silence and emotionless faces. She thought, "well, it didn't work, but I tried." Then, two weeks later, one of the most suave and sophisticated of the group, reclined in his chair, raised his hand and asked, " Hey, señora, when are you going to tell another story? That was cool!" Combining "cool" with valid learning experiences is the best a teacher can hope for. And when that learning experience is entirely cultural, we have done well indeed.

Notes

[1] The legends discussed in this article are available in Bacon, Humbach, Bikandi-Mejías & Courtad, 2000.

[2] *Syncretism* is the reconciliation or combination of differing beliefs or practices in religion, philosophy, culture, etc. See **Web Resources** for additional information and examples.

[3] The original grant was for K-8 teachers. In subsequent years we were able to expand the audience to K-12 and beyond.

[4] Professor Jiménez is best known for his collection *The Circuit: Stories of a Migrant Child (Cajas de cartón)*. He has won numerable awards for his stories, including the Boston Globe-Horn Book Award for Fiction, and the Americas Award for Children's and Young Adult Literature.

[5] Professor Bikandi-Mejías is a professor with Saint Louis University in Madrid.

[6] *The Legends of Mexico: Units of Instruction* is available from the University of Cincinnati. For more information, contact: Susan.Bacon@UC.edu.

[7] See **Appendix B** for guidelines on storytelling.

Works Cited

Bacon, Susan M., Nancy Humbach and Gregg Courtad, eds. *Legends of Mexico*. Compiled works of teacher/participants in the 1995-96 institute funded by the National Endowment for the Humanities and the University of Cincinnati, 1996. ED 400 675.

Bacon, Susan M., Nancy Humbach, Aitor Bikandi-Mejías and Gregg Courtad. *Leyendas del mundo hispano*. Englewood Cliffs: Prentice Hall, 2000.

Egan, Kieran. *Educational Development*. New York: Oxford University Press, 1979.

_____. *Teaching as Story Telling*. Chicago: University of Chicago Press, 1986.

National Standards for Foreign Language Learning: Preparing for the 21st Century. New York: American Council on the Teaching of Foreign Languages, 1996.

Rowling, J. K. *Harry Potter and the Sorcerer's Stone*. New York: A. Levine Books, 1998.

_____. *Harry Potter and the Chamber of Secrets*. Arthur A. Levine Books, 1999.

_____. *Harry Potter and the Goblet of Fire*. New York: Arthur A. Levine Books, 2000.

Appendix A
Resources for Teaching Legends

Web Resources

Note: Because URLs are prone to change, we offer only a few web sites here. However, a search for keywords, such as Puebla, Popocatéptl, *yerba mate*, yields many good sources.

La Llorona
http://cybernautas.com/webprize/llorona.htm
http://mexico.udg.mx/historia/leyendas/llorona.html
http://www.mexsa.com/llorona.htm

La Casa de los Muñecos
http://148.245.228.77/Diversion/museos/munecos.html
http://www.turista.com.mx/puebla/

La yerba mate
http://www.pampanet.com/jpablo/leyenda.htm
http://www.judithcorsino.com/elmate.htm)

Los novios
http://cbc.ca/news/indepth/background/volcano.html
http://volcano.und.nodak.edu/vwdocs/kids/legends.html#mexico

El ñandutí
http://www.geocities.com/TheTropics/Resort/2408/artesania.html
http://lace.lacefairy.com/ID/Nanduti.html

Sincretism
http://www.geocities.com/Athens/Parthenon/2104/syncretism.html
http://www.yale.edu/ynhti/curriculum/units/1994/3/94.03.02.x.html
http://anthro.palomar.edu/change/change_3.htm

Print Resources

Note: Many of these titles are available through the Interlibrary Loan Service. Check with your local library for further information.

Alvar, Manuel, editor. *Poesía tradicional de los judíos españoles.* Mexico, D.F.: Editorial Porrúa, S. A. "Sepan Cuántos…," 1979.
Anon. *Cuentos populares españoles.* Barcelona: Editorial Labor, S. A., 1980.

Anon. *Leyendas de Castilla.* Barcelona: Editorial Labor, S. A., 1984.

Anon. *Popol Vuh. Antiguas historias de los indios quichés de Guatemala.* México, D.F.: Editorial Porrúa, 1965.

Anon. *Relatos de Coyoacán.* Mexico, D.F.: Museo Nacional de Culturas Populares, 1988.

Anzaldua, G. *Prietita and the Ghost Woman; Prietita y la Llorona.* San Francisco, CA: Children's Book Press, 1966.

Aramoni, María Elena. *Talokan tata, talokan nana: Nuestras raíces hierofanías y Testimonios de un mundo indígena.* Mexico, D.F: Consejo Nacional para la Cultura y las Artes. Dirección General de Publicaciones, 1990.

Atienza, Juan. *Guía de las leyendas españolas.* Barcelona: Espasa Calpe, S. A., 1985.

Barlow, G and W. N. Stivers. *Legends from Mexico; Leyendas de México.* Lincolnwood, IL: National Textbook Company, 1995.

Barlow, G. *Legends from Latin America; Leyendas de Latinoamérica.* Lincolnwood, IL: National Textbook Company, NTC Publishing Group, 1995.

Bellpré, P. *Pérez y Martina.* New York: Viking Penguin, 1960.

Bierhorst, J. *The Hungry Woman: Myths and Legend of the Aztecs.* New York: William Morrow and Company, 1984.

Bierhorst, John, ed. *The Monkey's Haircut and Other Stories Told by the Maya.* New York: William Morrow and Company, 1986.

_____. *The Mythology of Mexico and Central America.* New York: William Morrow and Company, 1990.

Caballero, María del Socorro. *Costumbres del estado de México.* Mexico, D.F: Secretaría de Educación Pública, 1984.

_____. *Narraciones tradicionales del estado de México.* Mexico, D.F: Secretaría de Educación Pública, 1984.

Castañeda, O. S. *Abuela's Weave.* New York: Lew and Low Books, Inc., 1993.

Charles, D. *Chancay and the Secret of Fire.* New York: G. P. Putnam's Sons, 1992.

Cerero, Andres, ed. *El vuelo de la gente nube: narraciones zapotecas.* Mexico, D.F: Secretaría de Educación Pública. 1972.

Cordero y Torres, Enrique. *Puebla, ciudad de leyendas.* Mexico, D.F: Fotolitográfica LEO, 1972.

Davis, E. Adams. *Of the Night Wind's Telling: Legends from the Valley of México.* Norman: University of Oklahoma Press, 1946.

Delacre, L. *De oro y esmeraldas.* New York: Scholastic Press, 1996.

_____. *Vejigante Masquerader.* New York: Scholastic Press, 1993.

De Sauza, J. *Brother Anansi and the Cattle Ranch: El hermano Anansi y el rancho de ganado.* San Francisco: Children's Book Press, 1989.

Ehlert, L. *Moon Rope; Un lazo a la luna.* New York: Harcourt Brace and Company, 1992.

Flores Farfán, J.A. *El tlacuache Tlakwatsin.* Mexico, D.F.: Ediciones Corunda, S. A. de C. V., 1996.

Frías, Heriberto. *Leyendas históricas mexicanas y otros relatos.* Mexico, D.F.: Editorial Porrúa, 1986.

González Obregón, Luis. *Las calles de Mexico: leyendas y sucedidos, vida y costumbres de otros tiempos.* Mexico, D.F: Editorial Porrúa, S. A, 1988.

González, Torices, José. *Cuentos de la Castilola nuestra.* Simancas Ediciones, S. A. Valladolid, 1988.

Grifalconi. A. *The Bravest Flute*. New York: Little, Brown and Company, 1994.

Humbach, Nancy A. *The Crystal Serpent: Plays for Beginning Spanish Students*. Upper Saddle River, NJ: Prentice Hall, 1995.

Mariscal, B.L. de *The Harvest Bird*; Los pájaros de la cosecha. Emeryville, CA: Children's Book Press, 1995.

Martínez, José Luis. *Nezahuacoyotl, vida y obra*. Mexico, D.F: Biblioteca Americana. Fondo de la Cultura Económica, 1985.

Mena, José María de. *Leyendas y misterios de Madrid*. Barcelona: Plaza y Janes, 1989.

Meza, Otilia. *Leyendas del antiguo México*. Mexico, D.F: Edamex, 1985.

_____. *Leyendas prehispánicas mexicanas*. Mexico, D.F: Editorial Panorama, 1988.

Montejo, Victor. *The Bird who Cleans the World and other Mayan Fables*. Villimantic, CT: Curbstone Press, 1991.

Morales, Rafael. *Leyendas mexicanas*. Mexico, D.F: Editorial Aguilar, 1977.

Paredes, Américo. *Folktales of Mexico*. Chicago: The University of Chicago Press, 1970.

Parke, M. and S. Panik. *Leyendas de México y la América Central; Un cuento de Quetzalcoatl acerca del juego de pelota*. Carthage, IL: Fearon Teacher Aids, Simon and Schuster Supplementary Education Group, 1992.

Paz, Octavio. *El laberinto de la soledad*. Mexico, D.F: Fondo de la Cultural Económica, 1959.

Perea, Francisco J. *El mundo de Juan Diego*. Mexico, D.F: Editorial Diana, 1988.

Pérez, Martínez. *Cuauhtemoc*. Mexico, D.F: Populibros "*La Prensa*,"1957.

Peza, Juan de Dios. *Leyendas históricas, tradicionales y fantásticas de las calles de la Ciudad de México*. Mexico, D.F: Editorial Porrúa, S. A., 1988.

_____. *Memorias, reliquias y retratos*. Mexico, D.F: Editorial Porrúa, S. A. "Sepan cuan tos…,"1990.

Rael, Juan B. *Cuentos españoles de Colorado y de Nuevo Méjico*. Palo Alto: Stanford University Press, n.d.

Rivero del Val, Luis. *Entre las patas del caballo*. Mexico, D.F: Editorial Jus, 1989.

Robe, Stanley L. *Hispanic Folktales from New Mexico*. Ann Arbor: UMI Out-of-Print Books, n.d.

Rohmer, H. and M. Anchondo. *How We Came to the Fifth World; Cómo vinimos al quinto mundo*. Mexico, D.F: Children's Book Press. Panorama Editorial, S. A., 1988.

Sahagún, Fr. Bernardino. *Historia general de las cosas de Nueva España*. Mexico, D.F: Editorial Porrúa, S. A. "Sepan cuántos…,"1989.

San Souci, R.D. *The Little Seven-colored Horse*. San Francisco: Chronicle Books, 1995.

Scheffler, Lilian. *Cuentos y leyendas de México: tradición oral de grupos indígenas y mestizos*. Mexico, D.F: Panorama Editorial, S. A., 1989.

Séjourné, Laurette. *Pensamiento y religión en el México antiguo*. Mexico, D.F: Fondo de la Cultura Económica., 1987.

_____. *Supervivencias de un mundo mágico*. Mexico, D.F: Fondo de la Cultura Económica, 1985.

Sexton, James D. Mayan Folktales: Folklore from Lake Atitlán Guatemala. New York: Anchor Books- Doubleday, 1992.

Stross, Brian. *Demons and Monsters: Tzeltal Tales*. *Museum Brief*, No. 24. Columbia: The Curators of the University of Missouri, 1978.

Tapia, Francisco Xavier. *Leyendas y anécdotas de la historia de España.* Madrid: Editorial Anaya, 1987.

Las tradiciones de días de muertos en México. México, D.F: Dirección General de Culturas Populares, 1990.

Valle-Arizpe, Artemio. *Cuentos del México Antiguo.* Mexico, D.F: Espasa-Calpe Mexicana (Colección Austral), 1989.

_____. *Historias de vivos y muertos.* Mexico, D.F: Editorial JUS, 1981.

_____. *Leyendas mexicanas.* Mexico, D.F: Espasa-Calpe Mexicana (Colección Austral), 1982.

_____. *Personajes y leyendas del México virreinal:* relatos sobre la vida en la Nueva España. Mexico, D.F: Panorama Editorial, S. A., 1989.

Volkmer, J. A. *Song of the Chirimía.* Mexico, D.F: Panorama Editorial, S. A., 1990.

Weitlaner, Roberto J. *Relatos, mitos y leyendas de la Chinantla.* Mexico, D.F: Instituto Nacional Indigenista, 1981.

Wheeler, Howard T. *Tales from Jalisco,* Mexico. Philadelphia: American Folklore Society, 1943.

Zubizarreta, R.H. Rohnmer, et al. *The Woman Who Outshone the Sun; La mujer que brilla ba aún más que el sol.* San Francisco: Children's Book Press, 1991.

Appendix B. Procedures for Choosing and Telling Legends

The following steps may be useful in identifying legends for your students and developing them into units.

- Identify a legend or folktale that you like and believe would pique your students' interest.

- List the products and practices that are evident in the story and what they reveal about the perspectives of the legend's culture of origin.

- Gather background information and visual support to illustrate the context of the story:

    Time
    Location
    Characters
    Historical or political context
    Present key concepts and vocabulary in context.

- Give students a task as the read or listen (e.g., take note of the characters, the problem, the resolution).

If telling the story:

    Make a storyboard to cue your telling. Each frame should provide simple supporting information.

    Practice telling the story, allowing moments for listeners to supply some of the information or to speculate on what will happen next. Build in redundancy so that listeners will begin to anticipate and interact.

- Test comprehension progressing from receptive to productive activities.

- Go beyond the story with divergent activities: drama, debate, letter writing, poetry, etc.

- Explore connections with other content areas (geography, arts, mathematics…).

- Connect the story to present-day realities and ethics.

- Draw on the community to provide other stories.

- Have students present other folktales and legends.

- ENJOY!

Appendix C

Preparación

El contexto	**Los azulejos en la arquitectura**	**Algunos conceptos**
• Puebla	• la fachada	• el honor
• México	• la fuente	• la burla
• La geografía	• el patio	• el dinero
• La topografía	• la cúpula	• la vergüenza
	• el baño	• el orgullo
	• la cocina	
	• el vestíbulo	

Conexiones
- El arte
- La ética
- Las matemáticas
- La historia
- La sociología
- La gastronomía
- la cartografía

La Casa de los Muñecos

Comprensión
- Los personajes, el problema, la resolución
- ¿Quién habría dicho…?
- Ordenar frases
- Poner los sucesos en orden cronológico

Extensión
- Dramatizar los sucesos
- Escribir cartas al editor
- Diseñar una casa
- Invitar a los amigos a una fiesta en la casa
- Debatir los beneficios de sus acciones
- Buscar ejemplos modernos

Chapter 7

Building On Our Experiences

Núria Vidal
Education Office, Embassy of Spain

The project *Con la vida a cuestas* described here was initially developed for "*Tareas y Proyectos para las clases de hispanohablantes o nivel avanzado de español*," published by the Education Office of the Embassy of Spain as an important part of the "*Dossier de apoyo para la enseñanza en EE.UU.*" However, as the *National Standards* have been used as reference, the entire project can also be implemented in contexts of Spanish as a second or foreign language in advanced courses focusing on higher-level intellectual content. While the entire project is available on the web,[1] this chapter highlights the main objectives and content of the materials in the hope that readers will use them and adapt them to their own learners' needs. The activities are flexible and open to contributions from both students and teachers.

Since its inception, the project has been tested with most of the activities proving to be quite successful in their motivation of learners and in their development of the types of thinking skills that foster lifelong learning. We have found that the primary reason students get involved in the learning tasks described here is that the activities encourage them to reflect on their own experiences and to compare and expand their own views. Learners build self-esteem through a fuller and more respectful understanding of the rich and varied cultural heritages captured in their own diverse backgrounds while gaining insights into new socio-cultural aspects that broaden their awareness of the many different perspectives that enrich our world.

The major organizing principles of the tasks are the five Cs of the *Standards*: Communication, Cultures, Connections, Comparisons and Communities; all are integrated through the development of cultural and interdisciplinary knowledge, learning and communication strategies, critical thinking skills, and use of technology. This chapter provides a sketch of the project objectives, a general outline of the main content areas and products and progress indicators, and a sample illustrative lesson.

Project Objectives

The main objectives of this project are to 1) increase students' self-esteem by guiding them to identify prior experiences and relate them to the cultural products presented and 2) build learners' understanding and appreciation of different cultural heritages through critical interpretation of the perspectives underlying different cultural products and practices. **Table 1** presents the project objectives for each of the five Cs of the *Standards*.

Table 1. Specific Objectives

Communication	Cultures
To request, provide and obtain information on literary texts and songs. To reflect on feelings and memories and compare one's viewpoints with those conveyed through the voices of literary texts. To exchange opinions about past personal experiences. To contrast personal interpretations of literary texts with other partners. To produce and present a project considering the audience and the purpose.	To understand the Spanish cultural heritage expressed in literature. To interpret the underlying perspectives in different genres. To promote an understanding and appreciation of cultural diversity among the people from different Spanish-speaking countries. To adjust oral and written language to the audience, the context, and the purpose. To read, listen, observe, use and critically interpret and assess information obtained from different sources.
Connections	**Comparisons**
To acknowledge the importance of literature by relating our own personal experiences to distinctive viewpoints expressed in the literary texts. To recognize the distinctive viewpoints of the Spanish literature. To further one's knowledge of other subject areas through small-scale research. To identify the underlying patterns in different types of literary texts. To differentiate facts from opinions in written texts from difference sources.	To show awareness of the rich and varied cultural heritage in Spanish and Latin American literature. To identify distinctive viewpoints in Spanish and Latin American literature. To appreciate the different perspectives underlying literary works. To identify similarities and differences between Spanish culture and language and the mother tongue. To understand distinctive features of the varieties of Spanish worldwide.
Communities	
To present a project on their own memories and experiences to other classmates. To understand and critically assess the work presented by others. To use new technologies to establish links beyond the classroom. To use Spanish to communicate with other people outside the classroom. To use available resources to become a life-long independent learner in and out of class.	

Content and Progress Indicators

The project content consists of several sections or modules connected and unified through the theme of *memory* (**Table 2**). Each section provides an array of text types representing a variety of genres (literary and journalistic), authors, and cultural origins and perspectives. Section A consists of priming tasks to activate students' previous knowledge and experience of their past and is designed to engage them in reflection and sharing. The tasks in Section B, *El compromiso*, help students understand and define the most relevant literary genre they will be using extensively: autobiography. Through these tasks, students engage in and commit themselves to the objectives leading to both process and end products linked to the memories of their own lives. Two process-evaluation activities are included in this section: Revision of the progress indicators and guidelines for further investigation of the authors of the texts presented. These evaluation tasks will be used throughout the project as many times as the teacher or students find them necessary. Section B does not require texts or products since it is intended as a decision-making process to encourage students to take responsibilities for their learning and their own progress.

Table 2. Previous Knowledge, Definition and Commitment

Section A: Retomar la memoria
Subject-matter *Entre mis recuerdos* *El baúl de los recuerdos* *El territorio de la memoria* *Contar la vida*
Texts Song: *Entre mis recuerdos* by Luz Casal Excerpts from: *El territorio de la memoria* by Juan Cruz Ruiz *Historia de una maestra* by Josefina Aldecoa
Progress Indicators •Appreciate the importance of literature by relating personal experiences to the distinctive viewpoints reflected in the literary texts. •Read, listen and observe to gather information for carrying out the tasks. •Adjust oral and written language to the audience, the context and the purpose.

Section B: El compromiso
Subject-matter *Biografía y autobiografía* *Funciones de la autobiografía* *Nuestra autobiografía y nuestros objetivos* *Evaluación formativa* *Curiosidad por el autor*
Texts No texts (Learner decision-making)
Progress indicators •Read, listen, observe, use, and critically interpret the information obtained from different sources. •Acknowledge the importance of literature by comparing their own personal experiences to the distinctive viewpoints expressed in the literary texts. •Collect information from different sources. •Demonstrate awareness of and sensitivity toward the linguistic varieties found in all the Spanish-speaking environments worldwide. •Share and discuss individual interpretations of a given text to broaden, clarify, and confirm comprehension.

As can be seen in **Table 3**, Section C, *Activar la memoria*, offers a wider range of texts because it is in this stage that students are offered choices and different routes for carrying out the tasks assigned. From the varied subject matter, teacher and students may select the tasks most appropriate to their level and communication needs. In this section, the tasks need not be taught in progression and may be carried out by adjusting order and subject matter to the class needs. Section D, *Imaginación para el futuro*, is a short section that helps students develop creative skills by imagining their lives in the near future according to their expectations. Similarly to section B, section E does not contain authentic texts because it has different purposes: It is intended to study the works produced by the students and to review and assess the progress indicators by having teachers and students alike (individually and in pairs) rate the individual and the collective outcomes achieved.

Table 3: Activation, Imagination, Organization and Assessment

Section C: *Activar la memoria*

Subject-matter

La memoria de los míos. La memoria y la experiencia, la familia, las amistades, la Historia, los espacios, los sentidos, las tradiciones, las imágenes, los relatos y la creación.

Texts

Excerpts from:

Como agua para chocolate by Laura Esquivel
Una partida de ajedrez by Felipe Hernández.
La arboleda perdida by Rafael Alberti
Amigos íntimos by Nativel Preciado.
El chico de la moto by Susan Hinton
Recuerdos de infancia by Sapo Pareja Matute
Afrodita by I. Allende
Ana María Matute. La voz del silencio, M.L. Gazarian-Gautier
El arte visto por los artistas, Rafols Casamada

En busca del tiempo perdido by M. Proust
Dulce de por si by D. Maraini.
La vida oculta by Soledad Puértolas
Songs:
  Mi niñez by Joan Manuel Serrat
  El Mediterráneo by Joan Manuel Serrat
Poetry:
  Recuerdo infantil by Antonio Machado.
Article:
  "*Mientras ellos vuelven*" in *El País* 09/08/98

Progress indicators

- Use strategies individually and cooperatively when reading, listening and observing.
- Summarize main ideas in the text and draw conclusions; identify the author's objectives.
- Write and talk to inform; narrate and persuade to express ideas and feelings.
- Distinguish facts from opinions, reality and fantasy.
- Display sensitivity towards socio-cultural differences inherent in Spanish-speaking areas.
- Write and speak for different purposes in multidisciplinary contexts.
- Demonstrate the ability to adopt proper behavior in a culturally and linguistically diverse society.
- Discover patterns, establish links and make generalizations through key interdisciplinary content.
- Use creativity and reflect critical analysis; and use resources to conduct a research.
- Identify, analyze and interpret appropriate structural aspects to narrate, inform in written expression.
- Create and produce meaningful and informative writing that is well organized, coherent, and precise.
- Adjust production and the choice of vocabulary to the context, the audience and the purpose.
- Appreciate viewpoints other than one's own and those presented in the texts.

Section D: Imaginación para el futuro

Subject-matter

Plantearse el futuro
Inventar el futuro

Texts

Excerpt: *El buscón* by F. de Quevedo
Poetry: *Si volviera a nacer* by Nadine Stair attributed to Jorge Luis Borges

Progress indicators
- Understand the changing nature of the functions and forms of the language.
- Use technology to communicate with Spanish speakers all over the world.
- Share and recommend favorite texts.

Section E : *Organizar y evaluar los recuerdos*

Subject-matter

Formative and summative evaluation

El trabajo realizado: Mi autobiografía

Selección

Los trabajos de la clase

Los indicadores de progreso

Texts

Student-produced texts

Progress indicators
- Appreciate and respect the work done by others.
- Develop attitudes and skills for cooperation.
- Develop intellectual and aesthetic patterns to analyze and evaluate the means of communication.

Methodology

The methodological approach underpinning this project is in line with the ideas proposed by Ribe, Ribe and Vidal (1993, 1997) and Legutke and Thomas on tasks, frames and project work using the sociocultural aspects of Vygotsky's theories. The underlying philosophy of multicultural education is derived from Banks (1999, 2001), Nieto (1999, 2000) and Grant and Sleeter as well as from the notion of empathy constructed around self and community of Kanpol's *Critical Pedagogy* and Shor's work on negotiation and active student participation. Our aim through these tasks was to create a learning atmosphere that builds on learners' prior knowledge and encourages them to put hands on their experiences to develop further appreciation of others' differences. Through emphasis on real-life interactive and cooperative tasks that focus on both process and product, learners develop the types of skills, strategies and attitudes that foster lifelong learning. Considering that Spanish is a language spoken in many countries and which therefore conveys a rich variety of cultural heritages worldwide, we encourage the use of a wide array of literary works combined with technology applications that allow access to diverse information sources and the establishment of linkages beyond the classroom. A distinctive feature of our approach is the constant attention to learner opportunities for the exchange of opinions, the sharing of decision-making, negotiation and consensus building, the integration of different viewpoints and the development of respect for other perspectives. By guiding students to work cooperatively, we enhance the integration not only of all cultures represented in the classroom, but of all learning styles, skills and abilities. Further, students are constantly encouraged to focus on their learning process in order to achieve an outcome that follows the distinctive patterns and conventions of the language and its culture. When revising their final project before presenting to others, students will automatically bring into play various learning strategies and will be bound to develop new ones in order to achieve the desired goals.

Indeed, the educational value of this project lies in the fact that all students will achieve an outcome. The level of sophistication of this outcome, however, will depend on various factors: the student's age, background, linguistic proficiency, interest, effort, imagination and overall capacities; however, all learners will all be actively involved in the entire process—making decisions and developing thinking skills to achieve outcomes to be enriched by the viewpoints contributed by others. To illustrate our approach to tasks, we include in the following section some samples of the materials suggested in the complete project.

Sample Activities

The first activity described in this section, "*Adivina el paisaje*," uses pair work to activate students' previous experiences and create a positive learning environment while allowing learners the opportunity to get to know their partners better. As can be seen in the worksheet that follows, students are given prompts to help them get started, but they are free to make their own decisions on what to say and how to say it, thereby ensuring both motivation and a sense of autonomy. This activity is followed by the song "*El Mediterraneo*" by Joan Manuel Serrat, which is linked the matically and favors additional pair and small-group discussion. However, once students have listened to and understood the gist of the song, they are encouraged to take a step further, locating and retrieving information from the Internet that will help them make connections with other disciplines and fields of study.

¡ADIVINA EL PAISAJE!

> ***En parejas:*** *¿Qué paisaje nos rodeaba cuando éramos pequeños*
> *Se trata de que con preguntas cuyas respuestas sólo pueden ser:* SÍ, NO, DEFINE UN POCO
> MÁS, *adivinen el entorno de la infancia de su colega.*

Aquí tienen algunas sugerencias de los temas que pueden tratar. Añadan otros y confeccionen las preguntas antes de empezar a preguntar a su colega.

Temas	Preguntas
clima *(frío, calor, lluvia, viento,* *sol, nieve, templado, nublado...)*	
vegetación *(escasa, abundante, exuberante,* *variada, árboles en flor, arbustos...)*	
situación *(ciudad, campo, playa, mar,* *montaña, desierto, al lado de un río...)*	
colores dominantes *(verde, azul, marrón, ocre, gris,* *blanco, amarillo…)*	
acciones de la gente *(trabajando en el campo, en coche,* *corriendo, en bicicleta, a pié, bañándose...)*	
animales *(perros, gatos, caballos, ardillas,* *camellos, lagartos...)*	
otros elementos *(barcas, motocicletas, carros, tractores,* *bicicletas...)*	
Añadan otros temas...	

Terminada la sesión de preguntas y de respuestas cortas comenten todos aquellos pormenores que consideren importantes, clarifiquen aquellos aspectos que no han quedado claros y hagan otras preguntas si sienten curiosidad y quieren conocer algún detalle más.

El Mediterráneo

"…Yo, que en la piel tengo el sabor amargo del llanto eterno que han vertido en ti cien pueblos de Algeciras a Estambul para que pintes de azul sus largas noches de invierno…"

Joan Manuel Serrat

Lean y escuchen la canción de Joan Manuel Serrat, *El Mediterráneo.*² Después de su reflexión sobre el entorno de su infancia estarán más sensibilizados con los posibles detalles que escapan a la canción.

Ustedes son capaces de...

Individualmente:
Hacer un dibujo del paisaje donde vivió y creció Joan Manuel Serrat y colorearlo.

En parejas:

Hacer una descripción más concreta, ampliando detalles de su paisaje buscando información en Internet o en un libro de geografía.

En grupos de tres:

1. Preparar una entrevista, parecida a la que han hecho entre ustedes, para Joan Manuel Serrat.

Discutan en su grupo:

2. ¿Pensáis que el paisaje y el entorno afectan a la persona y determinan una manera determinada de vivir?

3. ¿Se aprecia en Joan Manuel Serrat una sensibilidad determinada por pertenecer a este mundo Mediterráneo que nos describe?

4. ¿Qué diferencias distinguirían entre el autor de la canción y ustedes?

Evaluation

Evaluation is understood as an integral part of the learning process and, therefore, students are responsible for their own progress from the very beginning. We draw on their prior knowledge and experiences and propose tasks that have a clearly formative and educational aspect in order to help students reflect on the goals achieved. Self-, peer- and co-evaluation are integrated into the entire learning process to favor a positive cooperative environment conducive to lifelong learning.

The worksheets that follow are just a few samples to illustrate the approach. First, students are encouraged to keep their own individual record of each of the tasks carried out, whether they are satisfied with them, what they can improve. Then, they must select the outcomes achieved with their favorite tasks and make a complete final document from the selection and edition of their previous work to present it to others. While they are reorganizing their productions, students have the opportunity to review and edit all the work done, select what they like, improve what needs to be improved, and discard what is not needed. In the next worksheet they must take notes on their partners' presentations, a task that will help them later in the next assessment task, "*el recuerdo colectivo.*" Here, students in small groups must make decisions about other students' work they particularly like and give reasons for their choices. Next, students are asked to look at the progress indicators and rate their personal achievement in light of the process and the final outcome—the accounts of portions of their personal and collective work on the tasks accomplished. Finally, they discuss their views with another partner and with their teacher before discussing the whole process and corresponding outcome as a group.

EL TRABAJO REALIZADO: MI AUTOBIOGRAFÍA

Escriba en la parrilla los títulos de todos sus trabajos de "*Con la vida a cuestas,*" estén terminados o no. Marque con una palomita (√) en las casillas correspondientes:

a. los que estén totalmente acabados,

b. aquellos a los que les falte alguna cosa,

c. los que más le gusten.

Título de los trabajos	a. acabados	b. inacabados	c. me gustan
[up to 20 boxes]			

¿Quiere mejorar alguno de sus trabajos? ¿Quiere terminar alguno de los trabajos inacabados? Anote todo lo que necesite hacer.

SELECCIÓN

Cuando haya completado sus trabajos, decida cómo quiere ordenarlos para presentar un documento único y explique el motivo de su elección.

Busque un título sugerente para su autobiografía. Escríbalo aquí:

Explique, a modo de presentación, su autobiografía. Cuente las satisfacciones personales, las dificultades, los retos, los miedos vencidos, el aprendizaje conseguido...

Ordene sus ideas en tres párrafos. Organícelos aquí:

1.
2.
3.

¿Ha terminado? ¿Le queda algún cabo suelto? Si ya está a punto organice sus documentos escritos o grabados. ¡Sea original!

Cuando haya terminado, explique su trabajo al resto de la clase.

EL RECUERDO COLECTIVO

En grupos de cinco

Seleccionen cinco autobiografías de la clase que no pertenezcan a nadie de su grupo. Con sus notas de los trabajos, y mirando la presentación y el contenido, seleccionen el apartado que más les gusta de cada autobiografía. Digan por qué.

Título de la autobiografía	Apartado (páginas)	Por qué
1.		
2. (up to 5 larger boxes)		

Grupo clase

Nombren a un coordinador para que anote en la pizarra las decisiones de cada grupo en referencia a los apartados seleccionados. Con los títulos en la pizarra, digan cuál va primero, segundo, y así sucesivamente. Ordenen los títulos de cada documento en la parrilla.

(up to 20 boxes)	

Negocien un título para su autobiografía colectiva

LOS INDICADORES DE PROGRESO

Valore personalmente de 1 (muy en desacuerdo) a 5 (muy de acuerdo) cada objetivo que negociamos al principio de nuestro proyecto.

A lo largo de este proyecto he aprendido a:

	5	4	3	2	1
1. leer y comprender distintos textos de autores que han trabajado en la autobiografía.					
2 planificar y llevar a cabo una pequeña investigación sobre mi vida pasada.					
3. compartir y comentar experiencias pasadas con mis colegas.					

4. respetar y valorar las decisiones de cada uno de mis colegas.					
5. ordenar y escribir los recuerdos de mi infancia y adolescencia.					
6. presentar mis recuerdos en un documento escrito, audio-casete o vídeo.					
7. seleccionar nuestros trabajos y juntarlos en un documento colectivo.					
8. apreciar y valorar las diferencias culturales de cada uno de nosotros					
9.					
10.					
Total					

- Realice este ejercicio de evaluación para el trabajo de un compañero y él a su vez que realice la valoración de su trabajo. ¿Coinciden en sus valoraciones?

- Realice este ejercicio de evaluación con su profesora. ¿Coincide con su valoración?

- Finalmente repitan la valoración de su trabajo como grupo clase. ¿Cómo consideran su trabajo colectivo? ¿Su producción final?

Notes

[1] This project is available as a PDF at: http://www.spainembedu.org/apoyo/contenidos.html. PDF documents are accessible by downloading Acrobat Reader.

[2] Available at: http://www.geocities.com/Paris/Cafe/6764/serrat.html#med

Works Cited

Banks, James and Cherry McGee Banks, eds. *Multicultural education. Issues and Perspectives.* NY: John Wiley and Sons, Inc., 2001.

Grant, Carl A. and Christine E. Sleeter. *Five Approaches for Multicultural Teaching Plans for Race, Class, Gender, and Disability.* NY: John Wiley and Sons, Inc., 1999.

Hernández, Felipe and Núria Vidal. *Con la vida a cuestas. Un proyecto interactivo para favorecer la autoestima y el respeto a la diversidad cultural de los alumnos.* Washington, D.C.: Consejería de Educación Embajada de España: http://www.spainembedu.org/apoyo/contenidos.html.

Kanpol, Barry. *Critical Pedagogy: An Introduction.* Westport, CT: Berguin and Garvey, 1999.

Legutke, Michael and Howard Thomas. *Process and Experience in the Language Classroom.* NY: Longman, 1991.

National Standards in Foreign Language Education Project. *Standards for Foreign Language Learning in the 21st Century*. Lawrence, KS: Allen Press, Inc., 1999.

Nieto, Sonia. Affirming Diversity: *The Sociopolitical Context of Multicultural Education*. NY: Longman, 2000.

Nieto, Sonia. *The Light in Their Eyes: Creating Multicultural Learning Communities*. NY: Teachers College Press, 1999.

Ribé, Ramon Coord. *Tramas creativas y aprendizaje de lenguas. Prototipos de tercera generación*. Barcelona: Publicacions de la Universitat de Barcelona, 1997.

Ribé, Ramón and Núria Vidal. *Project Work Step by Step*. Oxford: Heinemann, 1993.

Ribé, Ramón and Núria Vidal. *"Una propuesta de materiales para la enseñanza del inglés." Enseñar y aprender inglés en la educación secundaria*. Barcelona: ICE/Horsori, 1997. 107-199.

Shor, Ira. *When Students Have Power: Negotiating Authority in a Critical Pedagogy*. Chicago: The University of Chicago Press, 1996.

Vygotsky, Lev. *Thought and Language*. Cambridge, Massachusetts: The MIT Press, 1986.

Bibliography of Project Texts

Alberti, R. *La arboleda perdida*. Barcelona: Seix Barral, 1978. 11.

Aldecoa, J. R. *Historia de una maestra*. Barcelona: Editorial Anagrama, 1994.

Allende, I. Afrodita: *Cuentos, Recetas y Otros Afrodisíacos*. Barcelona: Plaza Janés, 1997.

Cruz Ruiz, J. *El territorio de la memoria*. Barcelona: Ediciones del Bronce, 1997.

Casal, L. *"Entre mis recuerdos"* in *Como la flor prometida*. CD Hispavox, 1995. Available at: http://www.guitarra.net/acord865.htm

Esquivel, L. *Como agua para chocolate*. New York: Anchor Books, Doubleday, 1997. 3-4.

Gazarian-Gautier, M.L. *Ana María Matute. La voz del silencio*. Madrid: Editorial Espasa Calpe, 1997.

Hinton, S. *El noi de la moto*. Barcelona: Editorial Empúries, 1989.

Maraini, D. *Dulce de por sí*. Barcelona: Seix Barral. Biblioteca Breve, 1998. 76-77.

Montero, M. *"Mientras ellos vuelven."* Madrid: El País, 9/8/1998.

Preciado, N. *Amigos íntimos*. Madrid: Ediciones Temas de Hoy, 1998.

Proust, M. *"Por el camino de Swann"* in *En busca del tiempo perdido*. Traducción de Pedro Salinas. Madrid: Alianza Editorial, 1976.

Puértolas, Soledad. *La vida oculta*. Barcelona: Anagrama, 1993.

Ràfols Casamada, A. *El arte visto por los artistas*. Francisco Calvo Serraller, ed. Ontario: Taurus, 1987.

Serrat, J.M. *"El Mediterráneo"* and *"Mi niñez."* Antología 1968- 1974. NY: RCA, BMG U.S. Latin, 1994. Available at: http://www.todomusica.org/serrat/disco7.shtml#1 and http://www.todomusica.org/serrat/disco9.shtml#1

Tamaro, S. *Donde el corazón te lleve*. Barcelona: Editorial Seix Barral, 1995.

Torrente Ballester, Gonzalo. *El oficio de escritor*. A. Ayuso, ed. Madrid: Ediciones y talleres de escritura creativa Fuentetaja, 1997. 30-31.

Other Recommended Texts

Arias Argüelles-Meres, Luis. *Último tren a Cuba.* Sitges, Barcelona: Editorial Premura, 2000.

Chacel, R. *Memorias de Leticia Valle.* Barcelona: Editorial Lumen, 1997.

Folkenflik, Robert, ed. *The Culture of Autobiography: Constructions of Self-Representation.* Stanford, CA: Stanford University Press, 1993.

García, Cristina. *Soñar en cubano,* New York: Ballantine Books, 1993.

Gruwell, Erin. *The Freedom Writers Diary.* New York, NY: Doubleday.

Lejeune, P. *El pacto autobiográfico y otros estudios.* Madrid: Megazul-Endymion, 1994.

Roura, A. *La mujer ante el espejo.* Barcelona: Thassàlia, 1997.

Santiago, Esmeralda. *Cuando era puertorriqueña.* NY: Vintage Books, 1994.

Acknowledgements

I would like to thank Carmen Fernández-Santás for her ideas and support in writing this chapter.

Chapter 8

Challenging Perspectives: Lessons From and For the Changing Spanish Classroom

Zena Moore
University of Texas at Austin

Although teaching culture has been one of the most heavily debated topics in the profession for over forty years, it was not until recently that teachers had access to national guidelines for culture teaching. The *Standards for Foreign Language Learning* urge teachers to design activities for student interaction with native speakers that can increase understanding of the foreigner's perspectives, values and beliefs. Yet, the "foreigners" in many schools (those of Texas, for example) happen to be of Mexican, Central American, or Caribbean Spanish-speaking ancestries who, because of the structure of the school system, often find themselves enrolled in Spanish classes alongside monolingual Anglo students. Thus, while the *Standards* contain very clear guidelines for the teaching of culture, the school population for whom the guidelines were meant has changed, is changing, and, according to the latest U.S. census report, will continue to change even more rapidly in the future. So, too, must our foreign language curriculum.[1]

In light of this drastically changing school population, what cultures and which cultural aspects should foreign language teachers select to teach? Will they highlight Mexican "mainstream" culture if the school population is close to the Mexican border, Puerto Rican or Colombian culture if they teach in Queens or in the Bronx? Furthermore, how should teachers of Spanish approach the teaching of culture, and what do we know of typical practice in culture teaching at the middle and high school levels? Years ago, Galloway (1985) reported four commonly observed approaches to teaching culture: 1) the "Frankenstein Approach" in which bits and pieces of unrelated information of the target culture are selected for learning, with the end result often being a distorted, even monstrous, depiction; 2) the "4-F Approach," which consists of festivals, food, folk dances and fairs, typically held on dedicated "culture days;" 3) the "Tour Guide" approach, in which the teacher presents information on monuments, rivers, cities, famous personages and their works; and 4) the "By-the-Way" Approach," in which the teacher presents sporadic lectures or anecdotes to highlight striking differences between two cultures. In these four approaches, there are several common features: a lack of structure and/or systematic planning for culture teaching; a tendency to exoticize the "other" culture, to cloak it in unexplained strangeness; the presentation of culture as novelty, incidental to the real tasks of language instruction; and, finally, the perception of culture teaching as mere "delivery of information," with the teacher being the guardian of its vault, deciding not only what to dispense, but when, how—indeed if—to dispense it. Granting as norm the existence of these four approaches raises several questions: Why do teachers select such topics for culture teaching? Are American students motivated more by food, music, and festivals than by any other stimuli? Why do teachers select what is "different" as a way of stimulating students' interest? But more importantly, if indeed culture and language are inseparable, why does the Spanish syllabus not reflect their integration?

This chapter is aimed at broadening the dialogue between teachers across school sites and across states wherever Spanish is taught. The data that form the basis for each of the "Cases" in this chapter come from three years of working with Spanish teachers in three public schools. To better understand the contexts in which the Cases emerged, I will provide a brief description of the school sites and populations where the data were collected. I will then use excerpts from seminar discussions, observations of classroom practice and examination of teachers' lessons and reflective journal entries as ways of introducing the challenges and problems of teaching culture in the real world of the U.S. high school Spanish classroom. The student teachers presented in the six Cases were given the specific tasks of documenting the culture lessons they observed during their student-teaching semester and writing reflective pieces on these observations. As reflective writing is one aspect of teacher education philosophy that aims at encouraging student teachers to be thoughtful and self-assessing practitioners, it was hoped that this experience would give them pause to assess and subsequently strive to improve their culture teaching.

As we will see, the concerns raised and discussed in the Cases essentially emerge from three pedagogic practices: a teacher-centered approach, a textbook-driven curriculum and a lack of reflection in teaching. A teacher-centered approach results in teachers perceiving themselves as dispensers of knowledge and sole decision-makers. A textbook-driven curriculum tends to discourage the use of supplementary authentic material and encourage an over-dependence on textbooks and an incorrect notion that completion of the textbook ensures learning. Finally, the role of teacher as sole decision-maker denies student input and autonomy and minimizes collaboration, thus negating three essential aspects of successful learning.

Lessons from the Real World of Teaching

The data presented in this chapter were collected while working with pre-service and in-service teachers of Spanish in the three Texas public schools that serve as professional sites for student-teacher field experience and observation. Two of these are low-income high schools and the third is a middle school where the majority of students come from upper-middle-income family backgrounds. In these settings, students carry out an 'internship' prior to their actual student-teaching experience. Thus, they are introduced to the school culture and to real school situations at a very early stage, witnessing students move from class to class, strolling the corridors, hanging out in locker areas, lunching in the cafeteria. Removing the methods course from the university to an authentic high school teaching site was one way of relating what students learn about teaching to what they actually do in the classroom. The weekly seminar component of this methods course was part of sharing these experiences. The student teachers generally are female, from Anglo middle-income family backgrounds. There may be a few native speakers from a number of Spanish-speaking countries, but these also generally come from similar middle-income family backgrounds and are also female in the main. The student populations of these schools, however, are very diverse—composed of Anglo, African American, and "Hispanic" origins, as well as recent immigrants from Eastern European and African countries.

Case 1. Famous Personalities

The lesson described here was taught by a cooperating teacher to an eighth-grade class composed mainly of native speakers of Spanish. Although the majority of these were from Mexico, there were several from Guatemala and Honduras, one from Cuba and one from the Dominican Republic. The "non-native" speakers were also from Spanish-speaking families but they themselves spoke very little Spanish. The teacher in this Case is a native speaker with over twelve years of teaching experience. Although she currently teaches Spanish, she was trained as an ESL teacher, a phenomenon that is quite common in Texas, according to a recent state survey. Most experienced Spanish teachers, in fact, were trained in areas other than Spanish; yet, because many of them are native speakers they were given Spanish classes to teach (Moore, Morales & Carel). This lesson was the teacher's sole attempt over an entire semester to include a culture component.

The teacher prepared a number of names of "famous people" and placed them in an envelope. Students were asked to draw a name from the envelope, conduct research on that famous person over a three-week period, and prepare a short presentation in English for the class. The project was worth thirty percent of the final grade; yet, in a class of thirty-five students, only ten completed the assignment. In fact, the same activity was used in all three of the teacher's classes with the same poor results: lack of interest and little motivation to complete the task. In their weekly seminar, the student teachers discussed these disappointing results:

Student Teacher 1:	They just don't care. You know, they just don't care. They are not interested in learning.
Student Teacher 2:	That's not true…I don't agree.
Methods supervisor:	Why do you say that?
Student teacher 2:	Why couldn't they choose whom they want to research? I mean, if you are a Mexican teenager, why would you want to know about a 14th-century poet from Spain?
Student Teacher 1:	Because they have to learn about famous people in the culture, that's why!
Student Teacher 2:	Are you saying they cannot choose famous people from their culture?
Student Teacher 1:	That's right! They don't know…that's why she (the cooperating teacher) prepared the list…

Student Teacher 2:   I refuse to believe that! Yesterday one guy in class was reading some newspaper the day before, or listening to the TV and he asked me, Miss, who is César Chávez? My goodness, some of them live on Chávez Street and they know Guadalupe and San Jacinto Streets. Why can't we begin with what they know?

Discussion of Case 1. This culture lesson is an illustration of Galloway's "tour guide" approach (1985). It was connected to the chapter in the textbook that dealt with "famous Hispanics." As is the case with public-school teachers across the country, the teachers in these schools are bound by the textbooks that the school district selects. Furthermore, in one of the schools, the principal had mandated that teachers include the completion of the textbook as one of their major instructional goals as, according to the principal, textbook completion was one way of ensuring both accountability to the parents and equality in learning activities. Completion of the textbook, however, does not mean that students must do all the exercises as set out in the chapters; rather, teachers can select those activities they consider most important and, typically, those activities dealing with culture are considered by teachers to be less important than those targeting grammar practice. In addition, the textbook's culture information is usually presented in reading passages accompanied by comprehension questions without further suggestion as to how the "culture topics" might be taught or expanded. The teacher in this Case thought that she was being creative in expanding on the textbook topic through out-of-class activity. In that way, she said, the students would not "lose valuable class time." Even though the class was composed of native speakers, the teacher said that she used the same approach in all of her other classes so that the "kids would not feel any different."

Several researchers have advocated a cross-cultural approach that begins with students becoming aware of their own cultural values (Galloway 1992; Heusinkveld; Kramsch; Ortuño). Over twenty years ago, Hanvey recommended the development of cross-cultural awareness for fostering insight into and, ultimately, empathy toward other perspectives; indeed, according to Seelye, empathy should be the ultimate cultural goal. The students in this class, in spite of being native speakers of Spanish, came from different cultural backgrounds. A cross-cultural approach, for example, that examined cultural patterns across various groups within one culture, may have served to develop their awareness that within Hispanic cultures there are differences as well as similarities, and that such similarities and differences vary according to geographical location, family income levels, age, gender, religious beliefs, ethnicity, generation, and so on. By encouraging students to reflect on their own cultural and personal values, teachers can pave the way for understanding the values in the "other" culture.

Taking into consideration the time constraints imposed by syllabus demands, perhaps teachers require more direct training in the design of activities that can connect to topics in the textbook through clearly structured lesson plans. For example, this lesson, instead of focusing on famous people as "cultural products," could have focused on *fame* as a cultural phenomenon, with a lesson objective stated thusly: "Students will develop an awareness of fame as a phenomenon in and across cultures." Having stated the lesson objective, the teacher can then design a number of group activities to achieve it. For example, students can be asked to select a famous personality from their cultural community and discuss why he or she is famous and what qualities and/or accomplishments they, themselves, admire about this person. The teacher can prepare questions as prompts to get the discussions going, such as: Who has the power in any cultural group to decide who is famous or to make people famous? Famous to whom and for what? How are the media used to promote fame in the U.S. and in other countries? Is importance given to sport personalities across cultures? Do poets and writers, scientists and philosophers in other countries enjoy as much fame and popularity as television and film stars in the U.S.? Why or why not? Students can then be asked to bring to class pictures from popular magazines or from the Internet and discuss popular icons from their culture with the objective of learning how the fame was achieved, how the person's fame reflects what is valued by a people, and what structures within a society help to create and promote "famous" personalities. Activities like these can help students develop a perspective for understanding what creates mainstream cultures and marginalizes others, and why marginalized cultures can be attractive to disempowered groups—topics that can be very appealing to students in high schools where cliques are popular. In short, students may come to understand what the French philosopher, Pierre Bourdieu, refers to as 'ways of knowing and understanding the world.'

First lesson to be learned. Begin with what students know. In the new foreign language classroom, the C1 will be very diverse. Instruction must first validate the individual's own culture, encourage investigation of students' own identity and, through sharing with classmates, guide learners to experience the diversity of identities in their own community. In addition, middle-school learners are at a developmental stage in their lives that makes the topics of fame and popularity very appealing. Even if the teacher uses the same approach to teaching culture with non-native speakers, the objective remains the same.

Case 2. A By-the-way Approach

The following lesson took place midway through the semester and was prompted by the fact that at that point the cooperating teacher had not given any attention to incorporating culture into any of her lessons. The group in this Case was a seventh-grade class composed of students from upper-middle-income families. The student population was mainly Anglo-American with a few students from Mexican families. The student teacher lived in a border town and was bilingual from a Mexican family. As a college student at an institution of predominantly Anglo population, she attended Spanish-for-native-speakers classes. She confessed to having learned nothing about other Spanish-speaking cultures as a student in classes that had focused on Mexican history and culture, and thus expressed surprise during the methods course that other Spanish-speaking countries did not celebrate "*el cinco de mayo*." From discussions in the methods course, she quickly realized that she was ignorant of other Hispanic cultures and, since the city in which she lived is nationally recognized for its musical promotions and abounds with salsa clubs, she thus decided to learn about *salsa* by going to dance classes. The following excerpt is taken from this student teacher's post-evaluation reflections on her own lesson.

I wanted to share with you that I had so much fun teaching this lesson. I decided to teach my students about culture. I feel that too often foreign language teachers concentrate on just teaching the language and forget the whole make-up about culture. I taught the students a little history about Latin/Spring celebrations. I also decided to teach them how to *Salsa* dance so I also threw in *Salsa* history. I explained its roots and how it got to be a big deal. I talked about Calle Ocho (in Miami), about Carnaval, Fidel Castro and the Marielitos...They took notes as I talked and I could tell that they enjoyed the activity because they kept asking and answering each other's questions. All this was on Thursday. Friday, I taught them to dance *Salsa*. I was real nervous because I didn't know how they would respond. BUT it was a huge success! Some kids came in after class to listen to the music and dance some more.

I think more teachers should concentrate on teaching culture. Kids love all that stuff, not just the part where you have culture day and bring some food...Students want to learn why things are the way they are! We need to give them more credit and allow them to explore other cultures. This helps them in life outside school. Now my kids can tell other people about a Latin experience that is very real to them.

Discussion of Case 2. An examination of the detailed lesson that the student teacher appended to her journal entry provided information that clarified her reflective notes. The student teacher had disseminated website notes that dealt with the widespread popularity of *salsa* and its Afro-Cuban influences. Even though she did not mention the word "perspective," she clearly felt that the introduction of information explaining why *salsa* enjoys such popularity was important for the students in understanding the phenomenon from the viewpoint of other peoples. She wrote that she "threw in some *salsa* history" as a way of providing background information, and her handout indicated that she had informed students that *salsa* originated in Cuba in the 1960s but that by the 1970s it had been embraced by Puerto Ricans, especially in New York—the city considered the cradle of *salsa* music in that era. *Salsa* has achieved popularity not only in Latin American countries but also in non-Latin countries such as Sweden and Japan.

The topic of *salsa* was selected by the teacher because she loved dancing and was motivated to share her interest with the students. She interpreted their response as one of lively interest when she wrote that students "loved all that stuff." The lesson was conducted in the following way: The student teacher provided handouts on the history of *salsa*, which students read and discussed in pairs. Then, using the overhead projector, she presented pictures of some *salsa* musicians. During this presentation, the students took notes and conversed with one another about the dress, instruments and physical appearance of the musicians. She also provided information on Fidel Castro and his invitation to exiled Cubans to return to Cuba and take back to the U.S. any Cubans who wished to leave. In May 1980 those who wished to leave Cuba, one hundred twenty-five thousand of them, gathered at the port of Mariel. These emigrants were mainly of African heritage and from poor areas and thus the phenomenon of *cubanía* emerged in little Havana, Miami as a preservation of Afro-Cuban culture. Listening to samples of *salsa* music and learning its dance were the following day's lesson activities. As part of the listening activity, the students listened to one *salsa* song and wrote down words they understood. This task was followed by discussion of the content and meaning of the song.

In her comments, this student teacher had expressed a slight but detectable impatience towards the common practice of having a "culture day" in which teachers "bring some food." In this regard, her attitude was similar to that of one of the student teachers of Case 1 who had expressed the belief that teachers do not challenge students enough. Yet, both her rationale for and approach to "teaching culture" in this lesson were not markedly different from the 4-F mindset that gives rise to the " culture-as-food-day" practice. For one, she had singled out a cultural product, *salsa*, but made no connections to the students' own cultural products. She could have approached *salsa* as an example of the expression of a marginalized group and had students suggest musical forms from their own cultures that they might consider as the voice of outcast peoples, such as that of jazz in its early history. Like *salsa*, jazz, blues, rap and hip-hop arose from the identities of their creators. Jazz and blues originated with African-Americans relegated to low status within the wider community whose ostracism took voice in their music. Likewise, *salsa* did not originate with the light-skinned Spanish-Cubans but with Afro-Cubans in poor rural neighborhoods; the rhythms and lyrics of *salsa* are heavily influenced by African slave songs and dances. Moreover, the importation-rejection-acceptance of *salsa* in Miami and other areas of the U.S. is a striking example of what happens when diverse cultures come in contact. The objective of such a lesson, then, could have been: "Students will learn that cultures are always changing, synthesizing and sincretizing, and people as culture bearers are the producers of these changes." Cross-cultural activities could have included comparisons of rap from Jamaica and its influence in the U.S., or the use of the accordion and the influence of German polka and vals on Mexican *corrido* and *conjunto* music. Students may have been interested in learning how African cultures have affected their own culture today, not only in music and food but in the oral art forms of "dizzing" and doing the "dozens" (Gates).

Although the students of this class had fun with the *salsa* activities—and much learning can take place in fun-filled activity—all evidence suggests that culture was not a structured and consistent part of the syllabus. The *salsa* lesson took place at the end of the week when entertaining activities relieve boredom. With such a random and casual approach, students may be left with some rather stereotypical impressions of the culture. Moreover, in this lesson, perhaps the most important cross-cultural aspect was overlooked: the different values associated with dancing. Students could have been given further tasks, for example, that focused on comparing dance across cultures. Most significantly, in spite of the fact that little culture was taught in this class, the teacher continued to perform the role as main provider of information. There was little attempt to have students develop their own research skills, to learn from each other, or to learn from the members of Spanish-speaking communities where they lived (see Heusinkveld, this volume).

In addition, how would such lessons be received by those shy, self-conscious students who do not wish to participate in dancing? For these students, the teacher could have planned alternative activity. She did include information of the history of *salsa* and the significance of Calle Ocho today in Miami; she also spoke of its Afro-Cuban origin. To expand on this, however, she could have introduced some fragments from the popular Hollywood film *Dance with Me* and had students compare the controlled, mechanical style of dancing the *salsa*, as demonstrated by Vanessa Williams, to the spontaneous, "authentic" versions witnessed in the clubs of Miami and in the style of Cheyenne, the Puerto Rican co-star of the film.

Second lesson to be learned. Middle-school students are synergistic learners requiring involvement of their total physical being in the learning process. Having students learn to dance *salsa* brought a new dimension to experiencing a cultural product and practice. Learning about the history of the dance, its origin and its increasing popularity can afford students the opportunity to capture perspectives underlying the product in practice. However, the students themselves had no input into the selection of the topic. The teacher did what so many foreign language teachers do with newly discovered cultural information and experiences that they cannot wait to share with their students: They teach the students the songs they know and play the music they like; they decorate the classroom with tourist posters they acquired on their visit to the target country. In sum, they create an exotic if not distorted picture of the culture. We must remember that the teacher's role is not to be the dispenser of cultural knowledge but to create, design and plan activities whereby students take ownership of their own learning. Making connections to their own cultures is critical to their identification, acceptance and ultimate appreciation of other perspectives.

Case 3: Multicultural Days That Exoticize the "Other"

In the three schools discussed here, there is an annual school-wide celebration of a "Multicultural Day" that constitutes an attempt to embrace and celebrate the cultural diversity of the student population. In one of the two high schools, this day provided the only evidence of culture "instruction" over one academic year. Apart from Mexican folk dances and pictorial displays, the emphasis of these events is always on food. Families and friends are invited to present short lectures on their countries and bring in samples of "ethnic" food for the students to experience. This practice of giving importance to food as a culture lesson created quite a discussion among the student teachers. Once again, commentary began with the complaint that there was a total disregard for the students' input in their learning. One student teacher opined that such food-events are not healthy practice when there are "so many obese kids" in the schools: "We are ignoring that fact...we keep focusing on food!"

Discussion of Case 3. The celebration of a multicultural day probably occurs in most schools as a public attempt to celebrate the cultural diversity of the student population. Most of the time, however, it is simply tokenism, as the word "ethnic" is used to describe anything that is non-Anglo and representation of Anglo cultures themselves is strikingly absent. Thus, while schools are to be applauded for recognizing and promoting cultural diversity, the highlighting of "ethnic" cultures may, in fact, simply serve to widen the cultural divide. Moreover, such an approach does injustice to Anglo-Americans, as all of our students have rich ancestral roots. Anglo students may welcome a culture lesson on the influences of Germany, Italy, Ireland and England on present-day U.S. culture or on the influence of foreign languages on North American English. Many high school students, for example, are unaware of the origin of such "typical U.S. products" as baseball, American football, the hot dog and hamburger, mistletoe and Christmas trees.

In the Case presented here, the student teachers agreed that they could not ignore the fact that obesity has reached epidemic proportions in the U.S. and suggested that teaching about food in the classroom must include treatment of health-related issues (see Galloway, this volume). Since many of their students come from other-than-Anglo backgrounds, they felt that they had an added obligation to make what they taught relevant to these students' needs. All the student teachers belonged to gyms, and regular workouts were very important to them—were they unwittingly imposing their own cultural values on the students? They, themselves, may have been unaware that they were responding to their own culture's middle-class values, that is, a preoccupation with weight. Indeed, full-bodiness in some cultures is considered an outward sign of family wealth and beauty; thus, what is considered "ideal" or "overweight" may differ across cultures. Seelye (54) offers suggestions for examining such culturally conditioned images without causing embarrassment to students. Once again, the language used to express size and weight should be incorporated into the lesson on culture, as words such as *flaquita* and *gordita* carry quite different connotations from those of the American English "skinny" and "fat." Students may become more aware of the total integration of language and culture when they analyze the influence of political correctness on the use of certain expressions dealing with body image. Examination of the diminutive "*-ito(a)*" can also lead to an understanding that these suffixes connote much more than size.

The fact that there was animated discussion of the appropriateness of focusing a lesson on obesity is a cultural phenomenon. With irrefutable evidence that obesity in the U.S. is increasing among younger children, a number of health-related issues rise to prominence, among them heart problems and diabetes. The student teachers discussed their role as language teachers and their response to the situation. They all agreed that they should include the topic as part of their teaching and suggested that the multicultural day could be improved if they used cross-cultural activities involving the cultural groups represented in the school. What would the cultural objective be in the Spanish classes? Seelye (59) presents an example of how food can be related to his broad seven cultural goals. He begins with behavior patterns associated with the production and consumption of food and concludes with the learner's interest in trying new foods and developing a taste for something new and different. High school teachers may find this model useful, as they can use the topic of food as the base for the lessons and integrate the other four skills in activities that involve students in designing their own daily menus, examining ingredients on food boxes, conducting surveys on eating habits in the school cafeteria, and suggesting healthier foods for young people, for example. Galloway (this volume) suggests having students compare food pyramids of U.S., Latin America and the Mediterranean; Ulloa Rodríguez provides a brief but effective lesson on nutrition in Spanish on her web page.

Spanish teachers can improve on the annual celebration of multicultural days in their school by designing the type of lessons that help students develop broader understanding of the interplay of such factors as religion, geography, economy and history in influencing cultural products and perspectives on healthy living. For example, in many Spanish-speaking countries, abstinence from meat on Fridays during Lent, a practice that originated in Roman Catholic teaching, has become part of everyday life. The influence of the Roman Catholic religion is widespread across Hispanic cultures and students could benefit from an awareness of how religion affects their own value system, lifestyle, and even the very school curriculum they follow.

Third lesson to be learned. This Case provides several examples of what teachers should avoid in their well-intentioned efforts to teach culture. First, teaching culture should not be limited to one day of the week, let alone one day per year, as this conveys to students that culture is not an integral component of language. Second, the study of food must go beyond "tasting" and "eating." Using Seelye's seven goals for cultural understanding as a guide, teachers can explore a topic such as food from many angles of product and practice. For example, what is the role and meaning of pan across the Hispanic world and how does this differ from U.S. associations with "bread?" Discussion of such basic food items can lead students to an awareness that what they eat depends largely on geographical location, climate, religious and historical influences and economic conditions.

Case 4: Expanding on the *Notas Culturales*

The lesson of this Case, planned for tenth-grade heritage language speakers, was taught by the cooperating teacher and documented by the student teacher in her reflective journal:

> I observed a culture lesson for Spanish Level 3 about the muralists in Mexico and why the government had asked these muralists during the 1920s and 1930s to paint murals on the buildings depicting important historical events of the country. The teacher began by giving the students an historical explanation of the creation of murals. Murals, according to the textbook notes, were a way of teaching an illiterate people. Moving from the general, the teacher then introduced three famous muralists. She showed pictures copied from the Internet and then focused on one particular painter, Frida Kahlo, the wife of one of the most famous muralists, Diego Rivera.
>
> There was a picture of Frida Kahlo in the textbook and the teacher asked the students to comment on it. To capture the students' interest, the teacher talked about the upcoming movie with Salma Hayek and the fight between Salma Hayek, Jenifer López and Madonna to play Frida…The teacher also brought in a short biography of Frida Kahlo (from the Internet). She divided the class into groups and each group got a different section of the biography, which was written in Spanish. Each group had to read its section of the biography and present five facts to the rest of the class.
>
> The students were very interested in the lesson because the teacher found so many ways to make the story come alive by mentioning details like Frida's accident, the fact that she was twenty years younger than Diego Rivera and she was able to tie the lesson to students' interest in movies and Hollywood stars.

Discussion of Case 4. The class was that of a low-income high school, but there were twenty computer stations in the library. The teacher planned for the students to work in pairs at the computers while she moved around the lab to provide assistance where needed. The librarian assistant was also available to provide technical support. Three simple steps to locate the websites were posted on the wall for all to see. To minimize technical problems and maximize class time, the librarian was asked to prepare all the computers to make connections to Yahoo and the students entered the lab to find the computers ready for use. The students were given the specific tasks of accessing a website on muralists in general and then selecting one painter who appealed to them. They were also required to print one of the paintings and explain why it appealed to them. What seemed to have captured the interest and admiration of the student teacher in this lesson was the attempt by the cooperating teacher to supplement the textbook information with materials taken from other sources including the Internet. The inclusion of additional material, such as information on the then-upcoming movie, made the topic interesting and relevant to students' lives at that moment. Having students work with the technology to carry out specific tasks was also a positive feature of the lesson.

The computer is generally underused in most public schools across the nation, for reasons ranging from teachers' lack of technological proficiency to a lack of knowledge of how to plan for the integration of technology into daily lesson planning (Moore, Morales & Carel). Computers are designed for individual work and the foreign language classrooms in the three schools described here are not equipped with computers for every student. Thus, one of the challenges teachers face is that of creating activities that can be completed by three or four students working at one computer station. Such activities, if not carefully monitored, can become very disruptive and noisy, two facets of classroom behavior that may be deemed undesirable. Although students can engage in meaningful conversations in Spanish while they perform the tasks, when teachers are pressured to ensure silence in the classroom, interactive learning is minimized.

Research tells us that teachers tend to rely on the textbook as the major source of cultural information (Moore 1996). Fortunately, however, computer technology—especially the Internet—offers a possible solution to the complaint of lack of time for culture. Lee and Osuna and Meskill provide examples of how students can increase cultural awareness through Web interaction with native speakers, for example. Yet, research on the use of technology to teach culture has been mostly limited to college settings where computers are used primarily to access information. Flipping through pages in a textbook or locating a book on a library shelf are tasks that are cognitively no different than surfing the net—the ultimate purpose is locating information. While it is true that more information is available at the click of a mouse and the access is speedy, the teacher must have clearly stated objectives, as what students do with the information is more important than the act of acquiring the information itself. Moreover, given that we now have information instantly at our fingertips, it has become increasingly important to teach learners how to evaluate the source of information encountered via the Internet. The cover or preface of a book may reveal where an author is "coming from," for example, but many times a website will not, and as students now have ready access to literally any information on any topic, the primary problem teachers face is that of teaching learners how to detect bias, how to discriminate between subjective and objective, how to screen fact from opinion or conjecture.

Aside from the information-access capabilities of the Internet, what are some other ways in which technology can aid the learning of culture? Among the few studies that focus on high school students learning aspects of the foreign culture is that of Carel, who designed a piece of software for teaching pragmatics. Although its focus was on learning French, the study showed that high school students can acquire an understanding of discourse styles of another language. Using clips of real-life conversations that take place in the home, at school, and in other public and private places, Carel created a CD-ROM to help students become aware of cultural differences in greetings, turn taking, interactive distance and gestures. These features of speech acts are generally not taught in high schools—nor at the college level, for that matter. Nevertheless, their neglect is one of the primary sources of intercultural miscommunication (see García, this volume). U.S. turn-taking patterns, for example, are very different from those of most Spanish speakers who can carry on several conversations at the same time, resulting in what Anglos refer to as "noisy" behavior (see González, this volume). Turn-taking behavior also differs within a culture—between genders, for example (Tannen). Many years ago, Edward Hall pointed out that ignorance as to the concept and use of space across cultures can lead to misinterpretation and rigid, negative stereotypes. Indeed, students from Hispanic cultures should be taught the differences in time, space and physical proximity in order to avoid misunderstandings with their Anglo teachers (see Humbach, this volume). Such misunderstandings can have serious emotional effect, as witnessed by one student teacher who moved from South America and placed her nine-year-old in a predominantly Anglo elementary school: The young child was accustomed to hugging her former teacher and kissing her farewell at the end of the day. But when she approached her new Anglo teacher with the same emotional spontaneity, she was gently pushed away. The child considered the action a rebuke and from that day became withdrawn, not only unsure of how to behave in the new classroom, but reticent in hugging and kissing even her own parents. Her work, in turn, suffered, and the parents were forced to change schools.

Fourth Lesson Learned. This lesson illustrates how teachers can employ computer technology in the teaching of culture, though admittedly the application of technology in this Case was limited and could be greatly improved. In addition, a focus on the life of Frida Kahlo could have integrated fragments of the film *The Two Fridas* (available on video) to invoke discussion of such themes as gender roles, coping with disability, and perceptions of body image and self-esteem. Topics such as these have great appeal for the students in this high school since they live in a city in which body piercing and imaging are becoming more and more popular. The use of multimedia with the computer as central tool can be of far greater advantage than the computer alone.

Case 5: Using Bloom's Taxonomy

A group of six teachers planned this lesson based on their belief that teachers do not challenge students sufficiently. They asked a middle-school seventh-grade teacher in the group to try it out with her class and report on what happened. The students of the middle school came primarily from the three major groups: Anglo-Americans, African-Americans and Hispanics. The teachers were interested in finding out if seventh-grade students could achieve the learning outcomes set out for them.

Using the Spanish bullfight as the case to be studied, the objective given to the students was that they would come to an understanding that "animals enjoy different status in different cultures." The students were given the task of arguing whether or not bullfighting represents cruelty to animals and should be stopped. The task was considered relevant because of the appearance of an article in the local newspaper that had denounced bullfighting as a "cruel cultural practice." The teachers decided to use a cross-cultural approach employing Bloom's taxonomy to guide the outcomes for each activity. They had discussed the *Standards* and the focus on products, practices and perspectives and believed that their biggest challenge was to create activities that helped students become aware of other perspectives. They had all learned about Bloom's taxonomy during their courses in Education Psychology and Instructional Material Design and were curious to discover if could be used as a practical guide for their lesson plan. They knew that taxonomy is a hierarchical classification such that one must reach the first level before the second. The stages are: a) knowledge of the topic; b) comprehension of the topic demonstrated in their ability to talk to a group of uninformed people about it; c) application as shown in their ability to write a rationale that reflects a certain philosophy; d) analysis or the ability to write a rationale to determine what the philosophy is; e) synthesis as exemplified by an ability to plan a lesson that reflects the philosophy and f) evaluation to see whether the activities achieved the intentions set out in the rationale. The students therefore created six activities guided by the levels in the taxonomy.

The class was divided into six groups. The first group was to use the Internet to locate information on a famous bullfighter. The teacher singled out one specific bullfighter because his was a rags-to-riches story not unlike that of many African American sports figures. The second group read the poem "*Llanto por Ignacio Sánchez Mejías*" by Federico García Lorca, which deals with the death of another famous bullfighter. The task of the third group was to examine three posters advertising bullfights to 1) identify differences and similarities in posters used in their own cultures and 2) create a poster of their own to advertise a bullfight that would appeal to audiences in those cities of the U.S. where bullfights are held regularly. The fourth group read a passage, with accompanying pictures and drawings, about the making of the matador's outfit. The fifth group prepared to talk about the different roles played by the various actors of the bullfighting spectacle. The sixth group's task was to collect recent information on bullfights as a tourist attraction. At the end of three weeks, each group shared what they had learned with the rest of the class. The students would then synthesize the information from all six groups and vote on whether or not bullfighting did encourage cruelty to animals.

Discussion of Case 5. The teacher encouraged students to locate and share information about bullfighting and to then use the information collected to reach a decision. Students learned that bullfighting had much in common with sports around the world: It is a way to achieve fame and honor; it requires a great deal of training and talent; it celebrates man's prowess, bravery and grace (as well as the bull's). It involved more than just killing a bull and many more "players" than the torero and the toro. Some students using the Internet retrieved information that dealt with the rearing and selection of the bulls and what is done with the bulls that are not selected for the fight. They learned that in reality only a few bulls are killed each year and that bulls chosen for fights are deemed to be as noble as their fighters in their strength and bravery. Some bulls exhibit so much bravery, in fact, that spectators plead for them to be spared (similar to gladiator fighting in which the bravery of the slave many times was the price of freedom).

Some students compared aspects of cruelty in their own sports and the injuries inflicted on boxers and football and basketball players. Others mentioned deer hunting, which is very popular in the state where they live; in fact, they spoke of the season prior to the hunt when the deer are fattened for the kill. The big difference they noted was that deer hunting generally is not criticized as a form of cruelty to animals, speculating that perhaps it is seen more as a private past-time and less as a public spectacle for which an entrance fee is charged. The main difference, some thought, was that it was not a commercial undertaking for profit—no one recalled ever seeing a poster that advertised deer hunting, for example, and no marketing efforts appeared to be involved in the sport. Some concluded that it is the outsider who in many cases creates the negative or distorted view of the cultural phenomenon and that it is easier to adopt an outsider's skewed view because of partial knowledge and experience of the phenomenon. The students' vote was that bullfighting *not* be declared a form of "cruelty to animals" as any sporting activity can be viewed from different perspectives. In addition, recent information on bullfights as a tourist attraction pointed to a changing pattern, that of providing spectacles for curious tourists who visit the countries with stereotypical beliefs and expectations.

There is no doubt that this lesson could be improved. First, there was an absence of information from the "native" perspective. This omission could have been avoided by using the Internet to access Spanish or Mexican websites dedicated to the topic of bullfighting, where the voices from inside the cultures could be heard.[2] The teacher had used a newspaper article as the basis for this cultural lesson; however, more recent newspaper coverage of the Fiesta de San Fermin provided yet another illustration of how media can promote similar stereotypes of a foreign culture through images of tomato-throwing, champagne-spilling and general wanton behavior (and if we look closely, the primary actors in Pamplona are no longer Spaniards, but American college students!). Indeed, the effect of the media on global thinking is a rich classroom topic for the examination of how stereotypes are born and bred, and also of how positive change can be triggered (recent attention to the cocoa industry in the Ivory Coast, for example, has made the public aware of child and slave labor). Carefully designed activities on the mass media and its role in transforming cultures can help students increase their knowledge of world events and this increased knowledge can lead to a decrease in ethnocentrism for greater cultural understanding.

Fifth Lesson Learned. The teachers used Bloom's taxonomy of educational objectives and found that it was a useful guide to check the learning outcomes of each activity. The tasks showed good variety and, in some cases, did indeed move students from the first level of gathering factual information to a synthesis and application of the acquired information; in others of these tasks, however, this progression was much less evident and may have been altogether non-existent: For example, some students read García Lorca's poem, others read various types of other information, but given the loose structure of the tasks, it is unclear as to what was done with the knowledge gained from these readings in terms of individual synthesis and application. Unfortunately, this stage of information retrieval is, in fact, where all too many of our classroom culture activities end.

This Case presents the challenge of accessing other perspectives through critical inquiry in the study of culture. Works by three major philosophers not commonly found in foreign language discussions on teaching culture—Gramsci, Foucault and Bourdieu—provide broad theoretical frameworks by which to understand how perspectives are developed. The work of Gramsci can help us understand hegemony and hegemonic influences on any culture—why some cultures experience greater acceptance and value over others and why others are marginalized. Gramsci's work can help students and teachers understand why some cultural products and practices are exoticized and others are demonized—rap music, for example, continues to be associated with negative stereotypes. Foucault's work has been introduced into many disciplines because it provides a solid framework for understanding the power of discourse specifically, and the power of language-users generally. Social formations, according to Foucault, are produced by collections of discourses and the discourses define, construct and position individuals within those formations. Bourdieu states that we come to know the world in the "spaces" or physical locations we occupy—where one is born, where one resides, where one is schooled, and so on. Moving in and out of our "spaces" and crossing "borders" into "other spaces" occupied by the "other" can provide ways of understanding the other culture.

With these ideas in mind, perhaps the most important point we can make about this lesson was that for all its varied activities, avenues of inquiry and opportunities for student debate, it did not guide learners to access another cultural perspective. Students expressed their own opinions, but because they were not guided to hear the voices coming from the other culture, they never left their own culture's frame of reference or even the realm of their own limited experience. They decided the bullfight was not "cruelty," but they did this by comparing a practice that is not of their culture to one that is of their culture and deciding the two were "similar enough." But would Spaniards compare bullfighting to deer hunting? And if students had ultimately condemned the practice, would this condemnation have been extended to the Spanish culture as a whole, even in the mind of one individual? To judge a practice without hearing the voices of the owners of the practice, without hearing it debated amongst its own people so as to know their versions of its pros and cons, is tantamount to comparing "yours" to "mine" solely on the basis of my criteria. In this lesson, students heard only the discourse of their own spaces—they never "moved out of their own spaces" to cross the border into the space of the "other" (Bourdieu).

Case 6. Using Popular Songs

This lesson was taught to a high school class of mixed students—Anglo, Central and South American—who were preparing for AP exams. The stated objective was that students would understand some cultural differences between North America and South America. The lesson was introduced using a song by the Guatemalan Ricardo Arjona, titled "*Si el norte fuera el sur.*"[3] The students had several activities to complete. They began by asking the Hispanic students what they knew about the U.S. and Canada, including stereotypical beliefs and where these beliefs originated. Most of the Hispanic students admitted that their notions about the U.S. and Canada had come from films and television. Some students had heard about NAFTA and that there was a recent decision to build a new highway connecting their state to Canada. The second task was to discuss in groups what they knew about Central American and South American countries and the stereotypes they held about countries of these regions. As most of the Hispanic students came from recent immigrant families of low-income backgrounds, their knowledge of U.S. culture was very limited, as was their knowledge of other Spanish-speaking cultures. For example, they were not familiar with "el Ché," so the teacher explained the references to the personalities mentioned in the song.

As the third task, the teacher then divided the class into groups to read special sections of the song. Since this was a mixed class of native and non-native speakers, students were grouped so that each group benefited from the input of the native speakers' language proficiency. The fourth task had groups discuss the meaning of the lyrics and for the fifth task students came back together to share their thoughts and opinions. Their final task was to create their own song in which they speculated on what would happen if the North were to become the South. Considering that this was an AP class, the last task was considered challenging, yet within the students' capability.

Discussion of Case 6. Along with folk-dances and food, songs are the most popularly introduced cultural products in the foreign language classroom (Moore 1996). Teachers typically select songs based on accessibility or personal taste and preference. Generally, they are used as background music or as an entertainment activity where students actually learn some of the lyrics. Some teachers use songs for listening comprehension purposes, employing modified cloze or gap-fill procedures; other teachers use songs for sound discrimination. Both of these uses are designed to focus more on linguistic code than on cultural meaning; however, there is much more that can be done with songs. Brooks reminds us that music is culture in its most appealing form.

> The human voice and the printed line are not the only vehicles of culture available in the language classroom. The element of culture that is closest to language is music...music is welcomed in the language classroom not because it teaches language but also because it represents other elements of culture in a most appealing form (Brooks 210).

Songs, like language itself, are bearers of cultural messages and values. They can offer social commentaries and can be used as historical markers (see Heusinkveld, this volume). For example, the popular *tejano corridos* and *romances* created in the early forties are folk songs that celebrate a patriarchal culture through images of women as saints or devils (Moore, 1999). In fact, the treatment of women in songs can be a very appealing discussion in any classroom for the purposes of cross-cultural comparison: Do American folk songs depict women in the same way?

Although "*Si el norte fuera el sur*" was used in a lesson that showed the inseparable link between language and culture, the use of music in the foreign language classroom has another valuable goal—that of forging links between the two largest ethnic minority groups in this country, the African-American and the Hispanic. In the schools mentioned in this chapter, the students hang out in groups largely divided along ethnic lines. Differences between these two ethnic groups are often highlighted, but similarities are more often ignored. This same approach to comparing two groups has been traditionally used to teach culture in the foreign language classroom; however, highlighting the differences and ignoring the similarities tends to create the negative stereotypes. There are common features in African-American and Hispanic cultures, probably as a result of African diasporic influences. For example, the love of dancing, the love of singing, and the global popularity of art forms from both groups can be further explored in culture classes. And there is the added linguistic advantage gained by listening to music: Students can begin to develop what Brooks calls the "rhythm" and "beats" of the language.

Sixth Lesson learned. Songs and music, on the whole, are appealing to most students of any age and gender. However, as teachers, we can do much more than we are currently doing with these samples of authentic material. Songs are cultural products and their introduction in the classroom as such is valid and justified. But teachers can move beyond simply presenting the product to help students understand that all cultural products—songs, art works, monuments, and so on—reflect the culture of the time when they were created and reveal much about their creators. In this regard, the stated objective of the lesson, "to understand some cultural differences between North America and South America," is too vague in expression, too hit-and-miss in direction, to be of any use either to teachers or learners. Presenting a cultural product is not the end goal; it is only the beginning. As teachers, we must not simply conclude a cultural lesson with mere study of a product or mere demonstration of a practice. If we do, we deprive learners of the opportunity to build awareness of other ways of seeing the world and to grow, as well, in their understanding of themselves.

Conclusion

This chapter has been directed primarily to teachers who work with changing school populations. Teachers of school populations similar to those depicted here may find it useful to immerse themselves in the cultures of the Spanish-speakers who fill their classrooms. Today, this may not necessarily imply a "study abroad program," as teachers can broaden their notion of immersion in the foreign culture to include not only a "visit to the target country" but also a visit to the corner store that is owned and run by Spanish-speakers, to flea markets that are organized by Spanish-speakers for Spanish-speakers, to clubs and restaurants where they can listen and dance to Hispanic music, to church services in Spanish, even to Hispanic "Bingo nights," and of course the Internet offers tremendous exchange opportunities through informal and professional multi-culture chat sites. The schools mentioned in this chapter are fortunate to have populations that reflect many Hispanic cultures, but all of us need only look into our communities to see the wealth of resources that await us not only for enriching our language and culture instruction but also for growing ourselves.

The need to give more emphasis, direction and planning to culture teaching is even more urgent if we as educators are involved in the humanistic endeavor of educating people to live harmoniously in a country that is evermore multilingual and multiculturally diverse. Moreover, we cannot afford to have an isolationist view of our role in this regard: We are teachers first, and we are foreign language teachers second. Now more than ever, we must strive to integrate into our curricula the general aims of education as expressed thirty years ago in the 1971 National Conference on Youth Report: "The primary goal of education should be self-actualization of all individuals served, not perpetuation of individuals to fit existing social slots."

Traditionally, foreign language programs have emphasized grammatical exercises, vocabulary–building and translation. More recently, with the development of computer technology, there is more audiovisual material available on CD-ROMs. However, the lessons and discussions reported here are probably not unlike what happens across the nation, and experience working with the three schools has taught us several lessons: that students are highly motivated to learn about their own culture and the cultures of other groups; that teachers need on-going training in teaching to changing populations; and that, although textbooks have improved over the years, teachers still need skills to develop the types of syllabi that will enhance the integration and teaching of culture. As teachers continue to rely heavily on the textbook, what is needed is a clearer definition of how linguistic aspects can be taught within a cultural context by using and supplementing this resource. Moreover, pre-service and in-service training must continue to include courses on teaching culture with specific emphasis on developing cross-cultural perspectives.

As pointed out earlier, the *Standards* were written for the traditional foreign language student in traditional foreign language classrooms. Therefore, how the profession thinks about teaching culture may have to undergo a pedagogic shift, with teachers exploring more avidly the types of approaches used in multicultural classes. Traditionally, teachers spoke of the target culture, and culture was taught by comparing the first culture to the target culture. Teachers may benefit from examining other approaches used primarily in the field of anthropology. For example, in 1953 Florence Kluckhohn published what she called a "values orientation model" to identify specific patterns of behavior that make groups of people different from others. She identified several factors that include Innate Predisposition, Person-Nature Orientation, Time Orientation, Activity Orientation, and Human Relations Orientation. The Florence Kluckhohn Center in Seattle, Washington, continues to use her values orientations as a tool to examine, compare and contrast worldviews. Foreign language teachers can use her values orientation model to help students develop the type of cultural perspectives recommended in the *Standards* (see, for example, Galloway 1999). For example, students can be presented cases of culture clash and invited to speculate possible explanations for the confusion caused by differences in perception.

Finally, changes in how culture is taught must begin with an examination of the terminology traditionally used to teach culture in Spanish classrooms. For example, the term "Hispanic," although efficient and politically expedient (especially in professional discussions such as those of this volume), does not capture the distinct identities of students who come from Honduras, Ecuador, Cuba, Dominican Republic, Colombia, Argentina, and other South American and Central American countries and whose skin colors make them indistinguishable from African-Americans, Mexican-Americans, Italian-Americans and Anglo-Americans. Even the term "Mexican" causes some blurriness in identity creation: It does not quite capture how the sixteen-year-old from Querétaro and the fifteen-year-old from Guadalajara see themselves. In fact, many of the students in the schools mentioned in this chapter are confused by the label "Hispanic" so often used to describe them and insist on referring to themselves as U.S. citizens or Mexican-Americans, Nicaraguans, and so on. As the high school population continues to change in ethnic composition, teachers of foreign languages in general, and of Spanish specifically, are in a favorable position to initiate the type of pedagogic approaches that better cater to the needs of the students and of the nation as a whole.

Notes

[1] For thorough discussion of heritage learners in today's classroom, see John B. Webb and Barbara L. Miller, eds., *Teaching Heritage Language Learners: Voices from the Classroom.* ACTFL Series 2000. Yonkers, NY: American Council on the Teaching of Foreign Languages, 2000.

[2] Some websites providing the insider's perspective on bullfighting, pro and con, are:
http://apps3.vantagenet.com/zsv/survey.asp?finish=Finish&id=1218163556
http://www.angelfire.com/on3/animales/toros.html
http://www.terra.es/personal/rjdrcf/famosos.htm
http://mural.uv.es/vicnagil/motxalo.htm
http://www.webinet.com.ar/wwwboard/messages/155.html

[3] The lyrics to "*Si el norte fuera el sur*" can be found at: http://www.lrc.salemstate.edu/spanish-lyrics.htm

Works Cited

Blyth, Carl. "Implementing Technology in the Foreign Language Curriculum: Redefining the Boundaries between Language and Culture." *Journal of Educational Computing Service* 20 (1999): 39-58.

Bourdieu, Pierre. *Distinction: A Social Critique of the Judgment of Taste.* Cambridge: Harvard University Press, 1984.

Brooks, Nelson. "Teaching Culture in the Foreign Language Classroom." *Foreign Language Annals* 1 (1969): 204-17.

Brown, Douglas. *Principles of Language Learning and Teaching.* Englewood Cliffs: Prentice-Hall, 1994.

Carel, Sheila. "Developing an Awareness of French Pragmatics: A Case Study of Students' Interactive Use of a Foreign Language Multimedia Program." *Journal of Educational Computing Service* 20 (1999): 11-23.

Finnemann, Michael. "The World Wide Web and Foreign Language Teaching." *ERIC/CLL News Bulletin* 20 (1998): 6-8.

Foucault, Michel. *The Archaeology of Knowledge and the Discourse on Language.* A.M. Sheridan Smith, translator. New York: Pantheon Books, 1972.

Galloway, Vicki. "Toward a Cultural Reading of Authentic Texts." *Languages for a Multicultural World in Transition.* Heidi Byrnes, ed. Lincolnwood, IL: National Textbook Company, 1992. 87-121.

Galloway, Vicki. As cited in Alice Omaggio Hadley. *Teaching Language in Context*, 3rd ed.

Boston: Heinle and Heinle, 1985.

Gates, Henry Louis. *Signifying Monkey: A Theory of African-American Literary Criticism.* New York: Oxford University Press, 1983.

Gramsci, Antonio. *Selections from the Prison Notebooks of Antonio Gramsci.* Q.Hoare and G.N. Smith, eds. New York: International Publishers, 1971.

Hall, Edward. *The Silent Language.* Anchor Press, Garden City, 1959.

Hanvey, Robert. "Cross-Cultural Awareness." *Toward Internationalism: Readings in Cross Cultural Communication.* E.C. Smith and L.F.Luce, eds. Rowley, MA: Newbury House, 1979.

Heusinkveld, Paula R "The Foreign Language Classroom: A Forum for Understanding Cultural Stereotypes." *Pathways to Culture: Readings on Teaching Culture in the Foreign Language Classroom.* Paula Heuskinveld, ed. Yarmouth, ME: Intercultural Press, 1997.

Kramsch, Claire J. "Culture and Constructs: Communicating Attitudes and Values in the Foreign Language Classroom." *Pathways to Culture: Readings on Teaching Culture in the Foreign Language Classroom.* Paula Heuskinveld, ed. Yarmouth, ME: Intercultural Press, 1997. 461- 485.

Lee, Lina. "Using Internet Tools as an Enhancement of C2 Teaching and Learning." *Foreign Language Annals* 30 (1997): 410-427.

Moore, Zena. "Culture: How do Teachers Teach it?" *Foreign Language Teacher Education: Multiple Perspectives.* Zena Moore, ed. Maryland: University Press of America, 1996. 269-289.

Moore, Zena, Betsy Morales and Sheila Carel. "Technology and Teaching Culture: Results of a State Survey of Foreign Language Teachers." *CALICO Journal* 15 (1999): 109-128.

Moore, Zena. "Post-colonial Influences in Spanish Diaspora: Christian Doctrine and the Depiction of Women in Tejano Border Songs and Calypso." *Sound Identities: Popular Music and the Cultural Politics of Education.* Cameron McCarthy, Glenn Hudak, Shawn Miklaucic and Paula Saukko, eds. New York: Peter Lang Publishing Inc, 1999. 215-233.

National Standards in Foreign Language Project. *Standards for Foreign Language Learning: Preparing for the Twenty-First Century.* Lawrence, KS: Allen Press, 1997.

National Conference on Youth Report. Washington, D.C., 1971.

Ortuño, Marilyn. "Cross Cultural Awareness in the Foreign Language Classroom: The Kluckhohn Model." *The Modern Language Journal,* 755 (1991): 449-59.

Osuna, Maritza and Carla Meskill. "Using the World Wide Web To Integrate Spanish Language and Culture: A Pilot Study." *Language Learning and Technologies* 1(1998): 71-92.

Seelye, H. Ned. *Teaching Culture: Strategies for Intercultural Communication.* Skokie, IL: National Textbook Company, 1991.

Tannen, Deborah. *You Just Don't Understand: Women and Men in Conversation.* New York: William Morrow, 1990.

Ulloa Rodríguez, Gloria. "Creating a Nutritious Diet." At: http://members.aol.com/classweb/ activities99/nutricion.html.

Walsh, Joel. "Meeting Standards for Foreign Language Learning with World Wide Web Activities." *Foreign Language Annals* 31 (1988): 103-14.

About the Authors

Susan Bacon is Professor of Spanish and Associate Director of the Institute for Global Studies and Affairs at the University of Cincinnati. In addition to her administrative duties, she teaches Spanish language and culture, second-language acquisition and teaching methodology. Her research interests include child and adult second-language acquisition, and the processing of authentic input. She is recipient of the prestigious Paul Pimsleur Award for Research in Education awarded by the American Council for the Teaching of Foreign Languages and the Modern Language Journal. She has been Project Director of a four-year grant from the National Endowment for the Humanities, and a Fulbright-Robles Scholar in Mexico. She is primary researcher for several empirical articles, and has co-authored elementary and intermediate-level Spanish texts including *Conexiones, ¡Arriba!* and *Leyendas del mundo hispano.*

Vicki Galloway is Professor of Spanish at the Georgia Institute of Technology where she also serves as Co-Director of the study-abroad intensive program in Spanish for Business and Technology. Her teaching responsibilities include courses in language, literature, culture and sociopolitical issues of Latin America and the European Union and she is currently involved in cross-disciplinary team-teaching initiatives. She is co-author of several foreign language textbooks for college, secondary and middle-school levels including *Acción, Visión y voz* and the Spanish-for-business text *Saldo a favor* and has published actively on a variety of topics in books and professional journals, including the *Modern Language Journal, Northeast Conference Reports, ACTFL Language Education Series* and a volume of the *American Educational Research Association.*

Carmen García is Asssociate Professor of Spanish Linguistics and Director of Lower Division Spanish Language Courses at Arizona State University. Her research interests include cross-cultural communication, oral discourse strategies of Spanish speakers, and the incorporation of discourse analysis in the design of foreign language teaching materials. She is author of three Spanish textbooks from basal to advanced levels: *Mosaicos, Interacciones* and *Mejor Dicho* and has published numerous articles on discourse analysis and foreign language teaching in *Journal of Pragmatics, Multilingua, Linguistics and Education, Hispanic Linguistics, Foreign Language Annals* and *Hispania.*

Olgalucía G. González is Associate Professor of Spanish and former Chairperson of the Department of Modern Languages at Washington and Jefferson College, Washington, PA. A strong proponent of study abroad, Dr. González has led student groups to Venezuela, Mexico and Spain and is co-founder of an exchange program between Washington and Jefferson College and CESA (*Colegio de Estudios Superiores de Administración*) in Bogotá, Colombia. Dr. González teaches Spanish language, Hispanic culture, and Latin American literature. Her areas of interest include Latin American women writers, Second Language Acquisition and Pedagogy, and she has presented papers and workshops on topics dealing with her research interests at regional, national, and international conferences. She is co-author of the intermediate-level textbook *De perlas* and of ancillary materials to accompany the basal *Visión y voz* program.

Paula Heusinkveld, Professor of Spanish at Clemson University, has presented numerous workshops on the integration of culture in the foreign language class, both in the United States and Mexico. She is the author of *Inside Mexico* and editor of the anthology *Pathways to Culture*. An accomplished musician, she performs regularly at multicultural festivals as well as in her own classes. In summer 2000 she designed and taught the course "Integration of Music in the Spanish Class" for the M.A. program of the University of Southern Mississippi in Morelia, Mexico.

Nancy Humbach is Associate Professor and Coordinator of Languages Education in the Department of Teacher Education at Miami University in Oxford, Ohio. Prior to her appointment at Miami, she taught Spanish, Latin American Studies and German at the secondary level in the Cincinnati area. A former Fulbright-Hayes Scholar in Colombia, she holds degrees from the University of Cincinnati and is a recipient of the Readers Digest/Teacher-Scholar Grant for Ohio. She is author or co-author of many textbooks, including the *Ven conmigo* series.

Zena Moore is Associate Professor in the College of Education of the University of Texas at Austin. Her published articles have appeared in *Hispania*, *Foreign Language Annals*, *Northeast Conference Reports*, *Calico* and the *Journal of Educational Computing Research*. Her current areas of research include assessment, teacher education and the teaching of culture.

Núria Vidal is Education Advisor at the Education Office of the Embassy of Spain where she has worked on several cooperative programs between the states of Maryland, Virginia, Pennsylvania and New York and the Ministry of Education in Spain. She has served as Director of the magazine *Materiales* and is now coordinating the "*Dossier de Apoyo para la enseñanza en EE.UU.*" In Spain she served as teacher trainer for the Department of Education of the Autonomous Government of Catalonia where she collaborated in curriculum design for the new School Reform. She is author of classroom materials and books on foreign language learning methodology and has served as investigative collaborator on research projects in language learning with creative frames and tasks at the University of Barcelona.